D1321202

C

On Our Own

SCEPTRE

Also by Anne Atkins

The Lost Child

Non-Fiction

Split Image – Male and Female after God's
Likeness

On Our Own

ANNE ATKINS

LIMERICK COUNTY LIBRARY

G 33474

WITHDRAWN FROM STOCK

SCEPTRE

Copyright © 1996 Anne Atkins

First published in 1996 by Hodder and Stoughton
A division of Hodder Headline PLC
A Sceptre book

The right of Anne Atkins to be identified as the Author of
the Work has been asserted by her in accordance with the
Copyright, Designs and Patents Act 1988.

10 9 8 7 6 5 4 3 2 1

All rights reserved. No part of this publication may be
reproduced, stored in a retrieval system or transmitted
in any form or by any means without the prior written
permission of the publisher, nor be otherwise circulated
in any form of binding or cover other than that in which
it is published and without a similar condition being
imposed on the subsequent purchaser.

All characters in this publication are fictitious and any
resemblance to real persons, living or dead, is purely coincidental.

British Library Cataloguing in Publication Data

Atkins, Anne
    On our own
    1.English fiction – 20th century
    I.Title
    823.9'14 [F]

    ISBN 0 340 67218 8

Typeset by Palimpsest Book Production Limited,
Polmont, Stirlingshire
Printed and bound in Great Britain by
Mackays of Chatham PLC, Chatham, Kent

Hodder and Stoughton
A division of Hodder Headline PLC
338 Euston Road
London NW1 3BH

For Alexander

Acknowledgements ∫

I would like to thank Sue for the wonderful lunches and nerveracking deadlines which frightened me into giving birth to a new book; and Gina and Murray for being such good friends as well as good agents. Also to Friedman for very generously giving me a computer to write my book on to, and Peter for quite generously giving me a laptop so I could write it in more interesting places (shame it doesn't work, but you can't have everything). To my brother Andrew, Gerald Peacock, and Andrew Hunter Johnston for their careful readings of the text, warm encouragement, and intelligent and invaluable corrections. To Stanley Sadie, for his expertise on Mozart. To my father for generously and graciously accommodating a changing, and probably deteriorating, world. To Hilary Wayment, OBE, for his advice on the stonework of the Chapel. To Professor Sir Owen and Lady Chadwick for letting Caz borrow their lovely cottage again. And a mention to Louis, simply in the hope that it might shame him into reading one of my books.

And of course I would like to thank Serena, Bink, Alexander and Benjamin, and my goddaughter Lara, for continuing so patiently with my education, and persisting so resolutely in trying to prevent my writing anything at all. And Shaun. For . . . um, well he made me a cup of tea a few weeks ago.

Anyone who knows Cambridge, and many who don't, will easily recognise the college with its Chapel and its choir. I have made no attempt to disguise it, and it is a distinguished and well-known establishment. However, although the place, the buildings, the institution, are much as I remember them – though they have had to change, of course, to keep up with the future, when my book is set – the people are not at all the ones I knew there. They are entirely imaginary. I have also taken one or two liberties with the geography of the countryside, the composition of the university, and calendar and time table of the college, and I would ask those who spot these to be forgiving.

One thing I am pleased about, and that is that I have realised a dream I know my father dreamt many years ago, and integrated girls amongst the trebles of that most beautiful choir in the world. Perhaps the future will catch up with me, and by the time we reach the date when my book is set, it will have happened. Too late for me, not that my voice was anywhere near good enough. And sadly too late now for my daughters. But perhaps not too late for my granddaughters.

ʃ

'Uns allen vielleicht war es beschieden, die erste sexuelle Regung
auf die Mutter, den ersten Haß und gewalttätigen Wunsch gegen
den Vater zu richten; unsere Träume überzeugen uns davon.'

'It is the fate of all of us, perhaps, to direct our first sexual
impulse towards our mother and our first hatred and our first
murderous wish towards our father. Our dreams convince us
that that is so' –

Sigmund Freud, *Interpretation of Dreams*

AUTHOR'S NOTE ∫

Extracts from Mozart's letters, and the quotation by Michael Kelly, were taken from *Mozart the Man and the Artist Revealed in his own words*, compiled and annotated by Friedrich Kerst, translated into English and edited with additional notes by Henry Krehbiel, published by Dover Publications, 1926. *Mozart*, by Charlotte Haldane, was published in 1960 by Oxford University Press, and is quoted by their permission. *King's College a Short History* is quoted by kind permission of the Provost and Fellows of King's College, Cambridge. And the quotation from Freud is from *The Standard Edition of the Complete Psychological Works of Sigmund Freud*, Vol. IV, p.262, translated by James Strachey, by permission of HarperCollins and A.W. Freud et al by arrangement with Mark Patterson & Associates. The observant will have noticed that the translation could be improved: a more accurate rendering of *gewalttätig* would be, not murderous, but violent.

'Dreams give me no concern, for there is no mortal man on earth who does not sometimes dream. But merry dreams! quiet, refreshing, sweet dreams! Those are the thing! Dreams which, if they were realities, would make tolerable my life which has more of sadness in it than merriment' –

W.A. Mozart

Ann Fitzwilliam turned in her bed and found, to her surprise and delight, that Alan was back. He was sleeping, his profile clear against the dim light of dawn, and the first thing she noticed, without being especially conscious of it, was his breathing, steady, and calm. She ran her hand over his chest and felt the silky hair and the warmth of his body. He made that gentle noise, that comfortable 'Mmmm . . .' that he always made if she caressed him when he was half asleep. She could never quite gauge his level of awareness when he was like that. Was he completely unconscious? He would say so, afterwards. Yet he would be aroused by a word or a touch, sometimes even reply to a question, apparently without consciousness: respond without wakening.

She was more exquisitely happy than she could remember being for a long time, such a long time, such a very, very long time. He was even more handsome, even more ravishing than she remembered, with his dark hair falling across his forehead and his fine bones and his clean-cut, straight nose. She rested her head on his shoulder and hugged her arm around him and wriggled her leg over his thigh and got into a thoroughly comfortable position. Then she nestled her face into his chest. His arms pulled her closer, he stirred, he slept on.

She didn't particularly want to wake him; not yet. He would wake with the morning and they would talk and make love and talk some more and read a bit and talk again and have breakfast together and even open some champagne because he was back, at last. There was so much she wanted to tell him about Theo, so much to ask him, so much to discuss and decide and make sure that she was doing all the right things. She needed his advice on everything. Had she been right to make him stay up the other night to finish his holiday homework? Did he agree that Theo shouldn't be allowed to learn the organ yet, however much he wanted to? Had she had coped all right when he fell off his new bicycle, and broke his front tooth, and shook and shook all the way to the dentist? Oh, if only Alan had been there then! She had missed him badly that night, and after she had warmed some milk for Theo and tucked him up and read to him and finally settled him for the night, she had gone down into the kitchen and cried and cried. But it was fine now: he was back, they could talk through all these things together, he would be pleased with her for managing without him, and they could go back to making joint decisions instead of Ann having to carry the burden for both of them.

She sighed with happiness and snuggled closer to him. She longed to tell him how much she loved him. But she knew, from long years of living with him, that, though he liked to know, he was sometimes embarrassed when she said so. When she said, 'I love you', he would sometimes brush her aside, though gently, as if she were a bothersome butterfly. But when she held him, like this, and stroked his smooth, freshly shaven cheek in the half light, he would quicken even in his subconscious, sleepy state, and hold her to him, and want her, and be content.

'Oh, Alan,' she said softly, smiling, and pulled towards her the cold, empty pillow in the bitterly cold and empty bed, and opened her eyes on to the permanent nothingness under the duvet beside her and a despair so bleak and overwhelming that her lungs pulled on the pain and she thought she must drown in the emptiness of it.

Dead. Alan is dead. There is absolutely and utterly no hope

and no point at all in dreaming he could return. She would never have him back again, and the never was absolute and really was never ever.

Suddenly, and with a stab in her side which took her breath away, she remembered him. She felt the palm of his hand, warm and strong against her cheek as he pulled her face towards his. She saw him, behind her closed eyelids, in the garden, kicking a football with Theo, his feet far too quick and nimble for his clumsy and unsporty son. She remembered how, with infinite patience when Theo was barely three, he had taught him how to sing his solfa accurately, and before very long how to distinguish a double-dotted quaver from a simple dotted one, and what the difference was between F double sharp and G natural. Then she remembered him, cross and grumpy after a bad rehearsal, taking a claw hammer to the kitchen door and ripping off the plywood façade, and how annoyed she'd been at the time.

She turned and looked at the clock. Just gone four. This time there had been no clues, no warning signs, no indication at all that it might not be real. At least last time she had said to herself, as she opened the door and let him in for tea, 'This is a dream; I must make the most of it and talk to him about everything while I have the time, before I wake.' But of course, in death as in life, in dreams as it had so often been in waking, they didn't have time. She had barely hugged him and said hello and put the kettle on while he took a telephone call and glanced at some work from his briefcase and hummed a tune which needed arranging before tomorrow, when she woke, long before she was ready, and her chance to talk to him was gone.

Rage: that was what she felt. Terrible but impotent rage at the beastly injustice of it. That she hadn't known she was dreaming; that she had woken so cruelly early and now wouldn't sleep again before tonight. And what do I do now? she asked herself, looking at the clock again. The luminous figures showed exactly 4.07.

She pulled the covers up to her ears and stared at the grey ceiling, dull like the ceiling of a cell, until her eyes hurt with the looking, and then she turned her face to the wall.

2

The little country bus stopped at the village green, opposite the pub, and Caz jumped out. She always travelled light, and virtually all she had with her was her computer, a hairbrush, and some clean underwear. She also had the confidence of the well-off, happy that if she really needed something she could buy it, though her brother Ben had warned her that Cley village might not have the software she was used to in Fulham.

'You'd better borrow the car,' he had said, as they were having tea the day before, 'to shop, and get about. I don't know how you Londoners think you're going to survive in the country. What d'you think you're going to do? Find a black London cab parked next to a fishing smack on the shingle, or what?'

'Take the car? Don't be ridiculous,' Caz had retorted. 'And I don't know how you country folk think you're going to have any countryside left, the way you keep running about in cars. You need one, I don't, and if I did I could hire one. Cley presumably has a garage somewhere, even if it doesn't have a computer showroom.'

'How are you going to buy a pint of milk? The nearest shops are a mile and a quarter away.'

'Good grief, Ben! When did you last read D.H. Lawrence or Thomas Hardy? People used to walk ten miles to get to work. Children walked two hours to get to school, and then two hours home again at the end of the day. It's not going to kill me to walk into Cley for shopping every few days. Anyway, don't they have delivery services?'

'There you are, you see. Typical. No, they don't. There isn't a supermarket that you can just ring up with your order. There's a local pottery, and a smokehouse for fish, and an expensive delicatessen and home bakery, and a couple of pubs. That's after you've walked into the village. No Sainsbury's. No milkman. No delivery. Take the car.'

'No.'

'Anyway, what about your condition?'

'Oh, for goodness' sake! I'm not an invalid!'

'I'm sorry,' he said, and Caz thought he sounded a little offended. 'Suki couldn't walk for more than five minutes when she was pregnant, that's all. Besides, I thought you were going to do some work, not spend all your morning shopping.'

'Walking helps me think. Abi, get off my knee; that hurts.'

They said nothing for a moment. Caz finished her slice of rather flat chocolate cake, with far too much butter icing, which Abi had made for her aunt that afternoon after Caz had turned up on the doorstep unannounced, having taken a taxi from the village station. She licked the butter icing from her fingers. Ben glanced at her sideways.

'Why didn't you go with Will to Italy?' he asked. 'It would have been a fabulous trip.'

'I have to work,' she said without looking at him. 'I'm a writer, remember?'

'Do you want to talk about it?'

'No,' she said rather too quickly. 'Thanks all the same.'

Ben was right, of course. It would have been quite wonderful. True, for Will it was a working visit. But since his brief was to look at some of the most stunning architecture Rome and Florence boasted, it would hardly have been onerous accompanying him.

It had seemed to Caz, when Will invited her, that she was faced with a clear choice. She could pack a bag with a little black dress and some scented soap, be dined on the banks of the Tiber, wined beneath a Roman moon, and shown around the remains of one of the loveliest civilisations of Europe by a man who understood it perfectly, staying in a friendly little hotel in Trastevere, and eating the delicious Italian food. Or she could stay at home, lonely and miserable, in a raw English October and a grey and soggy London, and produce a hundred thousand words. Nobody would reproach her if she failed to write her next book. Nobody, except she herself.

There was no choice, really. She was a writer. If she gave in now she might do so for the rest of her life. She had written nothing since the early summer. Now she had an idea for a book. She had even done her research. Will's absence was what she needed to make herself work again.

So she had kissed him goodbye, sat depressed in Fulham for a couple of days writing nothing, rung up the friends who owned the cottage in Norfolk, found it to be empty, slung her laptop in her bag, switched on the answerphone, and pulled the front door to behind her.

Any other reasons she might, or might not, have had were unimportant; or at least unexpressed.

Now, she shouldered her bag and crossed the green to the cottage next to The Three Swallows. It was as pretty as it had ever been, smiling and winking in the sun. The little window which looked out on to the green was the original Tudor window, with the tiny, irregular panes of glass, and the lead lattice. As Caz peeped in, it seemed that the house was welcoming her; as if it were inhabited, warm, friendly. She unlatched the heavy white wooden gate after which the cottage was named, and opened it wide over the cobbled courtyard. Opposite her was the old summer-house, through whose milky windows she could see canvas garden chairs and slatted wooden deck loungers full of long-abandoned cobwebs.

Built in the 1590s, and architecturally almost unchanged since, it was one of the sweetest houses Caz knew, and contained some of the sunniest memories of her childhood. This was where she had come with her mother, when she was three, and they had walked to the windmill which was still working in those days. This was where they had sat in the sunny, riotous garden and made daisy chains and smelt the wild roses and dozed in the sun. This was where she had paddled in the ford of the stream, shorts safely dry above her knees, while her mother sat with a picnic basket in the shade of the willow and read a book.

And this was where, years later and only last summer, she had come with Abi to find the same old pink scrambling rose above the study window, and the church green unspoilt opposite, and the disproportionately huge pre-Tudor church still dominating the same handful of houses.

This was where she would write her new book. She imagined the little study, with the painted wooden window seats and the threadbare carpet on the wooden floor. She had told herself that she would forget London, and the domesticity which she illogically felt was threatening to engulf her, and would lose herself in the plot and characters, the location and date of the story she now wished to write.

She considered the subject of her new book. She had been sitting in her conservatory, at home, listening to the radio while a delicate harpsichord minuet danced intricately and prettily through the notes. Very classical, very eighteenth century in its poise and light-heartedness. I wish I could play the piano like that, effortlessly, Caz thought to herself, resolving to practise for half an hour a day from now on. Then the commentator had announced the piece and its composer, mentioning in passing that he was six when he wrote it.

That was what had done it. She had pictured Abi, struggling to get a scale out of her school recorder, and thought, He *wrote* that? How could a child exist who could do something, aged six, that the rest of us could barely do if we trained for half a lifetime?

Then she started reading: biographies, musical commentaries, contemporary accounts. She knew there was a book there, waiting to be written, if only she could work out what it was, so she read and read and read. What she read fascinated her. The father, in particular – an ambitious musician in his own right, a successful, accomplished man – who put aside his career and achievements to promote his absurdly young son. The older sister, Nannerl, a child prodigy herself, an impressive harpsichord player before she was in her teens, who ended up slogging away teaching pupil after dunce-headed pupil to maintain herself in her old age.

The whole family intrigued her. Now, having done her research, she hoped, in the peace and quiet of Norfolk, to start the writing process.

As she put the key in the door, she looked up at the thatched lintel, where the wrens used to nest. There, under the straw-covered eaves, she could see a tidy little nest which looked as though it had been used that very summer. She remembered the parent birds, darting in and out with their beaks full of grubs, nipping about so quickly they could hardly be seen by the naked eye, except as a fragile flutter of brown. She struggled with the lock, and let herself into the empty house. It seemed dark and slightly chilly inside, and a bit too clean and tidy. She put down her bag in the hall and wandered about. The fridge was empty, the Aga cold. The cupboards had a few tins in them, and some scrapings of tea and a packet of coffee that smelt rather stale. There was no note for her on the kitchen table. She wandered into the large, low-ceilinged sitting room and sat down at the piano. She hadn't thought to bring any music. She tried to remember a little sonatina of Leopold Mozart's, but after the first few bars she got stuck on the bass line. Was it a tonic or a dominant chord under that lovely falling line in the right? Both sounded wrong. She searched in the piano stool for some music, but it was all fiendishly difficult, full of clusters of sharps and flats and clumps of demi-semi-quavers. She closed the piano lid and stood up again.

Then she remembered the letter.

The morning post had already come when she left her house in London the day before. She had looked through it quickly, and left most of it behind, unopened. One of the letters, though, she had picked out from amongst the others, and put in her bag. This wasn't in a white or brown envelope with a window to show the address. This was written by hand, on a mid-blue, thick, watermarked envelope. It had addressed her solemnly as 'Miss Cassandra Sanderson', followed by her publisher's address, which had been crossed out by someone in the office so that her own could be substituted. The hand which had written her name had looked like a child's hand, careful and very neat.

She put the kettle on and went to get the letter. There it was, in her bag, slightly squashed under her neat laptop. She stuffed it in her pocket as she made the tea then she sat down on the step, in the warm afternoon sun, took a sip of tea – too hot – and opened the envelope with her finger; it resisted her attempts to tear it tidily in a straight line across the top. She opened the matching, mid-blue sheet of paper, and was surprised at how short the letter was. At the top was the embossed address, in

dark blue, of a house in Cambridge. Before the address, the
writer had written, 'As from' – a rather unchildlike thing to put,
Caz thought. Beneath the printed address was the address of a
Cambridge prep school. Odd. If his home was in Cambridge, why
would he, or she, board at school? Perhaps it had simply been
written in a lunch break, or prep session, or hidden behind a
textbook during the maths period. Caz smiled at the recollection
of doing similar things herself.

Dear Miss Sanderson,
Thank you for writing the book. I liked it. I think I know how
you feel.
　Yours faithfully,
　　Theo Wedderburn
THEOPHILUS A. WEDDERBURN (Master)

Caz smiled. This was it; this was the reason she wrote books. The
simple appreciation of a child, an unknown person who liked her
work so much that he didn't just contemplate writing to her, but
actually did it, actually went to the bother of sitting down and
addressing an author he had never met and never would, for no
purpose other than to say he was glad that she had written. She
folded it up and put it back in the envelope. She would drop him
a note today.

Then she frowned. She took it out again and spread it
out on her lap. She reread it. She shook her head for a
moment, slightly puzzled, before putting the letter back in
the envelope. 'Oh, well,' she said out loud. Then she put it
down on the step beside her, and took her time finishing her
cup of tea.

There was no writing paper in the cottage anywhere, as far as
she could discover. Not in the desk in the sitting room, nor in
the little study at the end of the house, which overlooked the
village green through the tiny, hand-blown panes of Elizabethan
glass, nor in any of the bedrooms. The best she could find, in
the end, was a clean sheet of white A4, and a long brown
manila envelope. She had her fountain pen with her, which
she always carried, though she was the only writer she knew
who still used one.

Dear Master Wedderburn
Thank you for your letter.
  Which book?
  Yours sincerely,
    Caz
CASSANDRA SANDERSON

'PS,' she added: a genuine afterthought. 'Please feel free to call me Caz.'

It was past four o'clock when she set out to walk to the village.

She hadn't missed the post. She bought a pad of writing paper, some envelopes and a first-class stamp, caught the five-thirty, and had a drink in the village pub in the closing evening before going home to ponder her new book.

3

It was exactly two days later. He had replied by return, as she had. Everything – the paper, the two addresses, the careful hand – was the same.

> Dear Caz,
> Thank you. You may call me Theo if you would like to. The name of the book was *The Lost Child*. I started one of your books about the child Ariel, but didn't like it very much. But I thought *The Lost Child* was quite good. I have an idea for another book I think you should write. I wondered if you would like me to take you out to tea. I see you live in Norfolk, which is fairly close, I think. I have exeats on Wednesday and Saturday afternoons, and could take you to the Copper Kettle. Their cakes are home-made, I think, but they probably contain refined sugar. Fitzbillies cakes are brilliant too, but you can't eat there because it's only a shop. I don't know if you know Cambridge at all, but I could show you round a little.
> Yours sincerely,
> Theo (Wedderburn)

Caz smiled as she read the letter, then, as with the first one, reread it, this time a second, then a third time.

How old is a child who doesn't really know where Norfolk is? Ten or eleven? Yet he had read her novel, which was not a children's book. Though that meant nothing: some children can immerse themselves in the *Iliad* at an age at which others can barely cope with comics. If he was still at prep school, the oldest he could be was twelve, or at the very most thirteen. But that didn't seem right either: he felt younger, she didn't know why. She would have to wait and see.

She realised she was already assuming she would take up his invitation, one day. And why not? They might have a lot in common.

'I think I know how you felt.' Wasn't that what he had said in his first letter? Caz didn't bother to go and get it – she was outside, on a deckchair in the garden, eating a bowl of muesli – but she could remember the gist accurately enough. And what had he meant? Had he lost a younger brother or sister? Had he imagined a childhood companion, to whom he had said goodbye as he grew up?

I'm not an amateur psychologist, she reminded herself sharply. I'll see him when I next go to Cambridge: it would be quite fun. Even as she thought this, she realised that she didn't go to Cambridge any more, not since her grandfather had died, and Ben had gone down, oh, ages ago. And yet she had already made a couple of scruffy pages of questions and jottings which would need a few more days of research to clear up: half a week in the University Library wouldn't do her any harm at all. But she had come away to write. She mustn't give up yet. Research was always easier than writing, especially writing that was as painful and reluctant as hers was at the moment. She mustn't allow herself to abandon it so soon, however tempting the prospect.

It was clouding over, and chilly, and she went back inside to start her day properly. She washed up her bowl and put it, lonely as it was, on the wooden plate rack which hung on the wall by the kitchen sink. She poured herself a mug of grey tea from the cooling pot on the table. Her computer waited hungrily, impatient, in the study. She took her tea, which she knew she wouldn't drink but which was a necessary accompaniment to her writing process, and went back to feed her machine with the next couple of thousand words.

Half a morning later, Caz looked up from her screen and gazed through the window. She saw a dog running, wobbly in the uneven glass. She stretched. She rose, and took a turn about the room. She half yawned, then thought better of it. She turned back to her screen and read the numbers at the top of the page. Page 3, line 41, column 16. It would do. It would do till after lunch.

Inside the pad on the window seat was a four-page letter to Will, not yet sent. Caz was excellent at writing letters, lousy at posting them. Sometimes she would write every day for a week, then stuff all the letters in the same envelope and wait till she saw whomever they were intended for. She picked up the pad and went into the kitchen to make herself some coffee. Then she remembered the stale grounds and decided to go next door to the pub. Twenty minutes later she sat in the saloon bar with a cup of coffee and her letter pad in front of her, and wrote:

Dear Theo,
Thank you. I'd love to. But I'm busy writing another book at the moment. It might turn out to be a children's book, but it's not about Ariel. I think you might like it. Anyway, next time I'm near Cambridge I'll get in touch, and we can meet up at the Copper Kettle. That would be great.
    Yours, etc,
    Caz

She took another gulp of coffee. It tasted strong, almost bitter. She turned over the page of the pad and started again.

'Dearest Will,' she began.

I love you, she thought, but didn't write. Her existing letter to him didn't say any of the things she wanted to say. How could she explain that she went to bed every night, aching for him? That, every time she stopped to think of it, she longed for the dome of St Peter's, for Italian coffee, for the sight of his lean cheek in his native sun, with a sharper longing than that of any homesick child who has been sent away for the first time. That she would never forgive herself for not going with him. And, indeed, that it was only this which drove her to her computer every morning. That she couldn't bear to lose an Italian autumn with Will and not have a book to show for it in exchange, and it was this very loss which guaranteed that the words would be there at the end of the day. She didn't know how to put it: writer that she was, she didn't know how to tell him how much she loved him. She wasn't even sure that she wanted to.

She would post her letter to little Theo Wedderburn, in any case. The walk into the village would clear her mind for the afternoon stint.

That evening, five pages later, she sat at the same, now beer-sticky table near the window, overlooking the village green, thinking about her work. What should be the focus of her book? Should it be the child prodigy, the Wunderkind who had astonished half the crowns of Europe? Or should it be the insolvent, unsuccessful grown man, brilliant at any form of composition he turned his hand to, but unable to support his family on his inadequate income? Why had he died? Was it really Salieri who had poisoned him, or was that simply an excuse for an excellent film and better stage play?

Something was niggling at the back of her mind. She had read it back in London, she couldn't remember in which book, but she was sure of the detail. The composer had had a pauper's funeral. Everyone knew that. Barely a mourner to follow the coffin. Commonplace knowledge. Even his devastated widow had not walked behind him to say goodbye, though that was not unusual at the time.

But a handful of people had turned up and accompanied the body of the Viennese Kapellmeister, as far as the city gates at least. Süssmayr, his pupil who completed the Requiem for him. Baron van Swieten, his friend and supporter. And Salieri. She remembered it distinctly. Suddenly she could no longer believe that Salieri had been responsible for his death. If you had murdered a rival, would you walk behind his coffin? Would you be one of a small handful who distinguished themselves by paying their respects? It might be great material for a murder plot, but it was poor psychology. Nor did it fit that the successful and fashionable Italian composer would feel threatened by the struggling and indebted German one, however much he envied his talent. Or indeed that one creative artist would ever be likely to do away with another. Could she, Caz, an everyday writer, conceivably seek to end the work of a great one? Never. It was not credible. Besides, hadn't Salieri taken his rival's son, Karl, under his own wing, finding employment for him after his father's death? And yet the musician himself believed someone was poisoning him, and a few weeks later he died. Though, being truthful, Caz knew he hadn't really had such a shameful funeral. It was quite respectable and conventional, by the middle class standards of the time, and had been followed up a few days later by his own Requiem, performed in his honour.

She strolled round the green, contemplating the two-hundred-year-old tragedy under the gaze of the friendly cottage. The moon shone brightly, nearly full, behind racing clouds. It was an appropriate place to write, but it was very lonely. She longed for any kind of company, even a cat, to go home to after her evening drink. There was nothing, no one. Only the sound of old wood cracking in the night, and the windows creaking to the wind.

She strolled over to the cottage gate, raised its heavy latch and pushed it open with some difficulty, and went into the yard. The moon was now hidden behind the wall of the buildings, and it was suddenly darker in the old courtyard. She shuddered. For a moment she stood absolutely still, willing herself to stop breathing, and strained to hear. Silence. Her scalp tingled all over as she stared into the ungenerous darkness.

There is nothing but the echo of my own step, she told herself, and made herself turn again and walk to the door. A tree creaked in the churchyard nearby. Was it because she was pregnant that she was feeling so nervous? She'd never reacted like this before. She tried to picture little 'Itylus' as she had nicknamed the bump, though Will hated the reference, and wondered what other havoc their son was going to wreak with her life.

'Oh, Will,' she said, out loud. 'Oh, will, please come home!' Then she turned and ran up the stairs, tore off all her clothes except her pants and tee-shirt, and dived under the covers.

4 ♪

Eighty-four miles away, in Cambridge, Henrietta Davenport, known as Miss Henrietta to the boys, was making her final check of the dormitories. She had reached Mozart, the penultimate room of her round. The name had been changed from B to Mozart three and a half years ago, in an effort to give the dormitories more individuality. Tim Marshall, the new head master, had asked the children what they would like to call the dormitories, expecting the names of soccer heroes or film stars, or even, knowing the pupils here were bright and reasonably well read, perhaps some dashing role models from books. Charlie from the Chocolate Factory, perhaps, he thought, realising as he did so that he was hopelessly out of touch and old fashioned already, aged only forty-two. He would have to get into their culture, he had told himself, thinking that inviting them to name their own dormitories would be something of a first step. The last thing he had expected was Mozart, Beethoven, Scarlatti and Vaughan Williams. What will prospective parents think, he had asked his wife, dreading the accusation of 'pressurised', 'high-powered', or even 'élitist'. But he had told the children they could choose, and choose they had; he could hardly tell them he was vetoing their choice because he was afraid of being thought pretentious. Besides, at least they had settled for composers all the prospective parents would have heard of. He shuddered when he thought of the suggestions of one or two of the senior choristers: Janáček, Kabalevsky, and Howells.

Henrietta was oblivious of the head master's discomfort when she went through her mental checklist of the rooms still to be visited. Her appointment to the school had taken place after the dormitory's christening, so Mozart was how she had always thought of it. She put her head round the door and smiled at the sleepy heads on the pillows. She wasn't, of course, known as 'matron'. That was the privilege of her superior, Mrs Havent; she was simply Miss Henrietta, and preferred it that way.

The boys were, if not all asleep, at least all quiet. She crossed the room to shut the window a little: Mrs Havent would insist on keeping the dormitory windows wide open in all weathers, and it was now a fairly nippy October night. As she pulled the window to, she realised that there was no head on the pillow of Theo Wedderburn's bed. She sighed. She liked the little Wedderburn boy, but even she could not deny that he was a handful. He almost needed to wear a government health warning: This boy can seriously damage a teacher's mental state. She went over to give the bed a closer inspection. Where on earth could he be? Once he had been found in the Assembly Hall at nine o'clock at night, practising a new composition on the piano; several times he had been known to sit on the loo for half an hour or more, oblivious of the passage of time. That was probably where he was now. As she leant over his bed she suddenly jumped and cried out, then glanced round, worried that she might have disturbed the other boys.

'Theo! I nearly trod on you!' she said in a hoarse whisper which sounded rather loud and angry, and which she struggled to control.

'Hello,' he said, hardly looking up. He was squatting on the floor next to his bedside cupboard, contemplating something. Henrietta, who knew him well by now and was fond of him despite herself, recognised the worried, preoccupied tone. He was anxious about something, and until she could solve his problem – or rather, enable him, or wait for him, to solve it himself – she was unlikely to get him into bed and certainly would never persuade him to go to sleep. As her eyes grew accustomed to the darkness, she realised he was wearing shoes, though he was otherwise in pyjamas.

'Where are you going?' she asked, knowing as she did so that with any other boy she would simply have said, 'Get those off now and hop into bed.'

'To St Andrew's Street, I think.'

Thank goodness it's me, not Mrs Havent, Henrietta thought.

'Why?' she asked, quite calmly.

'The post will have gone from the pillar box in West Road. I thought I'd posted it, you see. I forgot I hadn't done it on the way back from Chapel.'

'Theo, you daft thing, it's gone eight o'clock.'

'Oh, I know that. But there's a late collection in St Andrew's Street. My mother told me. About eight forty-five, I think. I thought I'd probably be on time.'

'And what about school rules? Do you think you're allowed to go wandering about the streets in your pyjamas after Lights Out?'

'Oh.' He contemplated this. Incredibly, it didn't seem to have occurred to him.

'And do you think it's safe?' she continued. 'I mean, why do you suppose we have school rules?'

At this he frowned. The possible danger clearly worried him far more than the breach of school rules. Then he smiled at her, and not for the first time she marvelled at the genuine charm of his young face. She had to resist the impulse to hug him. 'Perhaps you could come with me?' he said hopefully.

She raised her eyebrows. 'Is it very important?' she asked him, wondering who the recipient could be. After all, his mother lived just round the corner, nearer than St Andrew's Street.

He considered. 'Not important,' he said, 'but urgent.'

'Could it wait till tomorrow?'

'I'd rather it didn't.'

Henrietta smiled. Well, she was going into the centre of Cambridge, to go to the cinema with a friend. She would be quite near St Andrew's Street. She had nearly finished her rounds.

'Give it to me,' she said, shaking her head at her own soft heartedness. 'I'll post it.'

'In St Andrew's Street?'

'Yes.'

'Before eight forty-five?'

'I'll try.'

'You won't forget?'

'I won't forget.'

LIMERICK
9 33474
COUNTY LIBRARY

'Thank you,' he said, and took off his shoes, got into bed, and turned over to sleep.

In the event, she nearly did forget. She got to the ABC Cinema early, at twenty to nine, and while she waited for the friend she was due to meet she felt in her pocket and found her hand closing over an unfamiliar envelope. Help, she thought, unlocked her bike again, pedalled furiously past Holy Trinity Church and down beyond Christ's College, and found a pillar box with the discouraging figure 1 on it, and the next time of collection: 8 a.m. the following morning. She sighed, and was about to post it anyway when she saw a post van on the opposite side of the road, with a postman just getting into it.

She dodged over the road, and tapped on the window. He wound it down.

'That's all right, love,' he said as he took the letter from her, and winked. 'He'll get it. Lucky chap!'

Consequently, it had gone ten to nine when she got back to the cinema. A tall and rather good-looking man in his early-thirties was looking at the clock above the Market Place and tapping his foot in a nervous manner.

'Hi,' Henrietta called as she locked her bicycle again.

'Henry, you're late,' he said without a smile, and then turned and went into the cinema.

Oh, stuff you then, she thought as she finished fiddling with her bicycle lock. At least I'll be able to look Theo Wedderburn in the eye at breakfast and give him a truthful answer when he asks me, which he's bound to. Suddenly she realised that her companion would never understand that her undertaking to post Theo's letter was just as binding as her arrangement to meet him at a quarter to nine outside the cinema – and of far more importance to Theo than it was to a man who had his pick of so many other, more punctual girls. Of that she was in no doubt at all. She would not go to the cinema with him again.

5

Caz woke, aching with fatigue. It was barely light. She looked
through the window expecting the trees of Parsons Green and
saw too small a patch of sky and the top of a horse chestnut
which she didn't recognise. She turned over to doze a bit more,
thrusting her head further under the itchy sheet which smelt of
someone else's laundry. The bed was cold, the mattress lumpy,
and the bedclothes inadequate over her feet. She had a vague,
throbbing headache. She also had no inclination to get up, and
felt as if she had nothing to get up for. She wished she had
brought a radio, and then, acutely, wished she were in her own
bed and not alone.

It was nearly nine o'clock by the time she eventually found
her way into the kitchen. It still seemed much earlier. And,
in the light of day, it was extraordinary that she had found
the friendly little cottage frightening the night before. She
wondered how long she would stay. Her book was not going
well. She was making herself write every day. But she felt
as if she had got stuck, like a twig snagged on the bank of
some gurgling stream, on the problem of his mysterious death.
If only she had some interesting and novel theory as to how he
might have died, she thought illogically and rather arrogantly,
then she would surely understand more about how he had
lived.

As she cut herself a slice of bread, she heard the old gate creak
on its hinges, then a little 'pat' as something fell on the mat.
Waiting for her toast, she went into the hall to get whatever
had come for the Anderson family, who owned the cottage.
It was unlikely that there would be anything for her. Will was

not a letter-writer by nature, and Abi had seen her a few days previously.

She recognised the envelope immediately, though it was face down, the handwriting hidden. Mid-blue, Conqueror paper. She smiled as she picked it up. He was prompt and persistent, at any rate.

The other post that had come with his letter was a postcard of Queens' Bridge, Cambridge. She took it into the kitchen to put with one or two other letters which had come for the Andersons, before she realised that the postcard, too, was for her.

My dear C,

I'm sorry to be such a bore, but Josh has just arrived from Reading with some friends, and they want to come to the cottage for the weekend. You won't be in their way at all, but I'm afraid you won't get much peace and quiet. If you want to come to Cambridge for twenty-four hours to escape, you're most welcome: it'll only be we wrinklies, so no loud parties late at night.

Love, Laura.

Damn, Caz said to herself. Damn damn damn. There was no earthly point in her staying at the cottage now. Apart from anything else, of course she would be in the way, whatever Laura Anderson said. And she certainly wouldn't get any work done. But then, she wouldn't get much done in Cambridge either. It would be pointless to go home to London, if she was planning to come back to New Gate Cottage in a day or two. She could go to Ben's, have a pleasant weekend off, and return to Cley on Sunday night.

She opened the second letter. 'Dear Caz,' she read, and at that moment the toaster popped. She made her tea, put her breakfast on a tray and went into the sitting room: it was now far too cold to sit outside. The butter dripped off her toast on to her fingers, and she tried to avoid getting it on the paper.

Dear Caz,

Why don't you come this weekend? I finish school tomorrow (Saturday) at one o'clock. I have to be back in Chapel at five, for Evensong, so don't be late. I will get permission from Mr Marshall for you to pick me up, and I'll wait for you under the Dead Slow sign.

   Yours sincerely,

    Theo (Wedderburn)

It was already Saturday. She would have to contact him immediately to tell him she wouldn't be there. But how? If she telephoned the school office, her message would have to go through a busy school secretary who couldn't go running around the school giving notes to individual boys, Miss, what did you say your name was? Cassandra Sanderson? Not the children's writer? Goodness gracious, we have some of your books in the school library. What did you say the message was? That you can't take him out after all? I'll pass that on. Don't worry; I don't suppose he'll be *too* disappointed.

Then she envisaged him standing beneath the Dead Slow sign, wherever it was, with his hands in his pockets and his socks round his ankles, waiting patiently minute after slow minute for the arrival of a lady he had invited out for tea.

She shook her head, and smiled again. She almost had a feeling of having been outmanoeuvred.

It took her only minutes to put her few belongings in her bag, straighten her bed, wash up and put away her mug and plate and the teapot, and leave a note and some money for the cleaning lady, in case she didn't return. She made a mental note not to arrive back at the lonely cottage in the dark. She locked the door and put the key back in the same old hiding place it had had when she was a child. She walked to the village. In the post office she bought a postcard with a watercolour of the mill, standing freshly painted and impressive, in the bleak bird-haven of the marsh.

Missing you more than you will believe. Or than I can. Hope I'm home before you get this. Don't tell me how wonderful it is there because I don't want to know. Itys fine. C.

6

'I can not write poetically; I am no poet. I can not divide and subdivide my phrases so as to produce light and shade; I am no painter. I can not even give expression to my sentiments and thoughts by gestures and pantomime; I am no dancer. But I can do it with tones; I am a musician' –

W.A. Mozart

Happily, Ann must have dozed. The next time she looked at the clock it read 7.53. She could turn on the radio without any fear of hearing Thought for the Day. There is a God in heaven after all, she thought, and smiled at the irony. If it were the holidays, Theo would have brought her a cup of tea by now, coming in in his funny pyjamas, which had been given him by a cousin and were much too long in the leg and looked like the girls' pyjamas they were, and kneeling on the floor by her bedside fiddling with the electric kettle and tea bags and milk. It was an office which he never allowed her to perform for herself, after Alan's death, and when he had been offered the choristership that meant he would have to board at school even though it was just round the corner, the first thing he had said to her was, 'Who will make your tea in the morning?' This simple little function symbolised his vast, almost dangerous concern for her, and his far too mature fear that she would not cope on her own.

And how am I coping? she thought.

She remembered the day of his voice trial vividly, and thought she would for the rest of her life. She and Theo had walked the five minutes from their house to the school, and had arrived last, later than boys who had travelled down from Glasgow and up from Kent and stayed in hotels in Cambridge to get there in good time for nine o'clock. For some days before, she had kept meaning to tell Theo that it was one of those occasions when he really must be on time; that he must get up an hour and a half beforehand to have time to dress; that he must have a decent breakfast and not be rushed. She kept telling herself she would tell him. But there was never a moment when she had the heart. Instead, she kept remembering how much Alan had looked forward to this day, thinking of his time as a chorister in Salisbury, and how he always said he would find Theo's trial more nerve-racking than any audition he'd ever had to go through himself.

She and Alan had talked about it often: how Alan would attach too much importance to the occasion; about the problem of being objective in assessing his own son compared with the other thirty or forty most musical children in the country; how Theo was bound to pick up on his father's nerves no matter how well Alan hid them. Theo was instinctive like that: as an animal is. He could sometimes sense the undertones of a conversation, or the antipathy of someone in the room, or the fact that someone most unlikely had taken a shine to him. Yet at other times he could be so extraordinarily insensitive, so completely deaf and blind to the most obvious things under his nose, that you felt you could almost pick him up and shake him and shake him until the teeth rattled, if you had to ask him just one more time whether he wanted toast for breakfast, or could he please get his socks on because otherwise you would miss the train and then the plane and then the whole holiday would be ruined.

In the end Ann and Theo had been so relaxed about the day that he hadn't even chosen the pieces until the night before, and then he had been three-and-a-half minutes late and the last candidate to walk into the hall. Ann had felt all eyes on them, the pitied young widow and the even younger orphan. She could sense the head master and the head of music and Alan's suddenly appointed successor all knowing they must bend over backwards not to favour Theo as a tribute to his father.

In retrospect, Ann wondered whether Amschel had made

allowances after all. Theo had been as difficult as only he knew how. He had insisted, time and time again, that his cello had not been properly tuned and that he couldn't play it until it was. Eventually, after the head of music had spent over ten minutes on it, he had given up and handed the instrument to Amschel, Alan's replacement. He had looked at the little, eighth-size cello with interest. 'I started on the cello too,' he said, turned the fine-tuners, held the strings up to his ear, and then handed the cello back. Theo had accepted it without a word, and, with only a few more minutes spent adjusting his chair and the spike and the music stand, had launched into a simple little piece of Bach, but with a tone and an interpretation that were apparently fairly impressive. The day was half an hour behind schedule, but the other parents were never told why.

After lunch they all gathered in the hall to hear the short-list. The others had spent the morning looking round the school and visiting Cambridge. Ann had gone home. She had hardly given Theo a thought, except to hope that he was enjoying himself. But when she returned, and heard the short-list called out without Theo's name on it, she was stunned. Not even short-listed! She had tried to prepare herself for eventual failure, for being asked if he could try again next year, but that he would not even reach the short-list was not something she had anticipated. The unsuccessful candidates were starting to disperse. Ann failed to feel pity for those who had come several hundred miles and been disappointed.

'Hello, darling,' she said, as Theo came up and threw his arms around her, and she wondered whether he genuinely didn't mind, or was simply covering it well. It was quite possible that he hadn't even noticed.

'Ann.' The head master came up to her. 'Amschel wanted a word with you, I know. He might ring you at home later on if you're going to be in.'

'Yes, that's fine,' she said. Then, as Theo was standing a few feet away and looking in the other direction, she couldn't help adding, 'Did he not do very well?' She hated herself for asking it, but she had to know.

'Um . . .' Tim looked momentarily flustered. 'Musically he's very good; very talented. As far as we could tell. We just had reservations about whether he'd fit in. But we'll ring and talk about it.'

'Thank you.'

By the end of the afternoon, they had appointed two children, a boy and a girl, though they had possible vacancies for up to four. But by then Theo and Ann had gone home, so they knew nothing about it. Ann had brightly made tea, and intended to ask him if he would like to watch television but had never quite got round to it, and was dutifully sitting in the kitchen with him and desperately trying not to convey her disappointment, when Amschel rang and asked Theo if he would come back and sing some more for him, the next day.

After lunch on Sunday, therefore, Ann had walked him over to the college and left him there, and Amschel had spent the best part of the afternoon with him, showing him how the vast Chapel organ worked, and explaining how to exploit the unique seven-second echo, and letting him fill the wonderful medieval space with his piping little untried treble.

And, as it turned out, Amschel had won. Tim, the head master, and Geoff, the head of music, had thought that such an eccentric and unbiddable boy would never cope with the rigours of the choir. But it was Amschel who would have to work with him. He wanted him. His would be the final decision. And of course they had, in the end, taken into account the trauma of his father's death, barely six months earlier.

Ann got up, showered, breakfasted, went round the corner to get a paper, and sat at the kitchen table till gone ten o'clock reading it and staring out of the window and looking forward to Theo coming home for the afternoon, it being Saturday.

Suddenly, and for no reason that she could afterwards discover, as if a cloud had lifted or a weight been taken off her shoulders, she went into the sitting room and picked up her violin from under the piano, took it out of its case and tuned it up. It was the first time for months. She played a couple of scales, and, though her fingers were stiff and clumsy and the scales were not nearly nimble enough, she felt the warmth of the sound under her chin and the voice of the instrument made her feel excited and alive again.

It was the way forward. She must practise, practise, work, work, work. She had loved her music once, and would again. No, she wouldn't be a world-famous violinist. But then, she probably wouldn't have been even if she hadn't married Alan. And if she hadn't met Alan she wouldn't have had Theo, anyway. She played a few bars of this, and a few bars of that, and eventually tried the Bruch, the concerto which had made her the toast of her year at the Royal College, for a few months at least.

The tune wound and leapt and sang, the fingers scattered about, the violin followed as best it could, and Ann was genuinely losing herself in the music and finding some of the relief that she had needed for so long.

And then suddenly, as if cold water had been thrown over her, she forgot the next note. She stopped. I must find the music, she thought, before I lose where I am. The telephone was ringing. Perhaps it was that which had broken her concentration. I shall answer the telephone, and then go straight to the music cupboard and find the Bruch concerto, she promised herself.

'Ann?' said a child's voice.

'Yes. Hello, Theo.'

'Hello. Um, Ann . . .'

'Yes. Guess what I've been doing,' she said in her excitement.

'Um. Dunno.'

'Playing the Bruch violin concerto.'

'Oh. What, on your violin?'

'No, on a jew's harp.'

'Oh.'

'*Dummkopf*. Of course on my violin.'

'Oh.' He laughed. 'Yeah. *Dummkopf*. What's a jew's harp?'

'Little twangy thing, I don't know. How are you?'

'Fine. How does the Bruch violin concerto go?'

'Yum te *tah* tjum! Diddle-iddle-iddle-iddle . . .'

'Oh, I know!' Theo cried. 'All double-stopping, isn't it? Really scrunchy.'

'That's it. I'll play it to you this afternoon.'

'Oh, Ann.'

'Yes.'

'I'm not coming home this afternoon.'

'Oh.'

'D'you mind?'

'Not at all,' she said, far too emphatically, trying hard to hide the yawning hole that had opened in her life. It was good, it was very good that he was becoming more independent. 'Are you doing something interesting?'

'I'm meeting a writer and taking her out to tea.'

'Really? Anyone I've heard of?'

'Cassandra Sanderson.'

'No, I don't think . . . Oh, wait a minute. Doesn't she write children's books?'

'Well, yes, but they're not very good.'

'D'you want to bring her here?'

'That's very kind of you, but no, thank you. So, I'll see you another time. Are you coming to Chapel tonight? Or tomorrow?'

'Would you like me to?'

'If you'd like to.'

'Okay. I probably will.'

'Oh, and Ann?'

'Yes?'

'The school says I have to have permission from you to go out with a stranger. Can you just tell Miss Jo that's it's all right? Here she is.'

'Hello, Mrs Wedderburn?' It still vaguely amused Ann that the school always called her by her married name, though she had never used it herself. Now what on earth do I do? she thought. I don't know anything about Cassandra Sanderson. She could be a child-murdering psychopath for all I know.

'Hello, Miss Jo. I gather Theo's going out for the afternoon with a Miss Sanderson.' Suddenly, and for no reason, Ann felt the tears coming. She held her breath, and could feel her eyes beginning to overflow. She felt instant humiliation, and could only be thankful that they were speaking over the telephone, so the other woman couldn't see her face. Why had she reacted like this? No one had mentioned Alan. There was no reason for him to come into her mind.

'Oh. We got the impression you'd arranged it. Is it . . .'

'Yes, that's quite all right, it's fine.' I mustn't cry, I mustn't. I mustn't let Theo down, she thought. He can't have his mother blubbing on the telephone to his teachers. What would the other boys say? she thought wildly, not pausing to ask how on earth they would ever know. I must get off the telephone quickly. Go away, go away, Miss Jo.

She also, urgently, wanted to be alone because she so longed to be able to weep, uninhibited. She knew the tears would be such a help, such a comfort, if only she could sob, uninterrupted, for ten minutes. She didn't need a friend with an arm around her shoulders. All she needed was the solitude to cry and cry, and then she would be able to bear Theo's not coming that afternoon.

It was a Sunday afternoon. It was May. Ann and Alan and Theo were going for a picnic. Ann and Theo had filled a basket with sandwiches and pork pies and tomatoes and bananas and a flask of tea for Alan and Ann, and a bottle of lemonade for Theo, and finally Theo's nature project from school, which Ann was going to help him with after Alan left them for work, when they'd had lunch. They were going to put the picnic basket in Alan's bicycle basket, which was large because he used it to take music and robes and things to Chapel. Then they waited for him to come home from Matins.

They sat on the doorstep of their house. Ann had on a wide, cream-coloured skirt, and a large hat to keep the sun off her eyes. Theo was wearing some new shorts which Granny, Alan's mummy, had given him the week before, for his sixth birthday. While they sat on the doorstep Ann was trying to explain to Theo a game she had played when she was a little girl. It was called 'Jacks', and as far as she could remember, you threw something in the air and called a number before the Jacks landed, and then she wasn't quite sure what you were supposed to do after that. She kept picking up some stones from their gravel path, and saying, 'All right, call a number,' and Theo would go, 'Three hundred and nineteen and a half – no, wait a minute, three hundred and nineteen and, er, point five,' and she would say, 'No, not that number. Four, or something like that,' and then she would say, 'Now, what on earth do I do now?' and Theo would shake his head, and then Ann would wrinkle up her nose and **giggle**, and then they put their heads together and gave each other a hug and laughed, with the sun in their eyes, utterly happy, and it was just when they were doing this that Alan's bicycle scrunched and turned on the drive and he jumped off, pulling off his bicycle clips and throwing his bicycle against the wall of the house.

'Hello. We were waiting for you.'

'Humm,' Alan said, getting ready to lock up his bicycle.

'You needn't lock it up.'

'Why?' he said, barely looking at them.

'We're going for a picnic. Remember?' It seemed to Theo that Ann tried not to show that she minded he had forgotten. They had spent quite a long time getting the picnic ready. Theo didn't mind, particularly, but he wondered whether it was the kind of thing that adults minded.

'Hell,' Alan said. 'Oh, hell.'

Ann said nothing for a few moments. Then she said, 'Come on, Tippy,' to Theo. Tippy is Theo's nickname. And, to Alan, 'It doesn't matter, if you're busy. Theo and I will go. It's okay.'

'What? No, don't worry, I'll come. What time can we get back?'

'Come on, Theo.' Ann took him by the hand and led him to her bicycle, which was already waiting propped against the wall. He was getting almost too big for the child seat, but he was far too young to ride a bicycle on his own, on the road. That was what Ann said anyway, and Alan agreed.

'I said I'd come, didn't I?'

Ann turned and looked at Alan. Theo wasn't quite sure whether she was angry, or just sad. When Ann gets angry, she goes quiet and a bit cold. She doesn't get cross or shout. She just goes very quiet. 'Yes, you said you'd come. But we don't want you to come as a favour. We've been looking forward to it, and we thought you'd enjoy it too. We don't want you to come and wish you were at home, looking at your watch all the time. If you'd rather be at home working, you stay at home and work.' Theo noticed that she was talking as if she knew what he, Theo, felt as well as what she felt herself, and he wondered whether she was right. Would he prefer Alan to stay at home? If they were going to have an argument, he would certainly prefer it. How did Ann know what he felt? he wondered. Or perhaps he simply felt it because that's what she said he'd feel.

He looked at his father's face and felt a knot tightening inside his stomach. Please, he thought. Please, please, don't. And he thought of the two of them, him and Ann, going around the kitchen with the basket open on the table in the middle, wrapping things in silver foil and boiling the kettle to make the tea, and smiling as they made the picnic. When they put the pork pies in, Ann had said, 'I think Daddy'll like these, don't you?' And then she had said, 'I wonder if we should put in a bottle of lager for him, what do you think? No, he's got Evensong. He won't want to drink anything.' And then, 'It's a shame we haven't got any cake. He would have liked cake. Do you think we should make some? Oh, no, look at the time. He'll be home in half an hour.' And Theo felt his eyes pricking, and he thought, please, don't.

And then, as he looked at Alan's face, he saw something go. It was like watching a puppet, and then having someone cut the strings. At that moment, he knew it would be all right. 'I'm sorry,' Alan said. 'I just forgot. I'm sorry.' Then he gave Ann a big hug, which opened after a minute to include Theo as well, and he kissed Ann, and said, 'Come on. I've had a foul morning and I'm about to have a worse afternoon, and what I need more than anything in the world is a lovely picnic in the sun with my wife and child.' He put his bicycle clips back on, and picked up the picnic basket from the doorstep and put it in his bicycle basket without them even telling him that was what he was supposed to do, and said, 'Where are we going? Grantchester?' and got on his bicycle without waiting for an answer, and Ann and Theo got on theirs and wobbled to the road behind him.

Soon he and Ann caught up with Alan, and they bicycled 'two abreast', which was something Ann was always telling him they mustn't do if the roads were busy, and Ann asked Alan about his morning, and he said something about his best tenor being sent down if he failed his exams, and the senior chorister breaking his voice, and Theo didn't really listen but simply sat on the seat on the front of Ann's bicycle with the sun on his face and his eyes shut and the wind blowing against him and cooling him. Sent down where? he wondered. He tried to think of somewhere that was down. The river was down. You had to scramble down the bank to get to the river. He imagined the best tenor, in his father's choir, failing his exams and being sent down from the Chapel to the river to fetch some water. He pictured the huge lawn in front of the Chapel, and the tenor walking round it to get to the river. He didn't know whether tenors were allowed to walk across the lawn. Alan was allowed to walk across the lawn, so when he was with him, Theo was allowed to walk across the lawn too, holding on to his father's hand and trying to keep up with him, as his black gown fluttered behind them like a crow flapping.

He didn't need to ask about breaking a voice. He knew all about that: when boys get to be teenagers, they break their voices and mustn't use them for a long time. That's when they leave the choir. If the senior chorister was breaking his voice now, it would be a nuisance for his father; he would have to bring in one of the probationers, and he had a recording coming up soon. Theo wondered why the senior chorister hadn't waited until after the recording before breaking his voice. It would be more sensible to break your voice in the summer holidays, so the new children coming in the next term could make up for the boys who were leaving. Theo decided that, when he became a chorister, he would break his voice in the summer holidays.

They had their picnic in Grantchester, sitting by the river. When they had finished, Alan put the basket back on his bicycle, and gave Ann a long kiss, and gave Theo a hug, and then went back for Evensong. Then Ann got Theo's exercise book from out of her big handbag and spread it on the grass.

'Right, now, what are you supposed to be doing?'

'Mmm. Dunno.'

'"See how much nature you can find near your house,"' she read. '"You may want to get an adult to help you. Can you find snails? Worms? Birds? Flowers? Draw or collect anything you like, and come to school on Monday ready to write about it." Okay. What shall we look at first?'

'Mmm,' Theo said again.

'Come on, Tippytips.' Ann looked around them. They were

sitting in a field, on the bank of the Cam, surrounded by cows, and cowpats, and cowparsley, and nature as far as the eye could see. It was hard to see anything that wasn't nature, except for a punt full of undergraduates coming noisily upriver towards them. 'What do you want to do?'

'Go for a walk,' he said, putting the side of his face on his knees and smiling at her.

'Well, that seems pretty reasonable,' she said. 'Come on, up you get. Let's fold up this rug and put it in my bag, and we'll see what we can see if we walk along this bank.

'There's a beautiful wood through some fields somewhere. Alan and I went there once, when we were students, visiting Cambridge. I wonder if I can remember the way?' So they had set off walking along the road, hand in hand, and Ann pointed out to Theo the banks of wildflowers along the way. He looked down at the bright buttercups, shining and smiling in the afternoon sun, and Ann picked one and held it under his chin, and said, 'Yes, you like butter,' which is silly because a buttercup will glow under anyone's chin, especially if the sun is shining – but then, perhaps it should, because everyone likes butter. Then Theo picked one, and held it under Ann's chin, and saw the bright yellow colour reflected on the darkness of her skin in the shadow, and smiled at her and nodded.

'It's like a medieval painting, isn't it?' Ann said, looking around them. 'Like a tapestry.' Theo wasn't sure, because he wasn't sure how a medieval painting differed from a normal painting, but there was a framed tapestry on the wall of Alan's mother's house, with a unicorn rearing and a girl with long blonde hair, and when he thought about it, he could see what Ann meant. The bank along the side of the road was green, but the daisies and buttercups were like white and yellow stitches, flecked on the grass, clumsily, like a tapestry. Not drawn, delicately and in detail, with a careful pencil, but scattered, like embroidery, wherever someone had managed to remember that they needed another colour.

They walked further on up the road, into a tunnel of light green, which reached up, up, arching above them like the walls of the Chapel, as delicate, as vast, as impossible to imagine how it was made. As in the Chapel, the fingers stretched above them, aching to meet and interlock at the top but never quite getting there, never quite grasping hands together, for ever just about to. Like the carvings in the stonework, the tiny leaves were made with the most delicate and careful detail, intricate, painstaking, as if someone had spent hours, days, over each one. Just so, different workmen in the Chapel, hundreds of years ago, had carved their own details in the stone, like the mother of Jesus hidden in the seed of a flower in the south-west corner. But when you looked casually you didn't see all this minuscule work that someone had put in; what you saw was the huge, strong trees, the strength, the bigness, the way it went on nearly up to the sky. What mattered was the whole thing, the white stone, the dappled green, stretching up to eternity.

They walked happily on up the road, through the light which filtered through the green stained glass of the leaves, and suddenly Ann's grip on his hand tightened. 'Look,' she said. 'Look at those lovely flowers.' There, in the gentle green shadow of the trees, on the bank, were tiny white splashes of flowers, like toothpaste flicked on the grass, and then a deep deep blue, which seemed to glow with a life that was more than colour. 'Bluebells,' Ann said. 'Aren't they beautiful?' And even as she said it, the sun came out from behind a cloud, and the bluebells became so much brighter they seemed to move.

'Look,' she said again, 'lords and ladies, I think.' She bent down and showed him a leaf, wrapped round a little purple finger, which didn't have anything to do with lords and ladies, as far as Theo could see. Toad in the hole, now; that would have been a good name for it. 'I haven't seen that since I was a child. It's got another name. A better one. Something in a pulpit. Can't remember. Come on; I think we'll find the wood this way.' And she let him climb over a wooden fence on to a little step, and they wandered through a field full of thistles and buttercups, towards some trees and a barbed-wire fence on the other side.

Then they heard an angry rattle, like a football rattle, amongst the trees beyond the fence, and an alarmingly large brown bird with brightly coloured turquoise flashes and a long tail came clattering out, low, towards them, before veering off to one side. 'Pheasant,' Ann said. 'And that clapping noise, up there, is a wood pigeon.'

'Look,' Theo said, and they stopped at an untidy pile of soft, grey feathers, whitish at the tips. In the middle of the pile was a dark, hard little mess, as if a giant child had been naughty and spat out his dinner, and large ugly flies settled and buzzed around it. Theo didn't ask what it was.

Suddenly, Theo heard thunder drumming the ground, and three huge and terrifying chestnut horses pounded over the crest of the field and bore down on them. They're going to kill us, Theo thought, and realised he had never before seen such magnificent creatures. They took no notice of Theo or Ann at all, but thundered up to the gate where a woman was calling, and where she put a halter on one of them and led him away, through the gate. The other two turned, affronted, their legs all wrong and off balance from the way they'd stopped suddenly. They stared at Theo and Ann as if it were their fault that they had been left behind. But in the end they simply snorted, and shook their ears, and loped off to eat the daisies and buttercups, as if they didn't mind after all.

When Theo and Ann got to the fence, they couldn't see where to climb under it or over it. Everywhere, there were tall, very stinging-looking nettles, and Theo only had shorts on, and Ann the thin skirt down to her ankles, and sandals. In front of them, suspended in mid-air, miraculously, was a tiny leaf, turning slightly in the breeze. How does it stay there? Theo asked himself. What is it doing? He went nearer, looking for evidence of a spider's thread, or anything that could explain this strange phenomenon, but there was nothing.

'I know there's a lovely wood somewhere,' Ann said. 'I know it's going to be worth it.' They wandered along the fence until they found a gap in the nettles, and Ann climbed over the wooden bar and Theo climbed under it, and she said, 'Here we are,' and stepped, half running, down a mossy bank so as not to lose her balance, and then suddenly cried out, and Theo's heart leapt to his head and he couldn't breathe and he lost his mother for ever in a pit of quicklime and didn't know what to do or where to run for help, and then his breath came back and he could see again and Ann was up to her ankles in wet black mud. And laughing. She was laughing, and holding her arms out towards him, and saying, What a twit I am and can you help me out but do be careful, darling, don't step too close. Theo's chest swelled with pride, and he stepped down the bank carefully, and stood on a dry strong log and held out his hand to her, and she squelched out of the ditch.

'Come on, let's see what we can find.' So they picked their way carefully through the elder, which crept along the ground, and under brambles, which tried to pull their hair, and over logs that were covered in slate-grey mushrooms, like shells, or like cockles clinging to old wooden breakers on the beach, and they passed deep burrows and tunnels dug underneath huge tree roots, which could have been Badger's den in *The Wind in the Willows*, or Bilbo Baggins's front drive, and Theo longed to be small enough to climb down them and pull the door knob. Eventually they reached a little lane through the wood which looked as if they might be able to follow it.

And then suddenly, as if they had landed on another planet, they saw them, like clouds and clouds of blue so intense it hurt the eyes; as if a painter had decided to paint a woodland scene with normal paints, and then had put one magic colour on which leapt out of the canvas, which was more real than the rest of the painting, which was three-dimensional on a two-dimensional picture. They were more real than real life. And they went on, and on and on, through the trees as far as the eye could see, beyond the slender tree trunks and the shivering leaves, and the drifts of last year's dead and rustling leaves, wave upon wave of bluebells like an ever-moving, ever-living sea. Theo thought he had never seen anything so breathlessly, frighteningly beautiful, swishing and washing over the velvety mossy banks, swimming over the pale green of the rest of the wood like oil on water. Here and there, there were other things to see: the pinky-purple of woodland campion, and the white of wood anemone and wild garlic, and the different kinds of moss, hairy, or soft, or springy. On the path there was the delicate skeleton of one of last year's leaves, pressed into the dry earth as if it were going to be a fossil in millions of years' time. Theo looked at its gently pale grey colour and wondered whether some future schoolboy, when the world was very different – if there were still schoolboys then, and not simply angels or Martians – would find it as a fossil in this wood, and take it to school on a Monday morning. Then he looked up again, and saw that the bluebells had multiplied even in the time he had taken to glance at the path, and were shaking and dipping and rolling with colour way off into the undergrowth.

He and Ann walked on, hand in hand, saying nothing. They must have been thinking the same thing. There was nothing else anyone could have thought, and it couldn't be put into words.

There was a rustling noise, over to their right – Theo knew it was his right, because it was the side of his bow-hand, which was the right – and they wondered what person or dog or whatever was going to disturb the wood. Then they saw a squirrel, noticing them and darting up a tree out of their way. A smaller rustling continued, and, without talking about it, they both stopped to see what would happen. There was a younger squirrel fiddling about, running around in the clean dry leaves. It was a baby squirrel. It must be: it was too small, and more finely formed than the other, and was not behaving as a woodland squirrel should. Theo had seen tame squirrels before, in the park, which come up to you and ask for bread, but this wasn't like that. This was like a wild squirrel which was so young, and so wild, that it didn't know it was supposed to be frightened of humans; not like a tame squirrel which has decided not to be because it likes having the picnic food. This squirrel had never had any picnic food, Theo felt sure.

They walked, without talking, through the wood and the bluebells and down to a little stream, where the thin trunk of a young tree lay across the trickling, singing water as if to provide a bridge for the little animals to run across. Down in the stream, nests of twigs had gathered together, put there by the water, perhaps, or by some animal which wanted to dam the stream. Do they have otters in England? Theo wanted to ask, but instead said, 'Who planted them all?'

'Who planted them? God, I suppose,' Ann replied, which Theo thought was the first time he could remember either of his parents mentioning this strange and mysterious person. He imagined Him, in gumboots and a jacket, slightly younger than Alan and with darker hair, going through the wood with a basket of bulbs and planting them everywhere. Theo knew the basket: it was a dark brown, old-fashioned-looking basket with a slightly crooked handle, which stood in their back porch, and Ann had once told him that, when he was born, it had arrived full of begonias from a friend. This basket never ran out of bluebells. Every time God planted them all the basket just filled up again.

Once Theo and Ann had walked into Chapel when the choir was rehearsing something. He and Ann had stood at the back of the ante-chapel listening, and someone, a boy called Harrington who was the senior chorister at the time, was singing alone. It was, quite simply, the loveliest thing Theo had experienced in his life. The sound rose, clear as a pipe but far more lovely, like a lark rising up and up, higher and higher into the heavens, and then seemed to show you the view and say, This is possible and dream it now and it is all there ever needs to be. Even the words of the song were soaring far over the horizon: *In the wilderness build me, build me a nest.* Theo thought, I never want anything in my life but this.

When he heard it, he realised, at the back of his mind, that it would have to stop eventually. But it doesn't matter, he thought; he will sing it again. He must. Nothing could be so wonderful, and not be repeated. *And remain there, for ever at rest,* Harrington sang. *For e-e-e-ver at rest.* The organ played a chord, softly, and tailed away.

In the silence that followed, Alan appeared from somewhere and told Harrington how to improve it next time. Then Theo knew he would never hear it again, ever, like that, in his whole life. Later Alan had said yes, some of Mendelssohn was tolerable and Harrington wasn't too bad when he put a bit of effort in, and perhaps Theo could learn it himself one day. Theo hadn't especially wanted to learn it. It was too beautiful for you to think, I want to do this. You were just happy that such beauty existed.

So that day, when Theo saw the bluebells, he knew he would never see them again, that he would never see such loveliness repeated, in exactly that way, if he lived for a hundred years. So he knew, too, that he would have to keep them, in his memory, to call on for the rest of his life.

They turned to go home, and walked back through the wood.

Theo had just thought he was getting used to the sight, when they reached a gate which led out of the wood, and they turned and saw a world of blue flooding and filling every crack and crevice of all they could see, and he gasped as if water had been thrown over him, and clung on to Ann, and wanted to cry.

And this was what Miss Susan wanted him to write about on Monday. In the few minutes she allowed for one lesson, which usually seemed to Theo to be over almost before it had begun, she expected him to capture the blue that danced before the eyes and almost sang out it was so loud, and the green chapel of ever-stretching leaves, and the tiny leaf suspended in mid-air, hanging by nothing, and the splattered paint of buttercups and meadow-vetch on the grassy bank. She expected him to compress it all into a bottle, and dip his pen into the inkwell of his imagination, except that he had to use a pencil at school because that was the school rule, and write it all on to the blank sheet of paper. She might as well have told him to climb out of the window, and jump to the moon.

His father might perhaps have put it into music. The tall trees could be a long high note on an oboe; and the squirrels would be scuttlings on a piccolo. The bluebells would be harps. Of course. Arpeggio after arpeggio on half a dozen harps. He didn't think Miss Susan would understand it, though, if he were to hand it in.

It would be cool to invent a computer which would photograph your imagination, and then print it out for you. It might be possible. If you turn your computer off by mistake, or wipe out a file, clever people can make the computer remember it again. It wouldn't be very different to remake something which you hadn't put on your computer yet. It was all there, in your brain, just as it was all in the computer's memory somewhere. It was strange that they had to learn handwriting at school, when a computer could do it so much better.

Theo thought of the endless sky of flowers deep in the wood, and looked down at his perfectly white, untouched, piece of paper. It expressed the walk as well as anything else could have done.

'Could you hand your work in now, please?' Miss Susan said.

When he was kept in during break that day, staring at his white sheet of paper, he tried to banish the beautiful wood from his mind. He knew that, if his mother hadn't taken him for that walk which he would never forget even to the end of his days, that if she had just shown him a picture of a daisy in a book, he could have done the work for Miss Susan. He could have said, 'A daisy is a flower with white petals and a yellow centre. It grows in lawns and you can make daisy chains out of it and it is usually a few centimetres high.' He needn't even have said that he didn't know whether it had stamens or how it reproduced. And he knew, if he had said this, if he had written these two or three stupid sentences, he would have got 'Top marks. Excellent', written in his book. He had seen it in other people's books, and if only he could have done this much for Miss Susan, he knew that she would have been very pleased with him. And if his mother hadn't taken him to the beautiful wood he might have been able to do it. Perhaps.

But he didn't want to blame the wood because of it. He didn't want it spoilt for him by Miss Susan shouting at him about his nature project. He had to keep them in separate compartments. If he could tell his mind that the wood, and the walk with Ann, had nothing to do with his biology homework and nothing to do with Miss Susan, then she wouldn't be able to get at it, and his wood would be beyond her reach, and still be beautiful.

When they came in at the end of break, his piece of paper was still blank, but his wood was all right. It was more distant in his mind – he had had to hide it away, and he wasn't sure whether he knew how to get it back – but Miss Susan hadn't touched it, and that was the important thing.

This time he was to stay in after lunch as well. Miss Susan said, 'I can't cope any more. You can wait outside Miss Jameson's office, and see what she says.'

Theo didn't mind. He liked Miss Jameson. She was tall, and handsome, and taught them interesting things in the science lessons. After lunch he asked Miss Helena, who was supervising, if he should go to Miss Jameson's office now.

'I don't think so,' Miss Helena said. 'Shouldn't you go out to play, with the other children?'

'He's supposed to stay in, Miss Helena,' the other children

said. 'He can't do his work. He can't even get his boots on in time. Miss Susan gets really cross.'

'That's enough,' Miss Helena said.

'Everyone gets really cross.' They were all talking now, explaining to Miss Helena. 'He can't do anything.' 'He's not really stupid, miss, it's just . . .'

'That's enough!' she said, and silence began to gather, again, around the corners of the room. Theo's ears hurt, as if they'd been scalded with too hot a bath. He had nowhere to look. Miss Helena was kind, and seemed to understand a little, and that made it very difficult. His eyes pricked and smarted, and he had to open them very wide.

'You wait here, Theo, and I'll go and find out what you're supposed to be doing,' she said gently.

When she came back, she said, 'I'm sorry, you're right. Miss Susan says you are to wait outside Miss Jameson's room until she comes out.'

Theo nodded dumbly. He told himself he was glad he didn't have to struggle with his shoes, and compete with the other children in the playground. He was also glad he didn't have to struggle with his picture of the wood any more. He would wait until they were all out of the building, and then he would remember his wood.

There was the noise and bustle of children packing away lunch and changing their shoes and talking about what game they would play, and then it was blessedly, blissfully quiet. Miss Jameson's door was shut. He could think about what he liked, now, and no one would interfere.

He had forgotten to go to the toilet after lunch. His parents called it the loo. It wasn't an unpleasant feeling, but he hoped Miss Jameson would appear soon so he could ask her permission to go. He held his legs together, and tried to remember the wood. It was the colour, wasn't it, that he had liked so much? The colour, and being with Ann, and if he were in the wood now Ann would say you can just go against that tree there, and then they could have gone on with the walk, though it wasn't that bad, really, he was sure he had needed the toilet worse than this before. He tried to conjure up the logs, the stinging nettles, the smell of crushed elder, and how hard it was to enjoy thinking about it while he had to keep his legs so tightly together, and concentrate so hard on not thinking about where Miss Jameson was.

Perhaps he could knock on the door, and see if she was in there. But he had been told to wait there. He could hang on, if he really tried and tried. He put his hands between his legs. What funny pictures they were, on the wall, not funny really, but he was just trying to think of anything, so he needn't think how much he wanted the toilet. There was a face, like a big red sun, why is it, I wonder, that they all hate me here? It's not hate, really, it's just, please come, Miss Jameson, it's just, please please, stupid stupid, am I really stupid, I can't, I can't stop, wet and warm down the inside of my legs, and on my hands, I need to wash my hands, and prickly and sticky and it will get cold now with the air on it, and what will I say to Miss Susan and she will shout again and all the class will laugh laugh laugh because I'm stupid stupid.

He didn't allow himself to cry until he was tucked up in bed under his duvet that night, and nobody knew he was there.

Then it came back to him, the humiliation.

He had had to change his trousers, and cope with Miss Susan's being kind and saying nothing about it, and everybody's being quiet and not shouting at him, which suddenly seemed worse because it was so odd.

He went home for tea that day in the wrong trousers, and Ann got a note in his satchel which simply said, 'Theo had a little accident in school,' and he said nothing and hoped the rest of the day would disappear quickly.

But when he finally got under his duvet and nobody knew he was there, he wondered about the person who planted all the bluebell bulbs; and wondered whether He, alone, saw Theo tucked up in his bed; and at last he was allowed, by that strictest of critics, himself, to cry and cry and cry. If you are there, planter of the bulbs, oh, if you are there . . .

*   *   *

When Alan came in from college, an hour or two later, he pulled his son's duvet off his face so he could breathe properly, and thought how happy and peaceful he looked.

Just as it should be, he thought. Not a care in the world.

7

'. . . throughout Mozart's youth and manhood it never seems to have occurred to anyone, that, slave as he was to his creative gift and to the exhausting physical work it entailed, he should have been shown some leniency with regard to the trivial matters he occasionally forgot or neglected' –
Charlotte Haldane, *Mozart*

Theo squatted on the ground, poking under the leaves with a little twig. He was comfortable. After morning school he had taken off his uniform and put on, instead, a pair of bright green corduroy trousers and a red sweat shirt and some very muddy trainers. Then he had gone outside and waited in the school drive for Cassandra Sanderson. As she didn't know the school, he thought he ought to wait at the end of the drive, near the road, so she would see him and know she was in the right place. She wouldn't know what he looked like, and of course, coming to a school, there were plenty of other boys there so she might get confused. He, on the other hand, would probably recognise her. She would look a little bit like the photograph on the jacket of her book. But not much like: people never look like their passport photographs, after all. She would be a woman on her own, not too old, looking around as if she didn't quite know where she was. So for the first few minutes Theo had looked down the road at every woman who came along, but none of them had caught his eye, and all had walked on past the school without a glance. One or two parents, or simply mothers, had come in their cars and turned into the drive, but you could tell the mothers:

they didn't hesitate; they didn't even think about what they were doing.

It had never occurred to Theo for a moment that Caz might not be coming.

But now he had forgotten why he was out here. He squatted, watching a worm bunch its body up thickly, and then pull it out again to a thin line, like pulling out chewing gum. He looked around for a suitable twig. The stalks of the fallen chestnut leaves were too flimsy. Eventually he found a bent little stick with the bark flaking off, dark with mud and dirt. It almost crumbled at his touch. He shuffled back, squatting, to find the worm and touch its side, to see it curl round in an automatic reflex. But it had burrowed itself into the ground and was disappearing. Theo was glad. If an earthworm stays in ultraviolet light for more than twenty minutes it begins to stiffen, and soon after that it will be dead.

'Hello.'

Theo looked up. 'Hello,' he said. 'Look, there it goes. You can just see its tail. Oop – gone!' He laughed, then became serious again. 'Do you call it a tail, if it's part of your body? I wonder what it's like. They don't have a brain, like us: just a kind of centre, for the nerves. More like a computer, I suppose. But they must feel, mustn't they? It must hurt when you tread on them.'

'I don't know,' Caz replied. She squatted on the ground beside him. 'What amazes me is the way other people think they know whether it hurts or not. People who like eating frogs' legs, or crabs, or lobsters. They say, "It doesn't hurt, if you're a crab, and you're put in cold water and brought up to the boil." But how could the crab possibly let them know if it did?'

'I've never had frogs' legs,' the child replied.

'They taste quite nice actually. Rather like tender chicken, in garlic butter. Do you like garlic?'

'I like it the way Ann cooks it. She's my mother.'

'Then you'd probably like frogs' legs. I used to, until I read about the way the French cut their legs off without even bothering to kill them, and toss them in a pile on top of a load of other, legless, twitching, living frogs.'

'I will never eat them. Never.'

'I didn't think you would.'

'I'm Theo.' Theo, squatting as he was, rested his elbows on his knees and his chin on his forearms, and smiled. She smiled back. They made no attempt to shake hands. 'I know who you are because I've seen the picture on the back of your book, but you've got no way of knowing who I am, have you?'

'Yes.' Caz considered for a moment. 'The way you speak is consistent with your letters. Also you're out here alone, so you're probably waiting for somebody. You've changed out of your school uniform. You're waiting near the end of the drive, as if the person you're expecting doesn't know the school. And you spoke to me as if you might know, or guess, who I was, as Theo would do. So . . .'

'I read a Sherlock Holmes book once and it was a bit like that. Perhaps it's because you're a writer. I didn't like it much though.'

'Why not?'

'Umm . . .' Theo was quiet for a long time, Caz thought probably a good half-minute or more. He was staring out, under the shade from the chestnut trees, through the school gates and over the road opposite. A car slowed and turned into the drive, but he didn't seem to be looking at it. Behind them, a chestnut fell, with the crackle and snap of breaking twigs before it reached the ground. One of the children shouted 'Ego!' and three or four of them ran and gathered round it to fight amicably for possession. Theo turned and looked at them, and then looked Caz in the face. 'Er, what did you say?'

'It doesn't matter.'

'Why didn't I like it? Perhaps because it was fiction. I'm not sure if I like fiction.'

'But my book was fiction.' Then, as he looked at her and frowned, she said, 'Well, it was sort of fiction.'

'I thought it was, what do you call it? That Greek word, like biology.'

'Biography. Autobiography. Writing about the life of the self.'

'That's good. Is that what it means? I'd like to learn Greek, but you can't until the Upper Fourth, and even then choristers can't, usually. Only if you're very clever. I'm quite clever, but I'm very slow.'

'Are you?'

'Apparently.'

Across the muddy football pitch a determined-looking woman with a no-nonsense bust was homing in on them. The word 'matron' came to Caz's mind, along with one or two epithets from Wagner, while memories of a hockey teacher she had endured a lifetime ago made her tense.

'Good afternoon. Have you come to take Theo out?' Caz hesitated. The arrangement had been that Theo would take her out, so this question caught her off balance. 'We usually ask for written notice from the parents: I'm sure you'll understand why. And we must see proof of identity.'

'I'm afraid I don't carry much.' Caz looked helplessly at Theo.

'Oh!' he said suddenly. 'Yes, I know!' And with that, he jumped up and started running towards the school.

'Huh! Now he's gone,' the size forty-four said unnecessarily.

Caz said nothing. She watched the little figure running across the gravel in front of the school and reaching the steps up to the main door. He is ungainly, she thought. I bet he's no good at football. I wonder whether it matters in a school like this.

There then followed an awkward silence for a couple of long minutes. I'm not going to break it, Caz thought. She can jolly well start the conversation herself. Eventually she did. 'You're a friend of Mrs Wedderburn, are you?'

'Never met her in my life,' Caz said with a certain amount of relish, and silence fell again.

Finally, just as Caz was about to weaken and comment on the conker season, they heard a cry of, 'I've got it! I've got it! Here we are!' and Theo was beside them again, with a copy of Caz's book in his hand.

'Theo, really! Where on earth have you been? You've kept everyone waiting yet again.'

'But you said we needed to prove who she was. This is the proof. You see: photograph. Cassandra Sanderson on the front. That's who she is. Why did you ask for it if you didn't want it?'

She chose to ignore this question, and turned, instead, to Caz. 'You'd better get him back by half past four. They leave for Chapel at five, and he'll have to change first.'

Caz waited until she was nearly out of view before saying, 'Yes, Attila,' and then asking Theo, 'Who the heck was that?'

'Oh, she's all right really. That's Mrs Havent. I think it's her husband's fault,' he added cryptically.

They went through college, past the Chapel, on their way to the Copper Kettle, and all the way Theo gave Caz a running commentary on what they passed, as if she were a tourist who had come especially to see Cambridge, and he her personal guide; which, after all, was what he had promised in his letter of invitation.

'Somebody committed suicide from this bridge once, in 1987 – or was it 1897? – because their exam results got mixed up with someone else's. She was a mathematician and her parents were very poor and had paid for her to come to Cambridge, and she was very clever and hoping to get some top maths prize, and when she sat Tripos, that's the exam you sit, because you used to sit it on a three-legged stool, you know, tri, like triangle, she got the results and was told she hadn't failed but she hadn't done that well, you know, got a two or whatever they call it, and she jumped off this bridge, and then it turned out she'd got the best maths result in Cambridge for, ooh, ever so long. And that's the organ scholar's room, Mr Ford, and he had too much to drink last Christmas and did midnight mass a bit, you know, drunk, with all the stops out and everything, at least we think he did because the Wachet Auf was twice as long as it should have been, and that's my favourite sheep there, with that funny black ear. Henry VI built this, well, you know, didn't build it personally, but got other people to build it for him, and he was going to put buildings on this lawn, going all the way down to the river originally, but they ran out of money or he died or something. Do you like that duck, with the turquoise, look, isn't it funny how the males are so much better looking because humans aren't like that really, are they? I mean, women have brighter dresses and things don't they?'

It wasn't until they were in the Copper Kettle and had squashed their way through the queue and had got themselves a tray with a pot of tea, a large fruit juice, a slice of apple pie for Caz, and for Theo, an éclair dripping with chocolate, and the largest scone Caz had ever seen in her life, full of jam and cream, and they had reached the check-out with about twenty-five people behind them also waiting to pay, that Theo said, 'Oops. I meant to get my post office book and take some money out. You wait here and I'll go back to school and get it. I won't be long. I can cross the road on my own, I think.'

'Hang on,' Caz said, as he began to wriggle his way through the larger adults on his way to the door. 'Theo, come back. Please!' she shouted after him, taking some money out of her back pocket and handing it to the bewildered cashier before abandoning their tray and pursuing him.

'One,' she said, putting her arm around his shoulders and propelling him back to the counter, 'it's a Saturday afternoon and the post office will be shut. Two, by the time you got back there would be a queue, all the way down King's Parade and back again, of people wanting to pay. Three, my tea would be cold. Thank you,' she said to the cashier as she took the change. 'Four, Mrs Thatcher back there would probably say it was time for you to change and leave for Chapel, and then she'd march me off to prison for letting you walk back to school unaccompanied. Five,' she said as she picked up the tray and they started to look for a seat, 'I fancy the window, don't you? Five, I've done enough waiting for you for one day. Lucky I had money on me, wasn't it?'

'Mmm. Your pie looks good,' he said, taking his scone off the tray and sitting down. 'We're lucky to get the window: it's usually full. At least, the time before when I came here it was. Thank you,' he added as she handed him the juice.

'Thank you. For the idea, if not for paying for it. You can pay next time.' They smiled, and addressed themselves to their food. Caz poured her tea. Theo picked up his éclair and took a bite. The cream erupted over his chocolately fingers, and dripped on to the plate.

'What's this book you want me to write?' she said, politely eating her apple pie with a spoon.

'A biography.'

'Who of? I don't really write biographies. I just wrote a story about myself, that's all.'

'My father.'

'Your father?'

'Alan Wedderburn. He was a famous musician.'

'Was?' Caz said, before she could stop herself.

Theo licked the chocolate off several of his fingers, and then picked up a paper napkin to wipe his hands before taking a drink of juice.

'You've got some on your nose,' Caz told him, rather unnecessarily, since he would have considerably more chocolate on his face before he had finished. 'Is your father . . .' she began, and then stopped. With an adult, she would have known how to proceed. A straight question is always best. Why should it be different for a child? Is he . . . what? No longer famous? No longer a musician? She watched him wipe his face with the inadequate paper napkin. His éclair looked tempting. 'Can I taste it?' she said, on impulse.

'Yeah.' He smiled, and handed her his plate. He has a lovely smile, she thought: it transforms his face. The éclair was surprisingly good. The cream was genuine, and the chocolate really tasted of chocolate. Caz rescued herself with her paper napkin too. 'Thank you,' he said as she gave it back.

'Why do you say he "was"?' she said at last.

Theo seemed to think for minute. Then he looked at her with his wide blue eyes. He hesitated. Eventually he lowered his eyes, and stared at her plate.

'Can I try yours?' he said.

'Of course,' she said quickly, handing it over. 'It's rather dull compared with yours. Just an ordinary apple pie, really. Your mother probably makes better ones.'

'Adults often choose dull things, don't they? You know, plain chocolate, instead of the nice milk chocolates with strawberry filling.'

'Yes, I suppose they do,' she admitted.

'It's quite a decent apple pie, though,' he said, handing it back. 'He was murdered,' he added.

8

'Young as I am, I never go to bed without thinking that possibly
I may not be alive on the morrow' –

W.A. Mozart, to his father.
Shortly afterwords, the latter died.

It was the day before the first day of the university term. It was
early October, and the school had already been back for a month.
Alan enjoyed those weeks before the Michaelmas term, when he
would be getting to know the new probationers and reminding
the others of all the things they'd forgotten in the hazy weeks of
the summer holidays, since the children all went home after the
few weeks of mock term in July which was known colloquially
as the Long Vac Term. It was a strange time, when the earth was
shedding and dying and slowing down, but the university was
coming alive and putting forth the buds of new undergraduates
and sprouting in all directions in preparation for the coming
year. The freshers had all been arriving that day, with their
proud middle-aged fathers who felt as if they had only just
gone down themselves, and were full of tips on how to punt
properly, as if anyone should want to do such a thing in the
winter term, or how to climb into Cats via the Master's Lodge
in the middle of the night, or how to fiddle the locks which had
chained up the Trinity Hall punts thirty years before.

'. . . my college, there. Bloody good college it was too. Had a
bedder called Susie, legs like bloody tree trunks covered in blue
creepers. She used to serve tea in the bar in the afternoon, so
we called her the Tea Bag!' Then raucous, self-satisfied laughter,

while the mothers gave Sensible Advice: Make sure you get reasonably early nights, never cut a tutorial, and do enjoy yourself, dear, won't you?

By and large Alan preferred the less assured ones, particularly the choristers' parents. Sometimes they hadn't planned their children's education at all, and stood back, bemused, watching their offspring overtake them. These were the ones Alan loved. Those to whom Cambridge was a complete surprise, who never would have dreamt of private education if some aunt, or teacher, or friend who had seen a recent documentary hadn't said, 'The child has a lovely voice and what about that school that was on the telly?' Then you would see a quiet couple in their forties being shepherded and bossed around by their young child of ten or eleven, for whom the six-hundred-year-old traditions of the university held no mysteries at all. Then, Alan would feel a deep excitement stirring in him. This was what the choir was for. This was what had changed his life, when he was a boy of eight, and it was open to anyone.

He had a lot of work to do in college that night, and had planned to dine in Hall. Unaccountably, he had forgotten that, either because or in spite of its being the eve of the beginning of term, dinner was to be a formal affair, with half a dozen courses and as many wines, and it would be nine thirty or later before he could decently slip back to his room. Apparently Henry VII had visited the college five hundred years ago and taken over the work of the Founder, and this event had to be celebrated regardless of the academic demands of the institution his predecessor had troubled to found.

Accordingly, Alan spent the meal in a distracted frame of mind, making mental lists of what he wanted to do before going home that night. He was seated next to the new research fellow in statistics, a woman who seemed so aggressively feminist that she struck Alan as twenty or thirty years out of date, and he found he had nothing in common with her politically, philosophically, or in any other way he could think of. Within the first couple of minutes she had boasted that she was tone deaf, a phenomenon so rare that in any other circumstances he would have found it fascinating. But she took such a delight in her handicap, as if it gave her a moral superiority over anyone else, that it seemed to

Alan she had probably cultivated it deliberately, perhaps with the specific purpose of annoying him. Even this, he might have borne, if she hadn't gone on to say she couldn't understand why, in this day and age, a purely academic institution could spend such a shocking amount of money on a variety of snobbish drinks, when it all tasted the same to her anyway. Just like music, she concluded triumphantly: I can't see how it improves the lives of a single person on this earth.

Any minute now, Alan thought, she's going to argue that the point of Cambridge is for the technological advancement of Europe, and once she's done that she'll abolish the Chapel itself and all its staff, not to mention the best chef in the university, all the college paintings, the lawn, and the entire Classics department. Half an hour before, he had been annoyed at the idea of having to waste his evening eating and drinking. Now he felt that the college was absolutely right to insist on a decent dinner on behalf of an obscure royal visit five centuries before.

'If it all tastes the same to you,' he pointed out, 'you need imagination to understand those who can discriminate between one grape and another. But perhaps I'm being unfair: I'm asking for something which probably isn't required for your particular discipline. I must confess, numbers look much the same to me. Of course, wine and music have always been able to transform the lives of the most downtrodden and wretched people to the lives of angels, if only for an evening. Which I have yet to hear claimed for statistics.' He saw her gathering up her mental weaponry, ready for the riposte.

Then he smiled, and disarmed her completely.

It amazed him how people could change because of a smile. One could say the most outrageous things, and then smile, and the insults would be taken as compliments, or jokes, or as nothing at all. Women, he noticed, were particularly illogical in this respect, and he took satisfaction in discovering that feminist statisticians seemed no exception. He turned away from her in the hope that she wouldn't talk to him again, preferably for several terms.

He was relieved when the Master stood up and announced coffee and port wines in the Senior Common Room. Now at last he could excuse himself. He dodged through the milling dons, up to the Master, and spoke in a low voice.

'Jim, I've got a fair bit to do before tomorrow. Would you mind very much . . .' The Master looked at him for a moment, and then nodded, and Alan gratefully made his escape, uncertain whether the stern look had been one of disapproval or understanding, and now beyond caring anyway. With any luck, others would have done their preparation earlier, or would by now have given up worrying whether it got done at all; Alan hoped he wouldn't be followed by half a dozen others slipping out as well.

He dashed up to his room, flung off his gown, and put the kettle on. Ann would be expecting him within half an hour or so. Perhaps he had better ring her and say that he might be delayed. He looked at the pile of papers on his desk, and weighed up how much was urgent, and what could wait. There wasn't a great deal, in fact, that absolutely had to be done before term started. Much of it was for the Service of Nine Lessons and Carols, which they needn't start work on for a couple of weeks yet. He had scribbled down the beginning of a new descant for one of the traditional carols. He took it over to the piano and tried out the first few bars with the other parts, singing it in a weak, absurdly high falsetto while playing the melody line and the alto, tenor and bass on the piano. Yes, it was good. It started unobtrusively, in unison with the tune, as a descant sometimes should, then in the third bar it parted, initially with a discordant second, and then climbed on up. It pleased him so far. He shut his eyes, standing as he was, stooping slightly, with his fingers hovering over the keys, hearing the different lines in his head. It could dip, there, in contrary motion to the tune, which the congregation would be singing, and then soar towards the end, echoing the chorus of angels in the words. Yes! He had it.

He dashed over to his desk for a pencil, and sat down at the piano, scribbling furiously before the ideas in his ear moved on. If he could get this right, he might be able to go on and write that new carol he'd been thinking about. It was wonderful when it happened like this, tunes coming thick and fast like birds flying into a garden and settling in the trees.

It was ten to eleven when he finally looked up from the manuscript, registered the time, and got up to go home. There was no point in ringing Ann now. He'd probably get her out of bed. And by the time he rang, he'd be there, almost. He pushed his bicycle clips over his ankles, picked up his coat and keys, and slipped out.

Ann was back home. She was on the beach at Kerry, holding a pony called Robin, and soon she was going to ride him, bareback, across the sands. She loved being in Ireland because you could ride along the beach without a hard hat on. Theo came up to her holding some shells, and asking if he could become an organist, like her father. Ann hadn't realised her father could play the organ. Suddenly she remembered that there was something unpleasant, a gloomy cloud, hanging over the day somewhere. Had her father told her off? It wasn't like him. She felt a sickening sense of despair.

Then it happened. Wendy, the best rider in the school, was riding out to sea on a pony called Trouble, striding out into the Atlantic, storming the white horses that tipped the waves. This side of the peninsula was rough, and wild, and had thousands of miles of ocean before it. Trouble began to swim. Wendy had no hat on, and Ann remembered thinking that she should have: she would have been safer. Trouble's body was later recovered, washed up on the shore, but Wendy's never was.

Somebody dropped a lobster pot in the boat behind her with a slap of wood on wood, and Ann woke up, and realised she had fallen asleep half waiting for Alan. Perhaps the noise had been the garden gate slamming shut.

As she sat up in bed, she remembered how, over twenty years ago, she and her friends had avoided Wendy's parents after that, unwilling to witness their awful grief. Then she remembered what the black cloud really was. She felt drained, and heavy, thinking of the way in which Alan had left the house. She rubbed her eyes. She wouldn't be able to get back to sleep now. Not for an hour or two. She was annoyed with herself for dropping off. She had planned to be awake when Alan came in. But then, she hadn't realised it would be so late.

She pulled the duvet off her legs, and put one of her feet on the rug by the bed. She shivered. She grabbed the jumper which was at the foot of the bed, and pulled it over her head. The book that she had been reading had fallen off the bed when she fell asleep, and lay, spreadeagled awkwardly where it had landed, as if it had dislocated something in the fall. She picked it up and smoothed back the pages and closed it carefully, memorising the page number. It was annoying: Ann looked after her books, and didn't like the pages to become creased. She listened again. This time she really did hear the garden gate.

She stepped out of bed and went out on to the landing. She could hear two clocks ticking. The little battery-operated alarm clock in Theo's bedroom, which she had bought to try to help him get up in the morning, sounded softly through his open door. And her parents' grandfather clock in the hall sent a heavy, warm tick up the stairs. Extraordinarily, the two clocks had ticks which seemed to be the same length. They fitted in with each other, taking it in turns to tick, perfectly syncopated. As Ann listened, she heard the back door open. She called Alan's name, but softly, so as not to wake Theo. Then she remembered that she had shut the kitchen door as she came upstairs. If she went downstairs quietly, in her bare feet, Alan would not hear her.

Good.

Theo held his breath.

His mother was on the landing. She had been asleep, he was sure of that. After about half past ten, or perhaps a quarter to eleven, there had been silence from her room. She had probably fallen asleep about then. Before that, he thought she had been waiting for Alan to come home. Alan was often late home, but usually Theo was asleep when his father came home this late.

Tonight he had not been asleep at all. Ann had put him to bed, and read him a bedtime story as she often did, and then she had kissed him and told him she loved him and said she was going to run a bath. That was at about half past seven. Normally he didn't go to bed till nearly eight. It's funny, isn't it, that sometimes, when you go to bed early, you then can't get to sleep for ages?

Theo had read to himself, after that, till nearly nine o'clock. Eventually Ann had come in, in her dressing-gown, and said she hadn't realised he was still awake. Her eyes were a little bit red, and she looked tired. She sat on his bed, and hugged him hard, and told him she loved him again. Then she said, 'Come on, Blue Eyes. Time for sleep.'

Ann often gave him nicknames. Sometimes she called him Blue Eyes, though in fact his eyes were green. He thought they were green, anyway, though he found it quite hard to tell exactly what colour they were. Sometimes she called him Handsome or Beautiful. Sometimes Egghead or Brainbox. His father sometimes called him Dipstick, or even Wolfgang. His favourite nickname of all was Professor. But tonight, Ann had called him Blue Eyes.

Then she had turned his light out, and gone away.

He lay awake for a long time, listening to the sounds of the night. Bits of a house creak, if you listen carefully. It's because the wood and stuff that the house is made of change size when the house changes temperature. Many things do. Water, for instance, when it freezes or boils. So when the water in the wood gets hotter or colder it must make the wood change size, and that's what makes it creak for no reason, in the middle of the night. It's not for no reason of course. When we say that, we just mean for no reason that we can see. Perhaps a miracle is something that happens in a way we haven't understood yet. But then there would be fewer miracles than there used to be. And walking on the water is still a miracle, for instance. Or the music Mozart wrote when he was six.

But why does the changing of the wood's size make it creak? Theo wondered. Perhaps it rubs against something as it moves. Perhaps it says 'ow' as it stretches. People think that materials don't respond in the same way as people, but in many ways they do.

He heard Ann make the sounds of getting ready for bed. Drawers opening and shutting. Shoes being put under the bed. Sighs. The bed creaking, and then pages turning, and then the sobbing.

She thought he was asleep. She wouldn't have let him hear her crying if she thought he was awake. If she'd realised, she would have cried quietly, as she sometimes did if she thought he might hear. He wondered whether to go and give her a cuddle. He did that sometimes. Sometimes, he would ask her what the matter was, and she would say 'Nothing', or occasionally 'Daddy'. He longed to cuddle her now. He longed to be big, and strong; so big and strong that he would be able to prevent her from getting hurt, again, ever. He wanted to put his arms right round her and keep her warm and make her happy.

He hugged his knees to his chest, and pulled his arms around his legs so hard that it hurt. He felt as if he were falling and falling and falling through the bedclothes, down to the centre of the earth, down to the land of shadows, and the not-dead, the Underworld, where that girl had eaten half a pomegranate and caused winter every year ever after.

Eventually the house became quiet. She had stopped. That was when he thought she must have fallen asleep. He still wondered whether to go and get in her bed. He didn't know why he hadn't gone to cuddle her when he had first thought about it. He listened to the tick of his clock, by his bed, and the fainter tick of the grandfather clock downstairs. The ticks were not quite the same. If you listened long enough, you could hear them get out of step with each other. He was cold without really noticing he was cold, his feet feeling like scraps of the night air at the bottom of his duvet. He wondered about the stars, and thought how strange it was that you feel they can look down on you when in fact they are nothing but huge balls of fire.

And then he heard Alan come in. He heard the garden gate swing back into position with a gentle clatter, and the scrunching of feet on the gravel. After a moment, after Alan had presumably locked his bike, he thought he heard the back door open and close. Alan hadn't locked the garden gate properly: Theo heard it bang again in the wind. Then he heard Ann on the landing. Sometimes, when he heard her on the landing, he would call out 'Ann', softly, and she would come and give him a cuddle. Sometimes she didn't hear. Occasionally, he suspected, she heard and pretended she didn't hear.

Tonight, he didn't call. He held his breath so that she wouldn't know he was awake, which was silly really, because you breathe when you're asleep, don't you? If someone's holding their breath, they're more likely to be awake than asleep.

Then he heard Ann going downstairs.

9

'Did I not tell you that I was composing this "Requiem" for myself?' –

W.A. Mozart

Alan locked up his bicycle in the passageway outside the kitchen door. He didn't bother to put it away in the garage. He used his bicycle so often that it usually wasn't worth putting it away, unless it was pouring with rain, or unless, for some reason, he wasn't going into college the next day. Ann put her bicycle away all the time, but then Ann was careful like that; almost fastidious. He smiled, remembering what she had been like as a student, polishing her violin, and putting it away in its case as if she were putting a child to bed, folding the piece of velvet which she always kept over it.

It was a shame she didn't play her violin more now. Women are funny like that: having a passion, as Ann had had for her music, and then simply putting it on one side, as if it didn't matter at all, when another priority comes along. She had been good on the violin. Very good. Amongst all the orchestral players Alan had conducted since, he hadn't come across many who were as good, as natural, frankly as musical as Ann. Perhaps she'd take it up again. He wondered whether she would be able to catch up. She'd never be the young star now, of course, but she could still be a pretty competent violinist.

He took off his bicycle clips and put them in the pocket of his coat, feeling, as he did so, for his keys. He took them from his pocket, singled out the key to the back door, and then took his lights off his bicycle. He must get a dynamo: it was a nuisance having to remove his lights all the time. He vaguely wondered why Ann hadn't done it for him. She usually did that kind of thing. If he remembered to mention it to her, she'd probably attend to it.

He put his key in the door before realising that Ann had left the door open for him. Of course she had. She always did. He always forgot that she would have done, and got his keys out anyway. Alan always locked doors. He had been brought up in suburbia, where doors were never, ever left unlocked. Ann had been brought up in the country, and was used to Ireland, and hated even locking the front door. She preferred to have it on the latch when she was in. Thank goodness Alan had put a stop to that, after the incident with her rings. He must remember to tell her that she shouldn't leave the back door open for him late at night. Someone could come in and attack her, or anything.

He put his keys back in his pocket and let himself into the porch. The door from the back porch to the kitchen was bound to be unlocked. He didn't shut it behind him.

He closed his eyes for a minute and rubbed them, wondering whether he wanted something to eat or drink, or whether to go up and see if Ann was still awake. Would she still be upset? he wondered. He found it hard to understand Ann's moods. Sometimes, if they'd had a disagreement, she seemed able to harbour it for hours, days even. It depressed Alan. He felt a failure at times like that; felt she was judging him, and he was failing, always. He could never come up to her high standards. He was not good enough, as a father and husband. However good a musician he was, he felt that he would always be a failure to Ann.

It was as he was shrugging off his coat that he heard the noise and started, then realised he was no longer alone in the room. He smiled wearily, and sighed.

He was too tired for a confrontation.

Theo was so frightened that he felt sick.

There were ropes inside his stomach, pulled tight, caught on things, tangled up like someone's knitting in a nightmare, like spaghetti made of elastic that had been stretched too far. He felt that he wanted to wee and throw up and have diarrhoea all at once. He lay so still that he seemed to be holding on to all his breath, for a long time.

He had heard his father talking, and to Theo he sounded annoyed. Inside Theo's head was a voice that kept saying, No! no! no! He wanted to scream and scream and scream, and yet he didn't want to make a sound.

He longed to be grown up, so he need never feel frightened again. Alan was never frightened. Alan's grandfather, Great-grandad, had been in the war, and even he wasn't frightened. He had gone into battle in a tank and all his friends had been shot to bits one by one, and he had never felt frightened at all. Theo knew, because Alan had told him Great-grandad didn't like to talk about the war, and when Theo was frightened about something he found it much easier if he could talk about it.

When he was big, when he was sixteen, the age Great-grandad had been when he said he was eighteen and went to war, he would never be scared any more.

He might as well practise now. He clenched his teeth, hard, and got out of bed. He got his towelling dressing-gown from the end of his bed, the one that had his initials on, TAW, which Ann had given him for Christmas last year, along with about six other presents, and he put it on. He heard Alan's voice again, and Theo was sure he was annoyed. It helped him to do what he wanted.

He went out on to the landing and listened for a while. Then he went downstairs to meet his father.

10

Caz looked at Theo across the table. 'Murdered?' she said, laughing slightly in embarrassment, and then felt the skin all over her scalp prickling. 'Goodness. Was he killed by a dangerous driver or something?'

'No.'

'Oh.' Now what? Do I ask *how* he died?

'He was hit on the head.'

'Ah.' She pushed some of her apple pie around her plate, smearing it in the cream. 'Mugging, or what?' This conversation is surreal, she thought. I'm glad the battle-axe can't hear.

'What's a mugging?'

'Well, um when you're attacked, you know, in the street, for your wallet or your money or something.'

'No,' Theo said.

The conversation lapsed. Caz took another spoonful of her apple pie, and felt she could hear her jaw working, deafeningly loudly, even in the crowded, noisy tea shop. Everyone suddenly seemed to be listening to them, or looking at them, or simply perversely silent, so that everything Caz and Theo did would be noticed. It was as if everything else in the tea shop were looming, larger than life, as in a bad dream or a surrealist picture: brighter, sharper, so that even their silence was louder. The walls were moving in on them when they weren't looking, and at any moment the woman with the odd poppy red pillbox hat at the next table, and the well-dressed man in a suit opposite her, were going to stand up and come over to their table and tower over them like enormous policemen with large nostrils.

Caz looked down at her hands, at the crumbs of her pie

gagging in the cream, the apple glistening in the artificial light. Theo's scone was gross in its proportions, like something in a John Wyndham novel, a vast mutant scone which would breed with other outsized and uncontrollable teacakes and eventually threaten to take over the world. So, she said to herself, the child believes his father has been murdered. And why not? Perhaps he has been. Why not? She answered her own question: Because I would have read it in the papers, that's why not. She looked up again, and found herself caught off balance by the intensity of Theo's gaze.

He stared at her for a moment, and then gave a little shiver, as if shaking the subject of his father's death from him like a dog shaking water from his ears. He smiled. Caz smiled back. Everything was normal again, the two of them enjoying a happy Saturday afternoon for the boy's exeat over tea in a tourist tea shop. He looked at his absurdly large scone, gave a theatrical shrug, picked it up, stretched his mouth wide, and bit down.

He was too vigorous. As his teeth closed over the two rounds of pastry, the cream exploded from the other side. Caz and Theo turned in unison, like cartoon characters, and saw the burst of cream on the tweed skirt of a fat passer-by. They stared at one another for a second in shock, waiting for the woman to turn.

Nothing happened. The cream continued on its way, wobbling on the bottom of the hound's-tooth skirt. The woman behind, carrying her own tray of tea, walked along with her eyes following the blob of yellow, staring at it as if transfixed. The tweed suit found a chair several tables away, at the back of the shop, and flopped into it like a bean bag being dropped into an armchair. Caz realised that she and Theo were still both holding their breath. She tried to let hers out carefully, so as not to giggle too much, and whispered, 'She's just sat in it!'

'What?!' Theo whispered back.

'She's just sat in it,' she said, much too loudly this time.

Then suddenly, and much too quickly, they both expelled all the air straining in their lungs, which came out like two corks shooting out of champagne bottles, spilling over in uncontrollable, frothing mirth, spraying both of them with laughter.

They ate the rest of their tea in silence, like naughty schoolchildren, occasionally glancing up at one another and giving surreptitious smiles. After they'd finished, Caz didn't feel like staying on to talk, with people and their trays hovering everywhere on the lookout for other customers on the move.

She stood up. 'Come on,' she said.

They went back out into the street. The sun had given way to a cloudy sky, and it was chilly and looked like rain. At last they could smile freely. They looked at each other, grinned, and glanced back at the shop. Caz tousled his hair, then found she was hugging him to her in spontaneous camaraderie. They leant against the wall, laughing, she with her arm around him, he imitating the action of the missile. 'Zoom . . . Splat!' he went. 'Right on her skirt. Then, kerflop, into the chair. Squishhhh.'

Then they realised they were still within view of the interior of the teashop, through its darkened picture window. 'Come on,' she said. 'Where shall we go now?'

'Um, I could show you the Chapel, if you like. If you're with me, we can get in for free. Thank you for tea.' And he began to lead the way back towards the college, going through the Porters' Lodge and round the smaller of the large college lawns, in the middle of which the statue of the saintly king stands, strangely blue, as if oxidised by the centuries, holding forth his hand in an everlasting pious gesture to generations of future students.

Theo said, 'I laughed like that once before.'

'Did you?'

'Mmm. It was a hot day, though, not like today.'

When they got to the Chapel there was a notice on the huge cast-iron gates saying, 'Closed for rehearsal. Next service 5.30'. 'That's odd,' Theo said. 'We're not rehearsing.'

'No, but your organist is,' Caz noticed, indicating with a nod of her head the powerful swelling and straining which seeped through the fabric of the building, as if wanting to burst the dams of white stone in a torrential flood of Widor.

'Oh, yes. That'll be Mr Ford, I expect. He plays even louder than Amschel. Though Amschel's jolly good of course. Let's go and look at the river. We should have brought some bread for the ducks. It's fun, doing that.'

It was as they sat on a forlorn bench, pulling their clothes about them as it began to drizzle, that Caz asked him, 'Why do you want me to write about your father?'

He turned and looked at the river, and put his arms around his knees, and Caz waited for several minutes. He hasn't heard me, she thought; or he's gone off on another daydream. She could only see the back of his head, not his face, and couldn't tell whether he was looking at the ducks, or thinking about something else. 'Theo?' she said softly, and gently took hold of his shoulder. She fancied that he made a slight movement, as if to shake her off. She let go, and pulled herself nearer to him, to try to see his expression. Something warned her not to say anything, or even touch him. It was almost – though this seemed impossible in so young a child, and one who was so winsome and attractive – but it was almost as if he might have dangerous moods, as if he might turn, and one would really wish something unsaid or undone. She could see the crescent of the side of his cheek, and wondered whether it looked a little red.

When he eventually turned back to her, she could see his face was flushed, and his eyes were bright and he was blinking hard.

'Are you all right?' she asked.

He nodded.

'Do you want me to take you back to school?'

He shook his head.

In the end he spoke. 'Ann says you have to talk about your feelings. I'm better at that now. You have to be in touch with how you feel, and you have to talk about it.'

'Uhuh,' Caz nodded. 'I could do with some of that too.' And then she took herself completely by surprise, by adding, 'I've been denying my feelings too, recently. It's not very clever, really.'

Theo blinked again, several times, and looked out towards the old college bridge, where he had pointed out to Caz, an hour before, the rooms of the organ scholar who liked his little Christmas tipple.

'And what are your feelings now?' she said. He turned his face towards hers, and she noticed the soft green-blue of his eyes under the deep blond lashes, and thought, He has the kind of eyes of which girls will say, when he's older, 'Why haven't I got lashes like that?' She suddenly felt as if she had known him a long time, and longed to put her arms around him and pull him towards her, deliberately this time, not just because they were laughing but because she wished to comfort him. Perhaps I should, she thought. But I don't know if that's the sort of gesture which prep school boys appreciate. Perhaps it would embarrass him horribly if any of his friends are passing, or even if they're not. In fact, she told herself, I don't know much about boys of his age at all.

'What are you feeling?' she repeated.

'Frightened,' he replied.

11

Later, when Caz looked back on that first meeting, she couldn't quite remember how or why they had gone to his mother's house. It was within easy walking distance; the problem wasn't that it was difficult to get there. It was just that it seemed such an odd thing to have done, to turn up at the house of a woman one didn't know, having taken her son out to tea without proper permission. But then, everything in her relationship with Theo so far had been unconventional.

Perhaps it had been something to do with the rain, which had now begun in earnest. Perhaps it was because she felt out of her depth with this bereaved child, and thought she should return him to a responsible adult, one who would know what to do. Or perhaps he had manoeuvred it because he genuinely wanted her to write a biography of an eminent musician whom she had never heard of.

Whatever the reason, twenty minutes later Caz and Theo stood outside a comfortable-looking Victorian town house in Sylvester Road and rang an old-fashioned bell-pull which caused a long echo to vibrate through the hall and beyond. Unexpectedly, Theo turned to her and seized her in rather too tight a hug.

'Thank you,' he said.

'It's a pleasure,' Caz replied, wondering whether it was, and exactly why she had agreed to come. They waited a moment, and then he pulled the bell again.

'She's all right,' he said strangely, as if to reassure himself. And then she came to the door.

Ann Fitzwilliam was a small, steady-looking woman with straight, shiny, chestnut-coloured hair and a freckled nose. Caz guessed she was the sort of person one would take to quickly; and also that the rather red, puffy eyes and weary look were peculiar to that afternoon, rather than typical.

The moment she saw Theo, her face filled with a smile so spontaneous and joyful that all three of them seemed to relax. Caz waited for Theo to introduce them, but he said nothing. She looked at him in silence for a moment, and almost wanted to nudge him as if she were a schoolgirl who had been brought home by a tongue-tied boyfriend. Then she turned to his mother and smiled. 'Mrs Wedderburn,' she began, but at that point Theo interrupted her.

'Miss Fitzwilliam really,' he said. 'Everyone calls her Mrs Wedderburn but it's not really accurate. Fitzwilliam is Ann's professional name, you see.'

'Please call me Ann,' she said, stepping aside to let them in. 'I'm hardly very professional at the moment, Tippy, so it doesn't really matter. And you must be Miss Sanderson? Cassandra? Do come in,' she added.

They followed her into the house, through the dark hall, and on towards the kitchen at the back of the house where windows over the sink gave on to a view of the lawn and large birch and chestnut trees filling the distant sky. She showed them straight to the kitchen table and put the kettle on without even asking them if that was what they wanted.

Within minutes they found themselves in the middle of a conversation they might have had if they'd known each other for years. What had they eaten? Had they got wet in the rain? Was it going to be a good conker season? What, darling? Mr Ford? Yes, he does play well: you're right.

And is the Copper Kettle the same as ever? Apple pie? No, it wouldn't be: scones and clotted cream would be much better. You *what*? You didn't! Theo, really! What a hoot. And what did you do: did you hide, or what? What about that Sunday lunch in Pizza Express, once, nearly Christmas time, do you remember, when Alan knocked over that bottle of red wine, and that look on the face of the people at the next table – remember . . .

And so they went on. Caz caught the look in their eyes, and the happiness at the shared memory, and the sadness that it had slipped out of their reach, long before she caught the sense of her own exclusion. Never again would the Wedderburns go out to a pizza parlour, as a family, the three of them, and be embarrassed by Alan knocking over a bottle and charming the waitress and ordering another. Because of a random few minutes, seconds perhaps, they had changed for ever. They were not a complete family any more, and never would be again. Caz lowered her gaze to the table, and waited for the moment to pass.

It did. They moved on. The conversation resumed. Soon they were talking again of Latin prep, and the Palestrina Mass the choir was doing that week, and the particular white mallard they had seen on the Cam, and whether it was a duck or a drake. In no time at all, it seemed, it was nearly half past four. Ann put her hand on Theo's arm, and glanced at the clock.

Suddenly, with no warning at all, he said, 'Caz might write a biography of Alan.'

Ann caught her breath sharply, and Caz turned to see on her face a look of such horror that Caz felt guilty, as if she herself had done something dreadful. 'No . . .' she started, and then turned to Theo. 'Wait a minute,' she said. 'You've got me into trouble three times today, and I've only just met you. I think if you do it a fourth time, I might blow the whistle.'

Theo gazed at her, all innocence, and said, 'What whistle?'

Ann seemed caught between alarm and amusement. 'Oh, Tippy,' she said. 'What have you done?'

'First,' Caz said, gathering momentum, 'you arrange for me to take you out without adequate permission, so someone called Mrs Hasn't, or Shouldn't, or something equally implausible, shows up and tries to turn me into recycled paper. Then, you invite me out to tea, encourage me to choose the most expensive item on the menu, and announce loudly at the check-out that you have no money and they'll have to wait several hours before you have. Then, you catapult clotted cream at the largest behind in the shop, and I think the rest of my bank balance is going to be mopped up in a law suit. Finally, you bring me home to meet your mother, and, instead of announcing our engagement as I expected you to do, you tell her I'm going to interfere in all your family's most private affairs, make them public, and make money out of them, without so much as asking her first. That's what Theo has done,' she finished up.

Ann nodded and laughed, as if to say she knew her son well enough to believe it. But Caz wondered why her eyes had been so bloodshot when they arrived, and why there was a wariness in her face now, even though she smiled, and why she said nothing. Did a widow need any particular reason to look red-eyed?

'Are we engaged?' Theo said.

'No,' Caz reassured him, 'nor likely to be, at this rate. Seriously,' she went on, turning back to Ann, 'it's true, Theo did mention your husband. The truth is, I don't really write biographies. Though, funnily enough, I'm working on something at the moment . . .' She hesitated. Caz never talked about work in progress, except the barest minimum to her agent and her editor to let them know what direction she was going in. Even Will only had a hazy idea of the work she was doing. Nevertheless, she went on: 'I'm working on a book about a musician. Which is why I came to Cambridge. I need to do some more research, but I'm not quite sure what I'm looking for.'

Ann remained silent for a moment. Then she said, 'I'm sorry if I reacted badly. I'm probably over-sensitive about it. I don't see Alan as public property, and perhaps I should. Anyway, Tippy, it's time to go back to school.'

Caz shivered. The light was drawing in, and the kitchen seemed less warm than it had.

It was when they were on the doorstep that Ann said, 'I won't come back to school with you, Theo, if Cassandra doesn't mind.' Caz was surprised. She had assumed Ann would walk back with them. She got the impression Theo had thought so too. Ann went on, 'Cassandra, if you'd like any help with your research, do call back, won't you? Alan had a very good reference library, and all his books are here now, though I'm afraid a lot of them are still in boxes. You're very welcome to browse.'

Caz was so pleased that she replied in a rush, unable to conceal her enthusiasm. 'I'd love it. When could I start? Tell me when I wouldn't be in the way.'

Ann said nothing. For an awful moment Caz thought she had asked too much: the other woman clearly longed for solitude, and had simply offered as a matter of politeness. Now she would have the embarrassment of telling Caz that she was too busy, that the books were inaccessible after all, that some time next week or the week after would be better. She stared over Caz's shoulder, as if she were alone, in a dream. Then she looked down at her son. His face broke into a smile, like the sun breaking through clouds. She turned to Caz and said, 'Tomorrow?' and added uncertainly, 'Perhaps you could come to lunch? If you don't mind something simple. Not a proper Sunday lunch. Bread and cheese.'

'I would love to,' Caz said sincerely, and wondered whether to add: If you're sure? But of course she was sure. She wouldn't have said it otherwise. 'Thank you,' she said. 'Thank you very much.'

It wasn't until she had left Theo at school that Caz started thinking about where she was going to stay. She knew Cambridge well, but had never before needed accommodation. The only Cambridge hotel she could think of was the Garden House. She had an idea there was another, smaller one, more like an inn, in Trinity Street, which was probably delightful if only she could remember its name.

After saying goodbye to Theo, she sat outside on a bench in the school grounds, under the dropping conkers, beneath the flaming autumn trees and rustling dried-paper leaves, and rang the directory. It was engaged. After five minutes she gave up, and decided to walk. It would be almost as quick, and far more pleasant.

As she put her telephone away in her handbag again, she saw the choristers coming out of the school, ready to walk to Chapel. The boys wore their Eton suits, black and white, several hundred years out of date and thoroughly incongruous, an absurdity which delighted the children as much as the tourists and guides to the city. The girls wore a less eccentric, sober black skirt and blazer, and a soft black hat like the one Caz could remember wearing for her finals.

Theo noticed her, and smiled in an embarrassed kind of way, forbidding her to wave with a look almost as nervous as if she had been his mother. She waited till the orderly crocodile was out of the school grounds, and then followed, a good fifty yards behind. She would part company with them at the Backs, and walk on to the Garden House. It would probably be far too luxurious, but it would do for a night or two. If she planned to stay longer, there were presumably landladies who could be prevailed upon to provide bed and breakfast.

12

The next morning Caz sat on the terrace of the Garden House Hotel, overlooking the river by the weir and the Fen, finishing her coffee. If I were at home now, she thought, Will and I would be reading the papers or having breakfast in bed or sitting out in the conservatory, and Gibbon would be doing his best to annoy us. No, we wouldn't be having breakfast in bed, not as late as this. And Will wasn't at home anyway. She would be sitting at home alone, cross with herself that she hadn't gone to Italy, hoping Will was having a good time but perhaps not too good a time.

Nearly eleven o'clock. She had missed Matins in Chapel. Theo had asked her if she would come, but she had had a strange reluctance to, she didn't know why. She had been to Evensong in the Chapel once or twice, as a child, with her grandfather, but since his death had forgotten about those services, with the vigorous resonance of Cranmer's prose, and the almost uncanny, almost divine sound of sixteen choirboys, or choirchildren as they were now, their voices shimmering, almost effulgent, in that vast, ethereal building. She had told the boy she might come. He had a proprietorial pride in his choir, and clearly longed for her to hear it.

If she stayed in Cambridge for another day or two, she would go. She would prefer Evensong to Matins. She had an idea, ill formed and illogical, that Evensong would be more of a celebration of music, whereas Matins, on a Sunday morning, was quite uncompromisingly a religious service, and she had no desire for that.

She considered her plans. She would need till Monday in

Cambridge, at least, and possibly Tuesday too. She wondered about Alan Wedderburn's books. Being honest, she was unlikely to find much among them, but on a Sunday she couldn't have done anything else anyway. It would be pleasant to spend the day with Ann, and Theo had seemed genuinely delighted that she had accepted his mother's invitation.

She closed her eyes and saw him again, sitting by the river, his face turned from her, and the side of his cheek burning red. It was an image which, strangely, had returned to her a number of times over the night.

Was Theo worried that his mother would die too, and leave him quite alone? Or was it simply, perhaps rather melodramatically, because his father had been murdered, rather than dying of some armchair ailment, that now he was frightened of a theatrically masked man in a night-time alley lurking with a knuckle-duster? Caz contemplated this. What did the boy mean, that his father had been murdered? He could hardly have been shot on the hearth-rug in the vicarage by the colonel's revolver because there was a flaw in the great-aunt's legacy, which was how one tended to think of murder, after all.

She felt an indecent curiosity about it. How often did one meet someone connected with a real and genuine murder? It was almost exciting. She imagined a tall, dark man, moodily brilliant, composing music in the conservatory overlooking the lawn while a shadowy stranger crept up behind him with a cosh and raised it above his head. The parallels with the subject-matter of her new book were uncanny. In her mind she heard the brooding, gloomy music of the Lacrimosa, with its persistent, knocking timpani, and envisaged the mysterious, unidentified visitor who had drummed on the door of that genius in his thirties in Vienna two centuries before, asking him to write the Requiem which he always knew would turn out to be his own.

She shivered slightly as she watched the mist above the Mill Pond hovering over the water. Involuntarily, she wondered whether she might be able to find out, over lunch with his widow, what had happened to Alan Wedderburn, without herself appearing to be too gruesomely nosy.

As she thought about her engagement with Ann, she remembered what the view over the lawn in Sylvester Road really looked like, and how the three of them had sat round Ann's kitchen table with no husband or father coming in for supper that night, and she imagined a small blond child lying awake in his bedroom above, while his father never came up to tuck him into bed any more.

Then she thought of Theo's young, courageous face, as he had sat beside the river determined not to cry, trying so hard to do as he'd been told and be open about his feelings, and she drew her coat round her more tightly.

13

'How I felt then! How I felt then! Such things will never return.
Now we are sunk in the emptiness of everyday life' –

W. A. Mozart

Ann sat in her garden looking at her pond. She loved her
garden. She was no gardener, and hated the feel of dirt under
her fingernails and the stooping and sweating of weeding, but
she loved her garden itself with a passion which almost hurt.

It was like having a baby, almost. The more trouble and agony
it was, the more you loved whatever had given you the pain. If
Theo had been an easier child, would she have loved him less?
She would never know: she would never now have another
child to compare him with.

The sudden misery caught her by surprise, even shocked her.
Ann was an easy-going person, everyone said so: she had coped
with Alan's death so remarkably well. Yet when she sat alone,
by her pond, on a Sunday morning and realised that she would
never have the little girl she had dreamt about – who would perhaps be two or three now, at nursery school, who would have
been talented and artistic and wonderful, of course, but not
highly strung like Theo, completely different in temperament,
easy-going, bouncy, sporty – her eyes pricked and her breath
caught on itself and for a moment it seemed worse even than
losing Alan.

How Theo would have loved her! He was so kind and loving
towards Katie, their two-year-old next-door neighbour, and so
clever with her, taking her down to the bottom of the garden,

and showing her frogs, and pigeons' eggs, and worm casts . . .
Ann pulled herself together. He would never have a sister. A
half-sister maybe. Was that likely? I will be thirty-five next year,
she told herself. And I don't want to marry again, not ever. She
hadn't realised, when she and Alan were happily together, when
he was still alive, how much of herself she was investing, and
had invested, in their relationship. One sorts out so many things,
gives so many things up, in fact, to make it work, that the idea
of starting again just doesn't seem worth it.

Like what? What had she given up? Her career, of course.

Ann shut her eyes for a moment and rested her face on her
knees. Why is it that one still feels sixteen, eighteen, even when
the years have long gone by?

It was her first day at the Royal College. She had been awarded
the place months before, but she still couldn't believe she was
really expected to turn up. As she approached the big front door,
hugging her violin case to her chest, she was convinced that, as
soon as she got inside, someone would say, 'Ann Fitzwilliam?
Ann Fitzwilliam? I think there must be some mistake? There's an
Anna Farringdon down on my list here, but we're not expecting
an Ann Fitzwilliam.' She had stood at the desk nervously, in her
best Laura Ashley frock and with her chestnut hair brushed till
it shone, and waited to be turned away. It hadn't happened, of
course. She was expected, she wasn't even the most nervous
there, and she was a real, training-to-be-professional musician.

She had never been so happy before, or even since, being
ruthlessly honest with herself. She had practised eight, nine,
ten hours a day; was never late for lessons or rehearsals; loved
sitting at the feet, metaphorically speaking, of her violin teacher,
inspiring, brilliant as he was. She was an almost perfect student.
But then, she was serious about her music. She imagined
herself standing by the podium of the Queen Elizabeth Hall,
the Barbican, the Albert Hall. Or, less grand, the Brighton
Pavilion or the Manchester Town Hall or the Sheldonian in
Oxford. She had never imagined herself at the second desk of
the second violinists, at the Cambridge University Music Society,
which was where she would be now.

Alan had so obviously been the rising star. So obviously the
conductor, the organist, the choirmaster of the future. He had

already done his three years as an organ scholar at Cambridge, helping train the choir and giving recitals and broadcasting on Radio Three. Anyone who had an eye for an up-and-coming career could spot that he would be a household name before long. Most of the girls at the Royal College wouldn't have dreamt of going out with him, he was so far above them. Ann, on the other hand, wouldn't have dreamt of it because she was so dedicated to her music. She didn't notice when he made a point of sitting next to her in the canteen. She hardly noticed when he came to her solo concert, and offered to take her out for a drink afterwards; she politely refused, because her parents were there, and didn't even wonder why he should have asked.

In the end he was forced to wait for her after her violin lesson one afternoon, and steer her unceremoniously into a greasy little tea shop on the corner of Gloucester Road, and tell her he was in love with her, simply in order to get her to notice him.

Then she did notice him. And she suddenly saw what everyone else saw. The aquiline nose, the shiny dark hair, the appearance of an Englishman with a romantic throwback to a Greek hero among his ancestors somewhere, the intelligent face and sensitive hands. Even, to the far-sighted, the look of a successful musician, Alan Wedderburn, OBE, Sir Alan even. Would he have been? Quite possibly.

And yet, for all that, she would have preferred to have been a musician in her own right. If she had been given a clear-cut choice like that – and of course if she hadn't fallen in love with him, so totally, so utterly that everything else paled by comparison – would you rather be Ann Fitzwilliam, violinist, or Lady Wedderburn, wife of the eminent, et cetera ... she would have chosen to be herself. But it never is a clear-cut choice. You are given the choice between staying in London, where you are on hand for auditions and orchestra work, or moving with Alan to Cambridge when he gets that wonderful job. Between doing the extra hour of practice in the evening, or stopping because Alan has come in looking miserable and needs cheering up with a good meal. Between doing your scales that day, or going to your crying baby, who seems so distressed even though the health visitor said: Don't worry so much, let him cry. Between taking on the session work, which is soul-destroying but helps the people who matter to remember who you are, and going to the parent-teacher evening at school and hearing yet again that your child doesn't fit in, and what are you going to do about it? Between trying to climb back on the ladder yourself, years behind all the students who are now jumping ahead of you, and spending hour after patient hour, day after patient day, year on year, as it turns out when you look back on it, sitting with your son trying to persuade him to start a scale, or finish it, or learn that difficult arpeggio, because you know he is frighteningly talented, and yet has such inexplicable problems of concentration and application that he won't even get a choristership in two years' time unless you pour your mind and soul and energy into getting him focused this afternoon.

He will, if he chooses, be a better musician than I could ever have been, Ann thought. Perhaps even than Alan, if he can survive whatever it is that separates him from other children, that won't permit him to do whatever it is he should be doing. And when he is as brilliant as he should be, when he is forty-something and married with children, and his seventy-year-old mother, who has never done anything with her life and never did become anything, is living with him in the granny flat, annoying his long-suffering wife, how will he see me then? And does it matter? How will I see myself? Will he mind that I am nobody, that I have nothing outside his happiness? Will he wish he had a more interesting, more independent mother?

A thrush hopped some distance from her on the lawn. He wanted to come and drink in the pond, but was uncertain how near to Ann he should go. Cocking his head on one side, he jumped a little nearer. It was extraordinary, she thought, how she could fill the days doing nothing. And the funny thing was, no one ever asked her what she did, no one asked her to justify all this time wasted. When Alan was alive, and Theo was living at home, when there genuinely had been more to do, Theo to ferry to this and that, Alan's tail coat to take to the cleaners ready for a concert, that sort of thing, she had done more of her own things too. Alan, to give him his due, had said to her from time to time, 'Shouldn't you do some practice? When did you last learn a new piece of music? Call yourself a musician?' he would mock, gently. 'If I had you in my orchestra I'd sack you!' So he had given her encouragement of a sort. But he had never offered to take Theo to the dentist so she could run through some scales just to remember what they felt like. He had never managed to help Theo get down to his pieces, or do his homework in the allotted twenty minutes, rather than the two or three hours it would take him without supervision. Alan had not mastered that at all. Within a few minutes of getting involved with his son, he would be shouting at him, enraged.

To be fair, Ann herself would raise her voice at him too, from time to time: she doubted whether Mother Teresa could have lived with Theo and not lost her temper. But she couldn't bear to see Alan do what she might have been doing herself if she were in charge. As soon as that happened, she could see the incident from Theo's point of view, and see how much it hurt, and see how he really had been trying but it actually was impossible for him to do the task he had been set.

Once he had been given a particular composition title which went: 'Where would you live if you could choose anywhere in the world . . . the bottom of the sea? The jungle? Even the moon!' Theo couldn't do it. He couldn't understand how his teacher could have been so stupid: how could she think the moon was in the world? Ann could have pleaded, explained, cajoled for a week: perhaps Miss Susan was tired; what did it matter anyway when the intention of the question was clear? Alan, on the other hand, would have promised a smack if he hadn't started within five minutes. And Theo's eyes would have gone watery and his face red, until he got another smack, and none of it would have made the slightest bit of difference. You could have punished him until he wept: he was simply incapable of it.

And Alan had started to see it too. He had begun to understand. You couldn't live with Theo for seven years and not change your view of children, and teaching, and the efficacy of punishment, and all the things which seem so simple until you have children of your own. If Alan had lived, he would have become more gentle with his child. She was sure of it. He had already changed towards Theo.

If Alan had lived. Things would have been so different, so very different.

If he had come home five minutes earlier, or later. If he had rung to say he was on his way. If they hadn't had that stupid quarrel. If, if.

She wandered back into the house and noticed it was half past eleven. Already. That writer, Cassandra Sanderson, was coming for lunch. She had nothing to feed her with. Perhaps the little Italian delicatessen in Newnham would be open. It was extraordinary how, even with nothing to do, she never seemed to have adequate food in the house. If it had been a weekday, she could have biked to the market and got some vegetables to make a thick, warming soup.

She sincerely hoped Caz didn't intend to write Alan's biography. Ann knew she ought to give more thought to it. If she commissioned an official book, she would be able to keep some control, and shape what was written. If she did nothing, someone would step in and write the thing anyway.

Ann gripped the side of the door on her way into the kitchen. It was coming again, the rising sense of panic, the breathlessness, the horror of that night, the moment when she had realised. The sound of somebody screaming and screaming and screaming. The awful, cold-blooded knowledge – despite this terrible thing that she understood, fully, instantly, and with none of that disbelief and numbness which is supposed to come with that kind of shock – the realisation that she must protect Theo, that at all costs she must protect Theo even though her life had just fallen apart.

Would Cassandra Sanderson ask her about it? Probably. Another day if not today. Ann must face it. If Cassandra didn't, then someone else, someone worse, less sympathetic, would.

'I didn't really have any intention of writing about your husband,' Caz said, apologetically, two hours later, as they sat in Ann's dining room with *pain de campagne*, and vacuum-packed Gorgonzola, and olive pâté. And when Ann, smiling, made no reply she foolishly felt obliged to continue, 'I'm afraid I hadn't even heard of him.'

'You're not a musician, then?' Ann asked.

'Only in an amateur capacity really. I mean, no, I'm not. I tinkle on the piano, that's all.'

Suddenly, Ann said, 'I must say, you're not like the rest of them.'

'Rest of whom?'

'The journalists. The would-be biographers. I'm sorry: I didn't mean that to sound so personal,' she added, as Caz, to her own annoyance, blushed and fiddled with her food. 'They're serious writers, some of them. You know, *Grove Dictionary of Music* sort of writers.' Ann took a deep breath, and looked out on to her garden. A large, fat magpie swooped down from a silver birch on the side of the lawn and took a few pogo steps across the grass.

'And why . . .' Caz began, and then couldn't think how to phrase it.

'Why don't I let them get on with it? I don't know. I can't face it, I suppose. Perhaps because it would seem so final. Perhaps I dread the endless questions, sorting out his papers, digging out photographs of him as a child, school reports, recordings he made as a chorister. I'll have to sooner or later, I suppose, or someone will just do it anyway, without my co-operation, and that would probably be worse. Tell me . . .' She turned to Caz, and brightened suddenly and almost artificially. 'Tell me, how did you come to be a writer?'

The rest of the meal was spent, rather incongruously, on small talk. In contrast to the day before, Caz now felt that Ann might actually be very difficult to get beyond a cheerful, easy acquaintance with. She seemed to have, at her very centre, a self-contained reserve, a distance that some people would call coldness, but that Caz suspected was a necessary part of her survival. Perhaps it had only been cultivated since her husband died.

It wasn't until they were having coffee that Ann asked her about her current book. Caz skated over the idea, tentatively, not wanting to give too much away. Ann listened, and pondered at length, and gazed out on her drear October lawn, and then, to Caz's great disappointment, said there was no point in Caz simply thumbing through Alan's books because they were all in a muddle, but she would see if she could find anything and let her know. And by then, Caz thought, I can be in the University Library where I can find everything I want. What a wasted couple of days. She should have worked out, when she was still in Cley, that all the libraries would be closed. She could have had a relaxed weekend with Ben and Suki and Abi, after all.

When she left Ann Fitzwilliam's house, her feet grinding the gravel as she passed between the tasteful laurel bushes which the press photographers must have delighted in capturing against the solid Victorian front of the house, Caz was surprised to find it was barely half past two. Evensong was at three thirty. She could have a pleasant stroll along the Backs, perhaps go as far as the Botanical Gardens, and still be back at the Chapel in time for the service. It would hardly be crawling with foreigners at this time of year, she reasoned. And she didn't really have an excuse to avoid it now.

She felt unusually tired. The backs of her legs were aching, and she wanted to sit down. She felt annoyed with herself, and tried to walk faster, before remembering that pregnant women are supposed to feel sick, tired and distracted. She had omitted to go through any of these experiences on behalf of her unborn baby. Will's baby. Their child. Ironically, Will was probably giving more thought to their new family, miles away as he was, than she, living with the little boy inside her.

She didn't feel particularly pregnant. She had friends who thought of their pregnancies all day, and felt they knew their babies long before they were born. Caz's experience was the opposite. She knew he was a boy, but only because the scan had told her so. Apart from that he was a stranger. Suppose they didn't get on? Perhaps she wouldn't like him? Or, worse, he might not like her. What did she know about looking after a child, after all? She might fail. She wondered whether it was because her body hadn't changed much that she felt so unprepared. Her breasts were sore, even acutely painful if she went swimming and got cold; and she felt nauseous when presented with soft-boiled eggs or strong coffee. But that was all. Perhaps once she was seriously fat and waddling about she would feel differently.

She had reached Queens' Road, and stood, looking towards the college gate and the river and Chapel beyond. As always, there was something surprising about the view: its elegance, its loneliness. The gate stood, solitary, impressive, with its strong white stone and intricate cast iron. The eye expects a solid wall around it, forbidding entry to the college. Instead, the meadow, and the bridge which swells like a woman's belly, and the path, bright with crocuses and aconites in spring, are all protected simply by a gentle moat, hidden by the surrounding grasses. So the uninterrupted view sweeps freely across the rough paddock and the ancient river and the beautiful, manicured lawn up to the exquisite Chapel, so delicate it looks as if it could be made of paper; and the beholder wonders, without consciously articulating it, why it seems unnaturally lovely, why he hadn't expected it to be so open to view, so generous.

Caz drank it in. Theo was lucky to grow up with this, taking it so for granted, possessing it with the air he breathed. The soft October sunshine seemed to be warming the stone, making it smile, as Caz stepped through the gate and walked along the path to the river.

She decided to walk round the lawn, past the Chapel, and

into the next-door college's gardens, and then stroll around for twenty minutes or so before returning for the service.

She found she had turned at the same time as a rapid-footed little man who was now walking alongside her. He was no taller than she, grey-haired with an impressive moustache, and was wearing a cassock and gown. A verger, she thought: he looked like a college servant, not a member of the teaching staff, and he was presumably going to open up the Chapel to prepare it for the service. She had a feeling he was looking at her, sideways. She glanced at him quickly, and found that he was. Smiling quickly, in a non-committal sort of way, she looked away again. She sensed that he continued to stare at her, and began to wonder whether he knew her. After a few more steps, he suddenly said, 'I've got it!' and stopped where he stood.

'Sorry?' she said, turning and stopping too.

'Miss Sanderson, isn't it?'

Ah, he's read one of my books, she thought, and smiled with satisfaction. She pretended to be above such things, but in fact she loved to be recognised, to be a household face. She glowed inside, and waited to be asked for her autograph.

'Ben Sanderson's sister, aren't you?' he said, and mentioned the date and college. 'I used to be his gyp. Frank's the name. Remember me? You came and stayed once, illegally, on his floor, didn't you? Least, he always said you was his sister, and I never had reason to doubt it!' And at his own witticism, he erupted into happy, infectious laughter, and Caz found she was laughing too.

'I certainly am his sister,' she replied in mock indignation, 'and I'm sure I could prove it, if only I could think how. Hello, Frank, how are you?' She took his hand with enthusiasm. 'I remember you well now. Ben still speaks warmly of you. He'll be thrilled that I've bumped into you. What are you doing here?'

'Redundancies,' he said, shaking his head. 'Redundancies! I ask you. Forty years I'd been at that college, man and boy, since I was a nipper of sixteen. Redundant, that's what I was. Every year, more students, fewer domestic staff. Every year. Now, if they got rid of some of the teaching staff, I could understand it. They sit on their backsides doing nothing all day. But you need the domestic staff. Don't even call them gyps any more, haven't for years. "Staircase supervisors" now. "Staircase supervisors", I ask you! You don't get looked after by a supervisor, do you? I started as a gyp, and finished as a gyp. That's what I was, and that's what I called myself.'

'So you got sacked?' Caz asked, genuinely shocked.

'Well, they found us all jobs elsewhere in the university, but it's not the same, izzit? Being thrown out of your own college. I don't know. Better off here, though. Lovely job. All that music. Lovely. I love music, always have. My wife loves coming to the carols at Christmas. We get tickets, you know. Walk past all those nerds and anoraks who've been queueing in the wind and rain all ruddy Christmas Eve, we do, straight in. Tickets in the choir, an' all, not the ante-chapel. Then a party: mince pies, mulled wine. *And* then we listen to it on the radio on Christmas Day too; hear ourselves coughing in the background! Not the same as being in your own college, though,' he added quickly. 'And what are you doing here? Coming for the service, are you?'

'I thought I might, actually. I met one of the choristers yesterday, Theo Wedderburn.'

'Sad business,' he said, shaking his head. 'Sad business, that was, wasn't it?'

'What was?' Caz asked carefully, ashamed to find that her heart had leapt with curiosity, and that she was now holding her breath to see if he would say more.

'His dad.' Frank clicked his tongue. 'Lovely man. What a waste, eh? He would have been Sir Alan Wedderburn before we'd all been in our graves. Well, before you'd been in your grave anyway. Don't know about me!' And the laughter burst out again, irrational, unexpected. Caz smiled.

'What happened to him, exactly?' she said, trying to sound only vaguely interested. She needn't have worried. Frank was dying to tell her, and was only too delighted to find someone who didn't yet know. He must miss all those eager freshers, anxious for any gossip, Caz thought, remembering the scout who'd been allocated to her rooms in Oxford, and who had happily spent half an hour every morning filling her in on all the under-stairs news in college, even though the regulations, by then, stipulated that he was only supposed to spend five minutes on each student, emptying the bin and running a duster over the mantelpiece.

'What happened to him? Beaten to death he was, in his own home. Bashed over the head. Never solved either. If you was a writer, now: make a fortune, you could. I'd do it myself if I had the time. Mind you . . .' And here he lowered his voice, and leant towards her, looking about him in a caricature of conspiracy. Caz looked around as well, and saw a few lone figures crossing the other side of the vast court. 'Mind you, they know who did it.'

'Do they?'

'Sure as Bob's your uncle. They know who did it all right.'

'But . . .' Caz frowned. 'Didn't they make an arrest?'

'Nah. Course not. Internal politics, that's what it was. Internal college politics. I could tell you a thing or two. Crikey, is that the time? I was supposed to open up ten minutes ago. There'll be a string of Frogs and Krauts outside that door before we know where we are. I must move it.'

'Frank,' Caz said, almost jogging behind him to try to keep up, 'I'd love to pick your brains about this. I've been asked to write a book about him, you see,' she explained, exploiting the truth quite shamelessly, 'and I can't find anyone else who knows anything about it.'

'Ah, well, Frank's your man. I'm your man all right. Tell you what, I'll let you into Chapel early. Not supposed to, but seeing as you're bonnerfeed . . . Come on. Now, if you catch me after the service, I can fill you in. You nab me later, I'll fill you in.'

Caz, wondering what 'bonnerfeed' was, watched Frank extricate from the folds of his ancient cassock an enormous iron key, and insert it in the huge cast-iron gate, which stood before the equally huge oak doors, which needed a different key. She had just worked it out, when he swung open the heavy oak.

He stood aside, and she stepped into the vast, hollow forest of stone and light and colour, stretching for ever to a white stone sky, yearning towards heaven. Involuntarily, as everyone's must who ever enters that building, her eyes flew upwards. Involuntarily, too, her mind flew to a God she had never believed in.

May you be forgiven, she rebuked herself. And may you be ashamed first.

15

'Wren went once a year to survey the roof of the Chapel . . .
and said that if any man would show him where to place the
first stone, he would engage to build such another' –
Edmund Carter, quoted in *King's College a Short History*
by Christopher Morris

Caz sat in the still quietness of the ante-chapel, surrounded by
the dim rustlings of vergers toing and froing. The Chapel itself
picked up the little noises they made and magnified them,
gently lobbing them from wall to wall to build up its notorious
seven-second echo. A sheet of music fluttering to the ground
was like the wind in the trees; a dropped hymn book like a
thunderclap. A soft footfall could be heard the other side of the
towering organ-loft, miles away it seemed.

It was pleasant, sitting in there, doing nothing in particular.
Her eyes rested on the tall stained-glass windows, and contemplated, without really engaging her brain, the stories depicted
there. One scene seemed full of giant snowflakes, though Caz
assumed it was probably supposed to be manna. She knew, in
a dreamy sort of way, that if she could be bothered to apply
herself, she could work out what the stories were. Her attention
wandered, further down the wall, to the heraldic design of the
first Tudor king. Here was the crown, here the gryphon of
Wales. And here, underneath, were the sixteen boys and girls
who were streaming in in their smart two-and-twos, just as the
choristers had for hundreds of years, to fill the Chapel with the
sound of human voices as ethereal as they were practised; at
the back of the crocodile were two younger boys not in Eton

suits, the two probationers. She saw Theo, but he hadn't seen her yet.

The Chapel began to fill with people, hushing their voices and slowing their steps as they entered the building. One or two took seats in the ante-chapel: most flowed on under Henry VIII's huge oak organ-loft into the choir.

As she sat there, Caz was reminded of a scene depicted in one of the many books of reference she had read for her research. An anonymous oil painting of a late-eighteenth-century Viennese masonic lodge. Candles burned, discreetly, on the walls by the carved emblems. Beneath them, men sat, whispering to one another. At the east end of the lodge, steps led up to an altar. Why was he a freemason? Caz asked herself. He seemed such an open, generous-hearted man; why would he become involved in a semi-illegal secret society? Through political conviction, perhaps? Though he didn't seem to be a political man; after all, he had been in Paris a mere decade before the French Revolution, and, in his letters home, barely mentioned politics. Religious conviction then?

At this point the choir, now fully robed, processed in from a side vestry, and the scattered worshippers in the ante-chapel rose to their feet. A few seconds later the congregation in the choir sensed the movement, and a sound, like that of a forest clapping its hands to the wind, rippled through the Chapel as hundreds of chairs scraped gently on the floor and hundreds of hymn books were picked up, hundreds of pairs of feet shuffled and hundreds of throats were softly cleared. The choir processed into the main body of the Chapel, and the congregation knelt and turned their minds to the bidding prayer.

As soon as the singing started, Caz rose to leave. The silver thread of the pure, English sound of sixteen choristers, the unbroken trebles and the fresh voices of the girls, rose over the lower three voices like thin smoke, cleared the organ-loft, and settled in the vaulted roof. She hesitated by the north door. She was troubled by her book: the thought of the masonic lodge had jogged something in her mind. Well, there are plenty more Evensongs, she thought, and left.

Caz unlocked the door of her hotel bedroom, noticed with

indifference that it had been cleaned, emptied her computer on to the inadequate surface which served as the nearest thing to a desk, and tried to marshal her thoughts. Masonry: surely that was the key. She ran her mind over the little she knew about the masonic themes in his music. *Die Zauberflöte*, of course. The stylised three knocks, the masonic key of E flat of the *Finale*. And the hopefulness of the philosophy: 'Soon the dawn will bring us light, and the golden sun will rise; soon superstition will disappear, and the wise man will be victorious.'

But he hadn't been victorious. Soon the wise man had been dead. Had his lodge mourned him? Or had there been relief that the impecunious embarrassment had gone? At least the brothers would no longer receive begging letters pleading for help to bale out his family yet again. One masonic brother, Michael Puchberg, received over twenty letters asking for help, along with repeated assurances that eventually his investment would be paid back, which of course it never was. Had Michael had enough? Was he someone who might not have felt undiluted sorrow at his fellow mason's death? Caz turned on her computer and started jotting down ideas. This was more like it; this was what she had become a writer for. The words were flowing now, and she found she even got physical pleasure out of the feel of the keys under her fingertips, and the clackety-clack as they registered her thoughts.

For twenty minutes or so she worked continuously, uninter-rupted, resting in the contentment that comes when the work pours effortlessly on to the computer. Searching for a thought, she glanced up for a moment and gazed across the fens. The cows were happily, silently, munching buttercups and nettles and tall grasses. Occasionally a don's wife, or a master from the nearby Leys School, bicycled precariously across the tiny wooden bridge by the Mill Pond. She wondered why on earth Theo had written to her. It was a strange thing for a child his age to have done. It seemed to be a cry for help, but why? Was it simply the overwhelming panic of a grief, a loss, he couldn't handle?

She turned back to her screen, considered a moment, and saved the file. She wanted to talk to somebody, to tell someone else about Theo, to share the burden of his bereavement with someone who could help her, understand her concern. 'Dear Will,' she wrote.

When she next looked up it was half past five; an hour and a half wasted. No, not wasted: she had written a long letter. She hadn't mentioned Theo Wedderburn, but she had sorted out a number of things in her own mind, in their relationship. She could E-mail it to him straight away. And yet she didn't. It could wait until she got home, and she would print it on to paper. E-mail would be too impersonal, or that was what she told herself. She crossed the room to put the kettle on, and forced herself to face the fact that she had not only missed going to see Frank, which didn't particularly matter; she had also written down barely half a page of ideas for her book before abandoning it again.

She exited from the programme on her computer and turned it off. She would go out for a drink and decide what to do. Suddenly, she felt acutely homesick. She wanted to be in her own house, in her own bedroom, with Will there, and a bottle of wine and a good cheese and perhaps something on the television. It would be a good idea to ring Will, she thought. He would want to know how she was.

As she strolled towards the Market Place she tried to remember which had been the fashionable pubs when Ben had been up. They hadn't been to pubs much: mostly, when he had taken her anywhere, it had been to friends' parties, or, once, the college bar. But she seemed to remember The Eagle. Wasn't it near the Arts Theatre? Sure enough, down Bene't Street, through an almost hidden Tudor archway which must be adored by such Americans as ever spot it, there was a little cobbled yard, open to the elements, with a gallery above and a drinking room to the side. It was still early, and the bar was not crowded. She bought herself a glass of wine and went and sat outside, where she was the only drinker.

She wondered whether she had been right to embark on the book she was writing. Perhaps it needed a real musician. Did she know the difference, after all, between an *appoggiatura* and an *acciaccatura*?

Perhaps, instead of what she was trying to do, re-create the life of a genius whom everyone already knew everything about, she should contemplate a workmanlike biography of Alan

Wedderburn: his professional achievements, his personal life. What he was like as a father, how his death had come about, the devastation of grief on his widow and young son. A book, sensitively written, about the life, and premature death, of a romatic young musician might well have a readership.

But she knew almost nothing of what had happened. Beaten to death in his own home, hadn't Frank said? Had Theo been there? Did he know the attacker? It seemed extraordinary that his assailant hadn't been convicted, if the police really knew who it was. Even if it had been an accident, there would surely have been a charge of manslaughter. 'College politics', wasn't that the reason given by Frank for some sort of cover-up? Come, come. What was Frank suggesting: that the Provost had got annoyed with the organist and whacked him one over the head? Such an idea was patently absurd.

Caz downed the rest of her drink and stood up. This was silly. She would go home, or rather back to her room that was very unlike home, and ring Will. She would tell him all about her book and he would tell her exactly what to do, where the book should go.

Nevertheless, she would love to know what had happened to Alan Wedderburn. How did 'investigative journalists' find out?

As soon as she got back to her room, she took out her telephone. She was not a natural maker of telephone calls. She was happy to use the telephone for business, when she had to. Otherwise she wrote letters. Will, on the other hand, tended neither to write nor to telephone. However much he might long to see her, she knew he was unlikely to ring. He was giving her the space she had said she wanted. She sat on her bed for a few minutes, preparing herself. She was getting ready to talk to him, to say the right things, to tell him how she missed him. She was pleased, so pleased, she had chosen now to ring. She dialled.

Will heard the telephone straight away. It wasn't the hotel telephone, but his mobile by the bed. He was just going out of his room. He stopped when he heard it. Could it be Caz? Hardly. He had dashed in from the bathroom several times, darted across his desk to pick up the receiver, broken off from architects' meetings and sessions with financiers, and fumbled with the catch on his briefcase when he heard the telephone ringing, and it was never Caz. He didn't want to be disappointed yet again. He was just going out for a stroll in the bustling Roman night. Without his telephone. He was lonely, he longed to be home in Fulham, he loved going back to Italy but it was no fun without Caz to show around. The door was about to close behind him. It wouldn't be her. Besides, it was nearly half past ten. What kind of idiot rings at half past ten at night?

Caz waited while the telephone rang. She knew Will would be there: he hated going out on a Sunday evening, because he liked an early night before starting the week. He was taking a long time to answer. He couldn't be asleep, surely? No. He was never asleep before eleven. She glanced at the screen on her telephone to check that she had the right number.

At last he answered. 'Hello.'

'Hello,' she said, 'it's me.'

'It's Will here,' he continued. 'I'm sorry I can't take your call at the moment. Do please leave your name and number, and any message, and I will ring you back as soon as possible.'

The answerphone had come on after the prescribed sixteen rings. It didn't sound like an answerphone: it was so bloody cheerful, it sounded uncannily like Will himself. Caz felt foolish for having replied to the machine. She put the telephone down slowly, wondering what gorgeous leggy Italian he was taking out to dinner.

16 ∫

Caz was sitting in the tea room of the University Library. Since breakfast she had entertained herself with a series of time-wasting activities: describing the reasons for her research, giving the name of her college in Oxford, waiting while the Master's secretary was rung up to check her identity, having her bag turned inside out, producing a driver's licence and bank cards and an old membership card of the Writers' Guild, ringing the Andersons to ask if Dr Anderson, as a senior member of the university, would vouch for her, and finally having a photograph taken of her which made her look a good ten years older than she actually was, which was then stamped into a piece of plastic which allowed her access to the University Library for the next twelve months.

It had left her feeling as if she had done a morning's work. She needed a break already, and she hadn't yet started. So she sat in the tea room, overlooking the churned turf of the back football pitch of Theo's school. The balding earth was a rich brown, almost navy blue, between the meagre wisps of dark wet green. She watched the children, rosy-cheeked and smeared with mud on knees that were bright with the cold, running in ragged clumps after a limp football and shouting cheerfully to each other. Every so often a young man with the chunky, track-suited good looks which depend more on youth and fitness than on any arrangement of features, blew a whistle, apparently at random, and regrouped the bunches of players.

Caz had not bought one of the famed University Library cheese scones. The tea room was out of cheese scones. She remembered, after she had ordered one and been told they were not available until teatime, that, in Ben's day, work in the UL had always stopped at around three twenty, when the scones appeared, as all but dons and third-year serious contenders for firsts had downed tools and streamed to the tea room in the hope of getting there before supplies ran out. Caz was relieved, actually. She hadn't really wanted a cheese scone. The breakfast at the Garden House had been more than generous, and she couldn't have managed one anyway. She had simply felt obliged to ask for the delicacy of the house.

And now that she was in the library, with the wealth of the world's English literature and reference at her fingertips, she suddenly found herself not the slightest bit interested in reading up her subject. The musician who had died so mysteriously in his mid-thirties a couple of hundred years ago seemed less interesting at the moment than the one who had done so a couple of years ago.

If she had shown some interest in writing a biography of Alan, she might have had a legitimate reason to find out what happened. She doodled on the scrap of paper in front of her, provided by the library for writing down computer reference numbers. She could remember reading, in some flimsy whodunnit she had picked up in a bored moment on a train or during a summer holiday, that the clue to the murder lay in the character of the victim. People get murdered because of who they are. Which was perhaps quite right for whodunnits, but did it happen in the real world?

Her doodle was turning into a right angle with a line at the base. Soon she'd be drawing a little rope with a loop in it, she mused. Most murders, as everyone knows, are domestic. So presumably most corpses are spouses, or brothers, aunts, children, grannies. But Alan Wedderburn? He was hardly bonked on the head with a blunt instrument by his wife or child. Frank said he had been in his own house. She didn't give much credence to his idea that the police genuinely knew who the culprit was. But perhaps he hadn't said 'the police'. Perhaps he had simply said 'they', and had meant the college authorities. What reason could a Cambridge college possibly have for hushing up a murder? A petty pilferer, perhaps, might be dismissed from service with a stern warning and no reference. But no respectable academic institution would turn a blind eye to a murderer.

She considered. Ann Fitzwilliam. Violinist. Irish, hadn't Theo said? Apparently quiet, unassuming. Still waters running deep, perhaps? Possibly Catholic, if she came from Ireland. Trapped in a loveless marriage to a man older than herself and far more successful; professionally jealous, and possibly more too? From what Caz had heard of him, Alan Wedderburn sounded the kind of man to whom adultery might come easily. So far so good, or bad, depending on how one looked at it. It was possible, even plausible. The college might well have suspicions in that direction, and not volunteer information to the police. A woman who kills her husband, for some desperate reason, is unlikely to be a threat to the rest of mankind, so the Provost and Dean might not feel a strong motivation to turn her in. And the reasons for remaining silent would be compelling indeed.

A brown sycamore leaf swirled past her window and drifted to the ground. Caz took a deep breath, clicked her tongue, and shook her head slightly before she remembered that she was in a public place. It was no good. If it were the plot for a prospective novel, Caz had to admit that she would not buy it. Why? Because she didn't believe it, that was why. It didn't fit Ann's character as it had been revealed to her so far. Of course, she had to admit that a real-life murderer didn't have to be quite as convincing as a fictional one, so the idea was still possible. But she didn't like it.

She must have been sitting there for ages. She was wasting time. If she was determined to muse all day over an event which had nothing to do with her, she would be better employed going to see Frank, and asking him what had happened. After all, he had promised to 'fill her in'.

The moment she thought of it, she wondered why she hadn't done it already. He would love to see her. He would also love to gossip. Once she had got this teaser solved, she would be able to get on with her book. She would telephone the college and ask to speak to him.

As she dialled the number, she looked out of the window again. She recognised a small blond head, a boy running clumsily, enjoying himself, but clearly not worrying whether he got to the ball before anyone else. He didn't. As half a dozen children clustered round it before him, he stopped running again, and stood, hands in the pockets of his track suit, gazing up at the library. For an odd moment, Caz almost thought he could see her, was looking straight at her, and wanted her to wave or acknowledge him somehow.

But of course he wouldn't know it was her. She would barely be a blob in the window to him, unrecognisable behind the glass that would be reflecting the dull sunlight.

Most homicides are domestic. Could a young boy, aged seven or whatever he was then, kill a fully grown man in the prime of life? Obviously not. Even if he could, no boy would ever want to. Not his own father. Freud nothing: even Oedipus did it by mistake.

Besides, Caz refused to harbour the thought that Theo Wedderburn would harm a fly. He was unusual, but he wasn't psychopathic. And he had the looks of an angel. He turned back to the game, and trotted dutifully after the ball.

She was through to the Porters' Lodge. 'Hello. Could I speak to Frank, please? I'm afraid I don't know his surname: he works in the Chapel. I think he's the verger.'

'Frank? Yes, of course you can, miss. I'll just put you through. Who shall I say it is?'

'Can you tell him it's Ben Sanderson's sister? He'll know who you mean.'

17

Caz was meeting Frank at half past two. Or so she thought. He had asked her to wait at the lodge, which she'd been doing for nearly fifteen minutes, and was now beginning to wonder whether he had meant the lodge of Ben's old college. Surely not: he would naturally mean the college where he had seen her last, where he was working now, unless he had specified otherwise. She told herself she would wait another five minutes, at least, before giving up.

She dug her hands in her pockets, and stared up King's Parade. It was a pleasant time of year, with few tourists, and a sense that the town belonged to the undergraduates and dons and their families, not the German and Italian coach companies. In a shop opposite, there was a 'Gentleman's Outfitters', displaying boating blazers, club ties, and college scarves, which Caz couldn't imagine anyone wearing after their first two weeks at the university. Further down, in Mowbrays Bookshop, a new Bible translation for children was on display, with various designs of church candle. The wind whipped leaves from the large horse chestnut in the front of the college, sent them somersaulting down the pavement, and twirled people's coats around them as they urged their bicycles against the buffeting October afternoon.

'There we are,' Frank said, appearing at her side as if from nowhere, and as if he were perfectly on time. 'Come along then, off we go.' And he set off, at a remarkable rate, clearly expecting her to follow, without a word of explanation. She dashed to catch up with him. He looked smaller without his cassock; better dressed, in an old-fashioned three piece suit, than any of the dons would have been. Caz wondered where they were going at such a pace.

'Here,' Frank said, steering her down a little alleyway she'd never noticed before.

A sudden gust of wind kicked the leaves up around their ankles, and persuaded Caz to pull her coat closer around her than before. Two undergraduates, coming towards them arm in arm, knocked into her, shoulder against shoulder, as they passed, and Caz was shocked at how young they looked. She and Frank twisted and turned through the narrow streets, bypassing the Market and appearing somewhere beyond the Corn Exchange, until they eventually found themselves at a little cast-iron gate set in an old brick wall.

'Here we are,' Frank said again, and produced from an inner pocket a shiny Yale key which looked far too new for the ancient, secret-looking gate in front of them. 'I've still got the key, you see. Once a member, always a member here.'

Caz looked about her, surprised. She hadn't recognised Ben's college from this hidden approach. They were in what looked like an ancient kitchen garden. It had an autumn bonfire smouldering in one corner and displayed neat rows of the early celery and late cabbages which were once seen in every middle-class Victorian household but were now to be found only in institutions like Oxbridge colleges and the occasional stately home.

She followed Frank as he wound his way through the garden and down some steps to a wooden door. Then he knocked on it, much as one might ask an old friend a polite, rhetorical question, and opened it without waiting for an answer. They went through another, inner door, and then Frank stood back to let her in.

'There,' he said.

Caz smiled, and looked around. They were in an enormous room, light and airy despite the fact that it was half under the ground. Along one wall was a vast range, hung with huge copper pans and great black kettles. The range was clearly not used, since along the other walls was every modern appliance one could expect: gas and electric cookers, microwaves, and a giant-size food-mixer. A large man, proportioned, as if deliberately, to match everything else in the room, stood, in his white coat and blue-striped apron and real chef's hat, at the gleaming stainless-steel table in the middle of the room where he was chopping something so tiny that Caz couldn't see what it was under his enormous hands. Another, younger man busied himself at one of the ovens.

'This is Miss Sanderson, boys. Famous writer,' Frank said proudly, as if he himself were responsible. 'Pete and Bill,' he explained to her.

'Hi,' Caz said, wondering what came next.

'Hello,' said Pete and Bill.

'There now,' Frank said, indicating the kitchen with a sweep of his arm. 'Unchanged since the time of Charles I. The range, the pots and pans, everything. Well, apart from the microwaves and that big table in the middle. Mind you, they still had the old oak table when I first came here as a boy. Sixteen, I was. Used to come on Saturdays, to begin with. Learnt the trade. The first thing I learnt was how to wait. "Soup from the left, wine from the right; soup from the left, wine from the right." I used to go into Hall muttering that under my breath. Terrified, I was, that I'd get it wrong. Students used to dress up for dinner in those days. Weren't allowed in without a gown, no sir. Ladies on Thursdays.

'And the second thing I learnt was the history of this kitchen. When Charles came back after the Reformation, back to England, this kitchen was just being built. And it hasn't been changed since.'

'Charles the Second?' Caz suggested.

'First. One with all the curls and the spaniels.' He thought for a moment. 'Or Second,' he added.

Caz smiled, and nodded. 'Gosh,' she said. She looked around her, trying to put a date on the room herself, but it could have been any time in the seventeenth century for all she knew. Or earlier. The fireplace reminded her of a line drawing in a history book she must have had before she even went to secondary school, of Lambert Simnel turning the spit in the king's kitchens after he had been discredited, and that must have been a good hundred years before either of the Charleses. 'It's, um – it's very interesting.'

'Interesting?' Frank said. 'I should say it is. And the most interesting thing about this kitchen is Pete's biscuits. They haven't changed much, either, since I was a boy here. Same recipe, passed from chef to chef. Best meringues in the university, and pretty well the best shortbread too.'

'Really?'

'You try 'em,' Frank said. 'You try 'em. I'm just going to show you upstairs, one or two things Mr Sanderson won't of told you about when he was here, and then we'll have a nice cup a tea and one or two of Pete's biscuits, won't we, Pete?'

'Fine by me,' Pete said, scraping whatever it was off his chopping board and into a large saucepan.

Frank was true to his word. Upstairs, in the deserted Hall, he showed Caz a stained-glass window which, whenever she had dined with Ben, she had always taken simply to be of the miracle of the loaves and the fishes. This time, however, when she looked under Frank's tutelage, she saw, for the first time, a little Tudor terrier defecating in one corner. On the opposite side of the Hall, in another window, he indicated to her, in the middle distance, a very unPalestinian cat chewing on some fishbones from the miraculous catch. And on the oak panelling behind the high table one of the carvings was discreetly picking its nose.

Having admired these random examples of college culture, Caz was taken back down to the kitchen where a stainless-steel pot of tea and a plate of home-made biscuits awaited them. 'Next time,' Frank said, 'I'll show you where the little boys used to climb up inside the chimney to clean the soot off.'

'Thank you,' Caz said, accepting the proffered cup. She had not long had lunch, and had no appetite for the strong, dark brown tea and more to eat, but she knew it wouldn't do any good to say so.

'Now then, Alan Wedderburn, wasn't it?' Frank said, as if her tour the other side of the green baize door had simply been a preliminary.

'Er, yes,' Caz said, and waited for more.

'It was Whistler,' Frank said.

There was a pause.

'Pardon?' Caz said at length. 'I mean, what do you mean, it was Whistler? What was Whistler?'

'Killed him. Common knowledge. Well,' he said, as if realising he had just debased his coinage, 'amongst those of us what knew. Common enough, if you know what I mean. Common enough.'

'Why didn't they lock him up?' Caz asked, wondering whether 'Whistler' was a euphemism she hadn't come across. For Aids perhaps? Or a new designer drug?

'Can't, can you? You know.' Frank pointed to his forehead and looked towards the ceiling. 'What they used to call simple.'

Caz glanced at Bill and Pete, wondering what they made of this conversation, but they were busy with their cooking and didn't seem to be interested, or even listening.

'Um, Frank,' Caz said. 'Who, or what, is Whistler?'

'Whistler. You know, Whistler. Well, that's what the boys called him. And it sort of stuck. Don't think he's got a real name any more. You've seen him around, haven't you?'

'Have I?'

'Bound to. Always around. Weekdays, usually. On his bike.'

'Around where?'

'College. You know.' He nodded encouragingly to her. 'Whistler.'

Caz had the feeling that the conversation had run full circle. She considered how to get it on to a new track. 'Is he a member of college?'

'No, of course he isn't!' Frank laughed at Caz's simplicity. 'At least, I don't think he is,' he qualified. 'It's because of a motor bike accident, so I suppose he could have been. Better than ever, these, Pete. Give Miss Sanderson another.'

'No, no really, thanks. Delicious though.'

They seemed to have reached an impasse. Caz found herself wondering again how those who made journalism their full-time career ever managed to get the information they wanted without becoming obnoxious. Frank seemed to have told her all he wanted to. The polite thing now would be to drop the subject, and talk about the weather, or his wife and children. But she wanted to know more.

'Er, Frank.' She hesitated. 'Why do you think . . . I mean, how d'you *know* this person Whistler killed Alan Wedderburn?'

'Well, generally known, innit?' he said simply. 'I say they should bring back capital punishment. I mean, why should a bloke like Alan Wedderburn . . . genius, in his own way. Not necessarily the easiest of men, but then why should he be? He was a genius, you know. And why should a nice lady like Mrs Wedderburn, and little Theo, who never did anyone any harm; I mean, I'm sure he's a monkey, they all are. But basically he's as innocent as the day is long. Why should they suffer, just because some trendy lefty politicians somewhere want to be all liberal and progressive about things? Why should they, eh?'

'Bringing back capital punishment wouldn't necessarily have saved Mr Wedderburn, though, Frank.'

'Course it would. You're not going to go bumping someone off if you're going to get hanged for it, are you? I mean, would you? Honestly?'

'No, but I wouldn't—'

'There you are then.'

'In countries where they've tried it, they haven't found—'

'Berrrh!' Frank scoffed. 'Load of statistics, that is. Besides, nothing would make any difference to old Whistler. He's nuts in the head, he is,' he concluded triumphantly. 'Well, can't sit here all day. Pete's got work to do, a'n't you, Pete?'

Pete merely nodded, without looking up. Perhaps this was the answer Frank wanted, because he made no attempt to move. They sat in silence for a while, before Frank said, 'It's the kid I feel sorry for. My mother died when I was a nipper. Thirteen I was. I was never the same again. Never got on with my dad after that, either. I blamed him, somehow. Poor bloke, don't suppose it was his fault. Anyway, there we are. That's life, innit?'

Caz hesitated a moment before saying anything. Then she plucked up courage. 'What happened, exactly?'

'She had cancer. People did in those days, didn't they? Mind you, they still do, I suppose. The Big C, they used to call it. As I say, it was hardly his fault. Though some people do say it's to do with stress, don't they?'

'Do they?' Caz asked without much enthusiasm. 'I just wondered, um, how exactly Alan Wedderburn died?'

'Coshed on the head, wasn't he? Bastard came in late one night and coshed him on the head. That Whistler's been hanging around for years looking for mischief. Not exactly looking for it: he's too daft to know what he's looking for. But, you know. Come on then, off we go.' And this time he really did get up.

'Thank you,' Caz said, rising to her feet. 'Thanks, Pete. The biscuits are lovely.' Pete looked up from his work for the briefest of smiles, and then resumed.

Caz followed Frank out into the dark October afternoon. The whodunnit was solved.

The anticlimax was complete. Alan Wedderburn had been bashed on the head by a brain-damaged lunatic who had been prowling around his house. The mystery was over, if there had ever been a mystery at all.

She had no excuse now not to work on her book.

18

'To please you, best of fathers, I would sacrifice my happiness, my health and my life; but my honor is my own' –
W.A. Mozart

Theo, Alan and Ann were on holiday. They had taken a cottage in the countryside, up a winding, deserted road, three miles out of the village, near the beach, behind high secretive mossy stone walls. It was called Pink Cottage. Theo loved it. They arrived early in the morning, having driven all night, and, as they looked through the gateway, the pink walls of the house were winking in the early sunshine and the honeysuckle was dancing around the doorway.

Theo scrambled out of the car and ran through the little wooden gate into the garden. It was a real country garden, with tall hollyhocks and blue delphiniums and bright, garish gladioli. The lawn was full of daisies and dandelions and clover, and the paths were overgrown with grass. Theo tumbled and somersaulted and rolled in the grass like a puppy, and when he was sick of that he ran back to the car, and found his parents had done nothing, and were still rubbing their eyes and yawning and sitting in the car with the doors open.

'Come on,' he said. 'Come and see the lovely garden.'

'Tippy,' his father said, 'give us a break.'

'I'll come,' Ann said. She hadn't been the last one to drive, so she wasn't as tired as Alan was. She heaved herself out of the car in that weary, heavy way that adults have, and held on to Theo's hand and followed him into the garden.

'Mmm,' she said. 'It's lovely.'

Then she sat on the bench and closed her eyes against the morning sun. Theo gave up. He went back to the car. His father was carrying boxes of groceries into the little kitchen. He looked tired and used up. Theo thought he needed help. He went to the boot and picked up a plastic bag with pillow cases in it, and then a small cardboard box with a loaf of sliced bread in a see-through plastic wrapper, and a jar of jam, and packets of butter and cheese, and a Thermos. His arms were nearly full. There was another plastic carrier bag with some of Alan's books in, so he took that with his free hand and went towards the house. As he reached the gate, he saw a blue flower wagging its head just above his. He stopped to look at it, and realised there was a ladybird crawling along one of the leaves. It had its black wings half showing, as they do if they've just been flying. Theo wondered where it had been.

Ladybird, ladybird, fly away home; Your house is on fire, your children all gone. Why does one think of ladybirds as she, always? You do, though, don't you? Though presumably there are male ladybirds too. It must be the name. Ladybird. If it were a gentlemanbird, you'd think of it as male. Theo realised he was in his father's way, so he moved on towards the house.

As he did so, his father said, 'Mind that bag, Tippy. Look!' He looked down, as best he could, over the box, and realised the plastic of the bag was tearing under the handle. Help. He could drop the box to catch the books, or he could let the books' bag tear and scatter books on to the ground. If he dropped the box, things would break. But if he didn't . . . at that point the bag tore some more and Theo let go of everything and gathered his father's precious books into his arms.

'Theo!' his mother screamed. 'Oh, for goodness' sake!' She sounded distraught. He turned and looked at the jam and glass all over the path. The Thermos would probably be broken too. Theo said nothing. He knew the adults would be upset. Adults often are. Often, they can't see the important things, because they're so busy looking at the unimportant things. Alan's books are far more important than jam and Thermos flasks. His books are part of his music, his work. You have to get that right, and then it pays for jam and Thermoses.

'Never mind,' Ann said. 'Thank you for helping. Go and pop those down inside, could you?'

Theo took his armful of books inside, then heard his parents talking.

'Couldn't you have helped him, Alan?' His mother was down on her knees, picking up bits of broken glass with jam on them. Theo hoped she was being careful, otherwise she would cut her fingers.

'I did,' his father said, walking into the house. This was true, in a way. He had warned Theo the bag was splitting.

'Please don't walk off like that,' his mother called. Alan put some things down on the table. His cheek was twitching. Theo felt a knot tighten inside his stomach. 'Alan, please!' his mother said.

It was his fault, of course. His parents would never say that, because they were too polite, and because it was so obvious. But if he hadn't dropped the box, nobody would be upset. He started to take the books out of the split bag. They were mostly books about music. He arranged them neatly on the kitchen table. He liked the kitchen. It caught the morning sun, and had clean white cupboards with nothing in them, and a gas cooker. Alan had gone back out to the car for more things. His mother came into the kitchen, but when she saw Theo, she didn't smile at first; not until she'd thought about it for a moment. Then she did, in a tired way, as if she didn't mean it.

'Have you seen a dustpan and brush anywhere?' she asked. Theo shook his head, and wondered where to look for one. Ann started opening the lower cupboards in the kitchen, and looking under the sink. It amazed Theo that adults often know where things might be kept, even in houses that don't belong to them. It must be to do with the fact that adults have lived longer, so have learnt something that he hadn't yet, but he couldn't quite see how that was. You don't get a class at school which goes, 'When you're in someone else's house, they will keep the dustpan and brush under the sink.' And yet Ann knew to look there, and Theo didn't.

Alan came in with some bags, put them on the floor, and said, 'That's nearly it.' Then he went over to Ann and put his arms round her.

'Why are you so annoyed with me?' she said.

'I'm not,' he said, breaking away from her, and looking annoyed. Then he saw Theo. 'Here,' he said, and put his arms around Ann and Theo both. 'Isn't Mummy silly?'

'No,' Theo said.

'No,' Alan agreed. 'Quite right. Thank you for looking after my books. Can't expect a woman to understand.'

Theo stiffened slightly. He was thrilled more than he could say that his father had noticed how he had cared for his books. But why had he been so rude to Ann? It made Theo very uncomfortable.

'Come on,' Alan continued. 'Let's have a bit of breakfast, then we need a long sleep. I do, anyway. You won't, because you were asleep in the car,' he said to Theo. 'You'll have to read a book, or explore the garden, while we go and have a lie down. All right?'

Theo had been mad with anticipation before the holiday. His mother had been looking forward to it so much, packing and planning and talking about all the things they would do, that he had built up a picture of the three of them on the beach, playing cricket, paddling, catching crabs, his father relaxed and idle as he seldom was at home. He imagined them blackberrying, unaware that blackberries didn't appear in June. And his father reading to him late at night. And cosy, unhurried family suppers.

And it was partly like that. On the first evening, Alan drove down to the village for fish-and-chips, and they sat in the garden in the late sunshine eating out of a newspaper. Theo went to bed late, in a little room next to his parents', and heard them pottering about long after his light was out, and the rustling of pages as one of them read in bed and the other got undressed, and the gentle murmur of voices.

A long time later, when they must have thought him asleep, he heard them moving in bed, and his mother giggling, and then saying, 'Just a minute,' and getting up and shutting his door. He was sorry she had shut his door, as it made him feel a little lonely and frightened, and he wanted to ask them to open it again. But he understood, not only that his mother thought him asleep, but also that she wanted him to be asleep, and he kept quiet. After the door was shut, he heard the noise of his parents having a long and vigorous cuddle, and knew that they wouldn't have wanted him there.

The next morning, when he woke up, he wondered what he should do. He wanted to go in and see his parents, but they might still be having the cuddle they were having the night before, and perhaps they would be embarrassed if they thought he knew.

In the end, he decided to rattle the door for a long time before opening it. He got up and went over to the door. He couldn't hear anything. They had probably finished their cuddle. Nevertheless, he took hold of the handle and shook it and shook it, to warn them he was coming in. When he thought he had given them a long enough warning, he tried to open the door. It wouldn't open. He turned the handle again and pushed again, but still it didn't open. Then he heard his father's heavy tread on the other side of the door, and the key turning in the lock, and his father opened the door.

Theo reddened with shame. His parents must think him very stupid, that he couldn't tell when a door was locked and when it wasn't. If he'd known it was locked, he wouldn't have rattled and rattled like that: he would simply have knocked and waited.

'Hi,' Alan said.

'Hi.' He could see Ann asleep in the bed. So they hadn't been having a cuddle anyway: they must have locked the door the previous night. Theo wandered over to the bed and climbed into it. His mother turned and put her arms around him, and then his father got in the other side and put his arms around both of them. They lay there quite content for what seemed a lovely long time.

When they were on holiday, Ann would buy special treats: peaches and cream to go on their muesli in the morning; Coca-Cola or tropical fruit juice for Theo for supper; and what she called 'local produce'. She would buy whatever she saw as the particular treat of the place they were in. Here, she told Theo, they must eat lots of fresh seafood and double-cream ice-cream. And Cornish pasties, of course. He wasn't sure why it was 'of course', but there are some things that adults know, magically, so he assumed it must be one of those.

That morning, after they had all had a cuddle in bed, Alan got up and made the tea for breakfast. Ann and Theo didn't bother to get dressed. They came down in their pyjamas, and found the breakfast all laid in the kitchen, and the top half of the front door open on to the little yard overlooking the gate into the quiet lane, and orange juice poured into three glasses and tea poured into three large cups. Ann smiled. 'Thank you,' she said.

After breakfast, Theo went out into the garden to explore. The sun came through the leaves in a pattern of pale green, full of secrets and promises locked under the shrubs and in the tree tops. Theo heard a tap-tap, tap-tapping noise, and turned to see a thrush knocking a snail against a stone. He stood, trapped in awful sympathy for the terrified snail, and the feeling of helplessness as it was smashed against the hard, smooth instrument of execution. Birds sang in the trees, and a woodpigeon cooed beyond the garden, in the trees on the slope of the hill below the house. It all seemed to hold a shimmering image of another world, a Narnia, an eternity which you might break into any time, almost by mistake.

Theo walked to the end of the garden. A low, tumbledown brick wall ran along the edge of the undergrowth, covered in brambles and foxgloves and deadnettles, with their sweet, honey-tasting flowers which promised that they wouldn't sting. He looked over the wall and down the slope of the hill, where sheep seemed pasted on to the landscape, silent and almost completely still. Suddenly, with a longing Theo had never experienced before, he wished, so hard that it hurt, that he had a brother or a sister. A dog, even. Someone with whom he could come here, and play, and know he or she would be his companion always. A hawk soared above the field with the sheep in it. Theo knew it was a hawk, because he had read about them in the encyclopedia at home, but he didn't know which kind. It looked too big to be a kestrel. With some excitement, he wondered whether it could be a kite. Just a dog would be fine. He would call it Rover, and tell it to fetch sticks out of ponds and streams, and they would watch the hawk together, to see whether it caught anything.

Suddenly, like a stone, it dropped. Theo caught his breath. There was a scuffle on the ground, and the bird rose with something in its claws. After a few seconds, it seemed to drop it again. It dived again, fumbled, then rose with its claws empty. Theo let out his breath. A baby rabbit was safe for another day.

He found himself back near the house. They were going shopping that afternoon. Ann had said so. 'As soon as we get organised, we'll go for a shop this afternoon.' Theo wasn't sure whether it would be the two of them, or the three of them. Probably all three of them. They did things together quite a lot when Alan was on holiday. It was quite nice, really. He stepped into the house by the back door. There was a strange sound. He stopped to listen to it for a moment. Because he'd been thinking about dogs, it occurred to him that the sound was a bit like the sound of a dog, snuffling. It made him smile. He went into the little sitting room at the back of the house.

Suddenly he felt that tightening in his stomach which made him feel sick, sometimes. The sound was of someone sobbing. But not a child. It isn't frightening when children cry: children are supposed to cry. Theo tiptoed through the sittingroom in the direction of the crying. He went into the hall, and suddenly, under the stairs in the hall, saw his mother crouched on the ground with her face red and blotchy and wet, and pulled down in an ugly expression. The sobs seemed to be coming out of her like huge gusts of wind tearing at trees. Theo stared in horror for a moment, then realised, as if he had suddenly woken up, that it wasn't a picture, it wasn't a film, that his mother really was upset and crying, just as he himself might if someone had been unkind to him. He sat down on the floor next to her, and tried to put his arms around her.

'What's the matter?' he said, as she sometimes said to him if he was upset. She shuddered again, and sobbed again, and then wiped her nose on her sleeve and her eyes with the back of her hand, and said, 'Hello, Tippy. Um. Nothing really. I'm just being silly.' Then she burst into tears again, and held on to him tightly, and leant her head against his. 'I'm sorry; that's a stupid thing to say. Of course something's the matter. It's just . . . Oh, I don't know. Alan needs a bit of time to unwind when we go on holiday, that's all. I'm not used to it. That's all.' She tried to smile at him. 'Silly, isn't it? I've lived with him for twelve years, and I'm still not used to it.' Then she took a funny kind of breath, and burst into tears all over again. Theo hugged her, and she held on to him tightly, and when she'd finished that bit of crying, she said, 'Oh, I do love you, Tippy.'

'What happened?' Theo asked her.

'Nothing really. He was just a bit beastly to me, that's all. He didn't mean it. He just gets very tired.'

Theo held on to his mother, and thought hard. When he was inconsiderate, his parents and teachers told him so. How often had he been told, 'We know you didn't *mean* to be selfish, Theo, but you have just kept twenty-five people waiting. You really can't treat people like that. Do you think you're the most important person in the world, or what?'

Even when Theo was selfish, like that, he didn't make people cry in the way his mother was crying now. His father ought to be told. In fact, he would *want* to be told. His parents often got cross with him, Theo, because they loved him. They said so. And Theo loved his father. Of course. He stood up.

'Where is Alan?' he said.

'I don't know. Gone out somewhere.' Ann rested her face in her arms. She seemed to have finished crying now, and was just tired.

Theo went and let himself out through the front door. The car was there, so his father couldn't be far away. He went to the gate and looked up and down the little lane. He wasn't allowed out on his own, and he wasn't allowed to cross roads on his own either, but it didn't matter any more. He went out through the gate and decided to turn right. There was no one on the road in front of him. It was hot, and the midges danced in the air. He wondered whether midges were ever frightened of their fathers, whether their mothers ever cried.

There was a rumbling somewhere. Was it thunder? Theo walked on, knowing thunder wasn't dangerous to someone his size: it's tall people, and trees and swimming pools and cathedrals, which need to be careful of thunder – well, lightning, really. The thunder grew, like a monster in a nightmare. Theo kept walking. Suddenly, with a terrifying roar like a lion jumping out of a cage at him, a huge lorry belted past, shaking the ground and frightening all the grass on the verge around so that it lay down in the blast. The dust and wind from the lorry hurled themselves at Theo, and before he had realised what the danger was, it was past him and thundering up the hill.

Theo knew cars were dangerous. The most dangerous things he was likely to meet, Ann said. Traffic was almost the only thing which made her angry.

He had heard her talking to Alan about it.

'If someone tried to introduce a drug,' she said, 'which was going to make everyone's life easier and do wonders for the economy of the country but kill several hundred children a year, there'd be an outcry. At least I hope there would. Three thousand people a year. A child a day. Think of it.'

Theo's knees were shaking so much, he had to sit down by the side of the road. He found himself saying, Thank you that he was still alive. Whom was he thanking? He didn't know.

He shut his eyes and buried his face in his knees. He remembered his mother, sitting like that with her face red from crying. He must find Alan. Alan would take him home safely, and make sure he wasn't run over by a lorry.

Still trembling, he stood up and walked on, stumbling a bit, keeping safely away from the road. He could feel his skin hot and prickly under his tee-shirt. A bird flew up in front of him, startled, calling as it went. As he walked on, he felt something burning, biting his legs, and looked down to find that he was walking through stinging nettles. He rubbed his legs, trying to catch the itching, and saw his flesh swell in lumps of scarlet spots all over his thighs and knees. His eyes began to prick. Suddenly, under a tree, he saw a figure sitting on a bench. It was Alan! It must be.

Theo had read about mirages in deserts, and knew that you can sometimes imagine the thing you most want to see. It had happened to him once in a supermarket, when he was with Ann, or rather, he wasn't with Ann but he should have been. He had run up to her and taken her hand, and she had turned into another woman altogether.

But this parent didn't seem to be turning into a stranger. As Theo got nearer, the man looked more and more like Alan. He was sitting on the bench, with sheets of paper and a pencil, and he was writing. He was composing, in fact. So it must be Alan, because other people's fathers didn't compose.

As he got near, Theo reminded himself why he had come. Alan must know. His legs were sore and burning from the nettles, and he was trembling from the shock of the lorry, but he had come looking for his father with a purpose, and he must deal with that first.

'You hurt Ann,' he blurted. 'You must say sorry.'

Alan looked up. 'What?' he said.

'You hurt Ann. You have to go home and say sorry to her.'

There was a long pause. Alan and Theo looked at each other. The grass whispered in the background, and the birds chattered and bustled about, but neither of them looked away. Theo noticed that the pupils of his father's eyes were small in the bright sunlight, and the muscles of his jaw were clenching and unclenching. He looked at him so hard that his father's nose went slightly blurred, but he didn't look away. His legs itched, but he didn't look down to scratch them.

In the end, Alan put his papers down on the bench beside him, and laid his pencil on the top, and spoke very quietly. 'How dare you?' he said. 'How dare you talk to me like that?'

'You talk to me like that,' Theo said. 'When I've done something wrong.'

Alan continued looking at him for a moment. Then he picked up his paper and pencil again, and continued writing. 'I think you'd better go back home,' he said, without looking up.

Theo didn't move. He thought of Ann, with her breath coming out of her in sobs, and he didn't move. After a while, Alan said again without looking up: 'Theo, I have told you to go back home. If you're still there in thirty seconds you'll get a smack. And it will be quite a hard one.'

'You didn't tell me to go home,' Theo corrected him. He found he was shaking again, and it was difficult to control his voice. 'You said you thought I'd better go home. I can't go home on my own, because we came here in a car, and I can't drive. And you've done wrong to Ann and ought to say sorry, because that's what you tell me to do.'

'How the hell d'you know what went on between your mother and me?' His father's voice was like a train coming at him through a tunnel. 'What gives you the right to interfere between us, eh? And what does she think she's doing, manipulating us both, sending you to talk to me like this, instead of coming herself?'

The injustice of this last remark stung Theo like a slap in the face. Did his father really think his mother would send him, down a dangerous road where he could have been killed, to talk to his father because she wouldn't come herself? Then it dawned on Theo, with a suddenness which took his breath away, that his father had tried to send him back along that same road, on his own. Did he not care if Theo were killed? He bit hard on his own teeth to try to stop the shaking, and refused to blink, and realised that his face felt hot.

'Hey,' Alan said, and his anger had dropped off him like a coat from his shoulders. 'Hey, come here.' Theo didn't move. His father would get cross again in a moment, because he wasn't doing as he'd been told. Soon he would be smacked, and then it would be like at school, as frightening as the outer darkness, where people gnash their teeth. He didn't move a millimetre. 'Come on,' his father said gently. He got up from the bench and put his arm around his son. 'You're right; you shouldn't go home alone along this road. You shouldn't have walked here either. What were you doing?' He led Theo back to the bench.

'Looking for you. You were horrible to Mummy.'

'Was I? How do you know? How d'you know she wasn't horrible to me? Mmm?'

Theo didn't know how to explain this. How could he tell his father that his mother was never horrible like that, never deliberately unkind, never made you feel small, as Alan could do. That she sometimes got cross, but was always gentle even then; and that she was never, ever, frightening. Theo said nothing. 'Come on,' his father went on. 'Let's go back home. Perhaps I was horrible. Sorry.' His father sighed, and shuffled his papers into a pile, and picked up his pencil. 'I'm writing a new anthem. I will lift up mine eyes unto the hills, from whence cometh my help.' Theo looked up at his father's face. He wasn't looking at any hills. There were none to look at. 'My help cometh from the lord.' Then his father started to hum a new tune. 'You'll like it,' he said. 'I'll play it to you when I've finished.'

People admired Theo's father's music. Ann didn't write music. She didn't even play her violin. But writing music counted for nothing, Theo told himself. Nothing, nothing, nothing. His mother was beautiful, and kind, and it didn't matter if she never played her violin again.

'Come on,' his father said again, as he took his hand. They walked along the road. Theo was safe now.

Theo loved his father. Of course. Everyone loves their parents. It's like parents loving their children. You sort of can't help it. Ann had said to Theo once, 'There's nothing you could do so naughty that I wouldn't love you any more.'

'What, murder even?' he said, expecting her to laugh and say, well, murder didn't count.

'Murder, even,' she said solemnly. 'You remember that. The day you think you've finally stepped beyond the pale, you come to me, and you'll find I still love you.'

'Beyond what pail?'

So Ann told Theo how the English had mistreated the Irish in the seventeenth century, and how the area around Dublin was called The Pale, and how anyone living beyond that was, well, beyond the pale.

'Is Alan English?' Theo had asked.

'As English as anyone ever is,' Ann replied.

He had often thought about that conversation since. But it was a long time ago, and even Ann couldn't have foreseen what would happen.

The choral scholars in Alan's choir did madrigals in the summer, on the river. They would sit in punts, and people would crowd along the Backs and on the college bridge and in their own punts, and listen to the contrapuntal lines of music weaving and tussling, disagreeing and agreeing again, the river carrying the music down to them as water always does. Contrapuntal, of course, is nothing to do with punts, but Theo didn't know that then.

One of the madrigals was about a turtle dove. It was Theo's favourite. It's not really about a bird, but about a man telling you how much he loves his girlfriend: *till all the seas run dry, my love, and the rocks melt with the sun*. The soft way the music swims and dips is just the way a turtle dove would, gentle and cooing and pale grey, with the tune singing itself in your head for days.

That was the way Ann said she would love him, like the turtle dove sitting on its branch singing to its love, and loving her for ever and ever and ever. Or that was what she thought then.

So Theo told himself that must be how he loved his father.

Yet there were times when Theo thought he almost hated him. That moment on holiday was a time like that. When Theo saw his mother crouching under the stairs with her face all red and blotchy, he realised afterwards he had not just wanted to tell his father because he thought his father would want to know. He has also wanted to hurt him, badly. He had clenched his fists and wanted to break something up so completely it would never be itself again, and the image he had before his eyes was the image of his father's face. He thought that, if he had been fully grown and stronger than his mother, as she said he would be one day, he might have picked his father up and shaken him and told him he was never to treat her like that again. But in fact he couldn't even walk down the road safely without his father's hand.

As they walked back along the road, it was as if the hurt Alan had inflicted on Ann were all forgotten. Alan hummed his new anthem, in all its four parts in turn, singing the bass line in his rich, resonating deep voice, which seemed to Theo to be more powerful even than the lorry that had roared past him half an hour before. His voice on the tenor part was thin, as he sang the higher notes, but when he got to the alto his falsetto seemed as vigorous as his low voice, startling the birds into fleeing before them, and causing a cow to stare over the high hedge in alarm. It was a good piece, the lines of music always going where the ear expected them to, resolving in the right places, and sounding sweet, like strawberry fool or syllabub would if you listened to it instead of eating it.

'Now, the best bit. D'you want to hear the treble line?'

'You can't sing the treble line,' Theo objected, smiling despite himself.

'Of course I can. I didn't spend six years at Salisbury Cathedral for nothing.'

'But that was when you were a little boy,' Theo pointed out. 'Your voice has broken since then.'

'Never mind,' Alan said. 'It's like riding a bicycle. Once learnt, never forgotten.'

It occurred to Theo that Alan was just saying these silly things to cheer him up. Nevertheless, as he put his voice into high gear again, and, instead of singing a decent manly alto, started singing the top Fs and Gs of the treble part, Theo found that he was unable to keep his solemnity. His father was singing frighteningly well, absolutely in tune of course and almost like a boy, a rather grotesque, slightly coarse but genuine treble, in the body of a bass, a real grown-up man.

'Daddy,' Theo said. 'Daddy, there's someone coming, look!' Theo hardly ever called Alan 'Daddy', but the embarrassment of seeing a man with a dog walking down the road towards them while Alan made that dreadful, nearly-respectable noise shocked him into it. The man was quite a long way off, the other side of the dip in the road, but Theo thought he could probably hear Alan already. Alan didn't stop singing. He waved his free hand at Theo, as if to say, 'Listen to this bit,' and crescendoed up to an outrageous A. Theo thought all the sheep for several fields around must be able to hear it.

'Daddy!' he said one more time. Then he began to giggle. The man with the dog bent down and busied himself with the dog's collar and lead. It was awful, the way Alan was singing so loudly; and of course that was what made it so funny. Theo couldn't stop laughing now. Alan winked at him, as he did a little run of semi-quavers and finally came to rest on the key note, and Theo pulled on Alan's arm to get him to stop but at the same time didn't want him to because it was so funny. The man with the dog was much nearer now, and had straightened up and was trying not to look at them. Theo controlled his laughter to a smirk and looked at the ground, and by the time they came nearly level with the man, Alan had stopped singing and was looking fairly normal, and Theo was hardly even giggling.

Just as they passed him, Alan said in a loud voice. 'That was very nice, Sebastian. Now can you do it in a different key: how about trying it in Fotherington-Thomas Minor?'

By the time they got back to the house, they were singing carols: Theo carried the tune – which is easy really – while Alan improvised new harmonies below, and sometimes even above him. It was odd, singing 'In the bleak mid-winter', while Alan sweated and Theo's forehead glistened in the heat. And as they sang that they wanted to '*Gi – i – i – ive my heart*', Theo thought how much more sensible that was than giving frankincense and myrrh. After all, if Jesus were as rich as all that, why would he need gold and things? Nevertheless it felt odd, singing it in the summer.

They rounded the corner of the wall, and opened the little gate which led to the house. And there, in the doorway, Ann stood with a smile on her face. In the first instant that he saw her, Theo felt guilty. He started to take his hand from Alan's, feeling that he had betrayed someone, somehow. But as soon as he saw her smile, he felt it was all right again.

It wasn't until they sat down over tea that he saw how red her eyes were, and that she wasn't really smiling behind them. She was just smiling on the surface, because she'd heard them singing down the lane and had wanted them to think that she was happy, too.

19

Caz didn't want to spend another night in her hotel room. It was expensive, and soulless, and, as she didn't allow herself to read when she was working on a book, there was nothing to do except watch the television, or drink too much, which she didn't want to do because of the baby. It made her feel very homesick. She had seen, when she stopped to browse in David's Bookshop round the corner, a little handwritten card advertising lodgings near the Arts Theatre. If she decided to stay any longer than the next day, she thought she would look for a room like that.

When she got back to her room she took a fresh sheet of Garden House writing paper and wrote a quick note to Ann Fitzwilliam:

Dear Ann,

Many thanks for lunch yesterday. It was very good of you to look after me on such a brief acquaintance, and it was delicious. Thank you.

I am planning to go back to London by the end of the week, and will probably move to a bed and breakfast till then. I wondered whether you found anything among your books which might be relevant to my research? I wonder if I could give you a quick ring later on to find out?

Yours,

Caz Sanderson

She frowned. She had used 'wonder' twice in two sentences. And the two its in the second sentence didn't make sense: she had made it sound as if Ann's kind gesture had been delicious. She took another sheet of paper.

Dear Ann,
   Many thanks for lunch yesterday, which was delicious and very relaxing . . .

It sounded sycophantic. She eventually settled on her third attempt, folded it, and put it in an envelope. Do all writers redraft their letters several times? she wondered. She had known herself spend half a morning on a letter to a bank.

It wasn't until she had sealed the envelope that she realised she was going home. She had written it three times, so it must be true. She put the note in her pocket and went out.

Twenty minutes later she was in Sylvester Road attempting to deliver it. As she struggled to push it through the cast-iron letter flap, which she found was sprung with far too strong a spring, she contemplated what she would do with the rest of her afternoon. The library would be open for a few more hours. She would go back and do the work she should have done that morning. The thought of it was beginning to make her quite enthusiastic, and when she finally got her letter through the flap and turned to go she was genuinely looking forward to getting back to work.

'Hello!'

Caz jumped, with a little cry, and put her hand on her chest. 'Oh! Hello,' she said lamely. 'I thought you were out.'

'I am,' Ann replied, and smiled. 'Please come in.'

'Aren't you busy?' Caz asked, meaning that she thought she herself ought to be.

'Not yet. Please come in.'

She followed Ann into the house.

'Tea?' she said, putting the kettle on before she received an answer.

'I've not long had some,' Caz started to say, and then added, 'but actually, yes, I'd love some more. Thank you.' As Ann put down her shopping and pottered about, warming the teapot and opening cupboards, Caz tried to fill the conversational silence. 'I met up with an old acquaintance, Frank – I don't even know his surname. He used to be my brother's gyp some years ago.'

'The verger?'

'Yes.'

'He'll have been giving you all the gossip, no doubt. Dear Frank.' Ann shook her head affectionately.

'Well, yes.' Then, so quickly that she had no chance to change her mind, she said, 'Who's Whistler?'

'Oh,' Ann said with a little laugh. 'Did Frank tell you Whistler killed Alan?'

Caz was taken aback, surprised that Ann could say it so lightly. But then, she wondered, how else would you say it? If anything happened to Will, for instance, how would she say, of someone she knew: That was the man who killed my lover. 'Yes, I'm afraid he did,' she admitted.

'He'll say it to a journalist one of these days, and be done for libel. Oh dear, you are a sort of journalist, aren't you? I wonder if Whistler's solicitor would do anything about it, if anyone did print anything.'

'I wasn't planning to write an article for the *Daily Mail*,' she replied, already feeling exposed and rather guilty. Ann nodded, as if in agreement, and said nothing while she poured out the tea.

'I just wondered who he is,' Caz persisted, despite herself.

'Milk, no sugar?'

'Please.'

Ann put the mugs on a tray, and fetched a cake tin from the larder in the corner of her kitchen. 'I only have fruit cakes now, I'm afraid. They have to be able to last from one weekend to the next; Theo takes several huge slices on a Saturday afternoon, then I forget the poor cake all week till he comes again. The number of sponge cakes I've had to throw away because they broke like a biscuit at the sight of the knife . . . Let's go and sit in the sitting room. It overlooks the garden. I love my garden. I think of it as a best friend, in a funny way. That and my violin,' she added after a moment's pause. 'I suppose my violin's a better friend to me than my garden, as it could provide me with a living. My violin's a bit like a lover: all or nothing. Whereas my garden's like a kind old parent. There for me when I want it; requiring a little attention, but not much; comfortable and comforting.'

'I'd love to hear you play,' Caz said, gazing out across the long shadows in Ann Wedderburn's undemanding garden.

Ann laughed. 'Well, maybe. Do sit down. The sofa's a lot more comfortable than it looks. Whistler,' she continued, sitting in the armchair near the empty fireplace, 'is, well, what is he?' She gazed into her mug. 'He's not a tramp. He's not destitute. He's a sort of hanger-on, really. I suppose he's a chorophile. He loves the choir, and choral music, and the Chapel. I don't know much about him, when it comes down to it. I believe he goes up to Ely, and Peterborough, and listens to the choirs there. On his bicycle, apparently. Perhaps he takes it on the train. He's unemployed. Technically, he's disabled. He lives in a council flat and just . . . does nothing. When I was young I didn't think people could do nothing. But I do nothing now. What do you do? I mean, I know you write, but what have you done today? Sorry: that was an impertinent question; you've probably written pages and pages before lunch, and looked up twenty references in the University Library this afternoon.'

'No,' Caz said. 'I've done nothing, actually.'

'There you are then.' Ann smiled. 'Alan was completely incapable of doing nothing. He couldn't sit still for five minutes. I think that's why I'm so inactive now. I sort of reacted, when I met him, and slowed down, and I don't seem able to speed up again now he's gone. He had so much energy, I think it used to spin off him, on to us. Or on to me, anyway. I didn't need any energy of my own, because he had enough for three. And now there's nobody around with any energy any more.'

The two women sat, comfortable with one another, demanding nothing, with their hands wrapped round their tea mugs, looking out across the lawn.

'On holiday,' Ann said, 'on the beach, everywhere, Alan would come out of the sea and take a pencil and paper out of my handbag and write down a new setting for a psalm, or a descant for a carol. Coming down the ski slope he'll be composing a new cantata.' Caz observed, intrigued, that Ann had slipped into the present tense. 'And then, if you talk to him at the café over lunch he'll get really annoyed, because you're interrupting him at his work. But he won't say, he won't tell you . . . I mean, you wouldn't realise why . . . Look,' she said suddenly, abruptly turning to the window.

'There's a thrush with a snail. It distresses Theo dreadfully when they do that. He thinks it must hurt so much. The snail, I mean. I once asked him why he didn't stop the bird doing it; chase it away, you know. He said it would only make it worse. He has a theory that you shouldn't interfere with nature, unless you know exactly what balance everything has with everything else. Theo has all sorts of theories. He's usually right. It's the result, I suppose, of spending so much time apparently doing nothing. He thinks, you see. Alan used to believe he was backward, when he was two or three years old. He thought he was seriously stupid. You ask him if he wants an egg for breakfast, and he doesn't answer you for five minutes. So you ask him several times, and eventually he says, "Sorry, what? Would I what? What did you say?" So the tendency is to think, This child is really stupid. And what you don't realise is that he's been sitting there all along working out why honeysuckle grows clockwise in the northern hemisphere and anti-clockwise in the southern hemisphere, and why it doesn't work in the same way with water going down the plughole. It's lucky he is bright, because Alan always hated stupidity more than anything. He could never have lived with a stupid son. Though I suppose it wouldn't have mattered, as it turned out.'

Caz took a drink of her tea, before saying gently, 'It would, though, wouldn't it?'

'Yes. Yes, of course it would.'

'It will always be important to Theo, what his father thought of him.'

'Yes. Though—' She stopped. 'Though I wish he'd lived. I could always tell he'd think more of Theo when he became a teenager.' And as Ann looked out over the garden her face crumpled up to weep, and the tears ran down her face and fell into the hands which lay, unnaturally immobile, on her lap. Before she knew what she was doing, Caz put her mug down on the coffee table, and came and sat on the arm of Ann's chair and put her arms around her, awkwardly, trying not to fall off the arm into Ann's lap. 'Sorry,' Ann said conventionally, wiping her nose on the back of her hand.

'Here,' Caz said, fishing in her pocket for a handkerchief. She found one that was a bit squashed and crumpled, but clean.

'Thank you,' Ann said, and blew her nose. As she did so, the tears began again. 'He's so clever, you see,' she said at length. 'I know he's difficult, and his teachers find him a pain in the – I'm sorry. I mean a pain in the neck.' She wiped her face. 'But one day he's going to be so clever. A mathematician, or a scientist, or a musician. Probably a musician. And he's going to be a brilliant organist, and Alan would have been so proud, and that day when he gets up and plays his first recital at Westminster Abbey, Alan's not going to be there, and he's never going to know, and he would have been so proud he would just have died. Sorry. Didn't mean to pun. And he would have been a much better father to him when he was older, much better even than he was when Theo was tiny, and . . .' She clenched her fists angrily, and the tears poured down her face, distorted by the crying. 'And now it's only me, and it's all wasted.'

'But it's not, though, is it?'

'It is. Because I love Theo no matter what he's like. I won't care what he's good at. But Alan would have loved him *because* he was good at music, you see.'

'Yes. I see,' Caz said. She stroked the other woman's hair. It had a beautiful chestnut sheen, and was soft.

'Even so,' Caz said as it occurred to her, 'Theo will grow up knowing, somehow, that his father would have been really proud of him if he'd lived. He'll know that Alan would have approved. It's not the same, I know . . .'

'No.'

'. . . but it is something.' And Caz wondered how Ann coped with the injustice of it. Did one make oneself see it as inevitable, as fate, as something that was always preordained, that one's husband should be killed before one's child reached his eighth birthday? Or did Ann accommodate the terrifying thought that it might actually be random, that if he had come home via a different route, or if it had rained that day, or if the policeman who would normally have been passing the house hadn't stopped to adjust his shoelace . . . And if so, how did she live with that without going mad?

Ann sat up, and wiped her eyes, savagely, on the screwed-up handkerchief, and blew her nose again. Caz took her hand from Ann's hair, and wondered whether now was the least embarrassing time to get up and go and sit on the sofa again. 'I don't know why one always apologises for crying,' Ann said. 'It's silly, isn't it? I suppose it's because I've imposed on you, in a sense. You're not a close friend, but I've made you behave like one; I've made you look after me, and I had no right to do that.'

'Nonsense. It's because we've lost a sense of corporate responsibility. There are certain things we owe one another, and shouldn't need to ask or apologise for. You don't need to know someone in order to pull him from a burning train. We owe each other comfort when we need to cry, whether we're friends or not.'

'Thank you,' Ann said, and smiled at her. 'I do feel a little better, I suppose. It doesn't help in the long run, though. That's why I don't do it much. Nothing's going to bring him back, and that's what hurts.' She stood up. 'I'd like some more tea. How about you?'

'Yes,' Caz said, standing up too, next to her. 'I didn't finish that one. You sit down. I'll make it.'

'Thank you,' Ann said, landing heavily in her chair again, and suddenly looking exhausted, so that Caz was glad that she'd offered.

As she walked away from the house, some time later, Caz realised she would never have made it as an investigative journalist. She hadn't found out anything more about Alan Wedderburn's death. And she didn't really care.

She had not been walking more than ten or fifteen minutes – in fact, she found herself walking behind the choristers, in their smart suits and scruffy crocodile, and was just crossing the college bridge – when her telephone rang. She felt embarrassed answering it in college: she felt sure there must be some rule against it. Like, 'No cycling, no dogs allowed, do not answer mobile telephones'. She pulled it out of her bag and scrambled down the bank towards the river. Hiding under the large willow which has wept, every summer for generations, over numerous love affairs in punts, she finally answered the call.

'Cassandra Sanderson.'

'Cassandra, it's Ann here again. Ann Fitzwilliam. Sorry, did I catch you at an awkward moment?'

'Oh, not really. I just had this absurd idea that one shouldn't answer a telephone going through college. You know, like you're not allowed loud radios. In London, people are talking on their telephones all over the place: pavements, theatres, restaurants. But no one in Cambridge does it much.'

Ann laughed. 'You're right. Perhaps things are less urgent here. Listen, I'll tell you why I'm ringing: I've just read your note. You said you might look for a B and B?'

'Oh. Yes, I'd thought about it.'

'Well, why don't you come here? I mean, it's only for a few nights, isn't it?' she added. 'You said you were going back to London soon.'

'Probably. That's very kind of you, but I don't want to impose. I must pay you, and everything.'

'Nonsense. You'll be near the library, and I'm going to look through Alan's books this evening to see if any would interest you. To be perfectly honest, it would be nice to have some company. I know you'll be working, but it's so long since I've had anyone to stay, I've almost forgotten what it's like! Why don't you pack your things, and come back in time for supper?'

Caz considered for a split second. 'Thank you, Ann,' she said. 'I'd love to.'

It took Caz barely ten minutes to collect her few belongings from her hotel bedroom and settle her bill. With everything stuffed back into her handbag, she stepped out on to the Fen, by Scudamore's Punts, and gazed into the weir. It held a morbid fascination, suggesting boats out of control, and watery deaths; Ophelia sucked under the surface by the fingers of greedy weeds jealous of her virginal beauty; the half-remembered final scene from *The Mill on the Floss*, with the sad and lovely, ill-fated Maggie and Tom twisting round and round in the boat on the evening water, before going into the ever-night.

She left such gloomy thoughts, and started walking towards the Mill Pond, through the munching cows and long grasses.

Would Ann expect to feed her all the time she was there? Or should she offer to go out for her meals? But Ann had suggested Caz was to come as a guest, not simply take a room with her instead of taking lodgings somewhere else. She wondered idly whether Ann Fitzwilliam struggled financially, and what her source of income was.

When she answered the door, Ann welcomed Caz as if they were old friends who hadn't seen each other for a while. It seemed much longer ago than that same afternoon since she had been here.

'Go on up,' Ann said. 'First on the right. I've just got something on the stove, then I'll come up and make sure you're all right.'

'Don't worry,' Caz said. 'I'm sure I won't get lost. If I do, I'll Morse Code the SOS signal on the radiator pipes.'

Her hostess smiled. 'All right,' she said. 'I'll have supper ready for seven thirty or eight. I'm assuming you're free this evening and want to eat with me?'

'Please. It's very kind of you.'

'I'm enjoying it. I haven't cooked properly for ages. Come down if you want to, but don't worry if you're busy and have things to get on with. Help yourself to the bathroom, all that sort of thing. Appear when you're ready. Help, I think it's boiling over!'

Caz went up and found her room. There was a wash basin in one corner, and a four-foot wide bed with a hand-made patchwork cover over the eiderdown, and in the corner, by the window, a small Edwardian lady's-wardrobe. There was also a kind of home-made collage, with photographs of what looked like the garden outside, one of the Chapel, and several with Ann, and Theo, and a very good-looking man in his thirties with an aquiline nose and dark hair. Caz looked at the collage for a long time, till she began to feel as if she herself had experienced the happiness on those faces, blown with sea spray, or laughing on a hillside, or rapt in concentration above the baton or behind the diminutive cello. There was one of a beautiful young girl with a violin – so beautiful that the picture drew one's eyes to it again and again. As Caz looked at it, she felt the sharp stab of envy and admiration that any woman feels when she sees another, more beautiful than she has ever been or ever will be. This was a different Ann from the widow in her thirties who was running to deal with burning sauce downstairs.

Caz shrugged her bag on to the bed and looked out over the garden. The long shadows had gone, and the lawn was darkening even as she looked at it. Late birds chucked home to bed, and dark shapes fluttered in the trees above. Caz turned back to her bed, took her telephone out of her bag, and rang Will's number.

It was nearly an hour later when she came downstairs.

'Sherry?'

'Thank you. Tell me where the nearest off-licence is, and I'll nip out and buy some wine.'

'That's kind, but don't worry. Another night that would be lovely. I've opened some already.' Suddenly, with a flicker of a frown, vulnerable like a child's, Ann added, 'I hope it's the right one. D'you know, that's one of the most annoying things. It's so silly, it makes me cross. Alan knew a bit about wine, you see. Not much, admittedly, but more than I do. So he always used to choose what bottle to open. I mean, I can't even tell the ten-pound bottles from the real plonk; not even by the label. And I couldn't care less about the wine, but every time I go to the cellar, it makes me cry.'

Caz stared at her. She had driven her knife into the kitchen table, and was gouging a hole in it.

'I'm sorry,' she said, angrily, through her tears. Then she looked at what she had done. 'It's probably because you're here. I usually just swear. I don't know why. I never used to before Alan died. He used to comment on it: I never said anything stronger than "bother," he said.' She tried to laugh, but it turned into crying even as she did so. 'Now I do it all the time. I don't seem able to stop. Specially when I think about him. It never makes me feel any better.'

'It's all right,' Caz said. 'Really. You're allowed to be angry. If you weren't swearing, you'd probably be smacking your child, or getting drunk, and that might make you feel a lot worse. For what it's worth,' she picked up the bottle and studied the label, carefully avoiding looking at the table, 'this bottle is medium-priced, but tastes much better than that, and has just been reviewed as being eminently suitable for drinking with' – she looked at the hob – 'new potatoes and ratatouille and turkey . . . or is it veal? Not European, I hope . . . for two people who want a civilised evening talking and looking out over a pleasantly quiet garden on an autumn night. There. It doesn't make up for Alan, I know, but it's the best I can do.'

'Thank you.' Ann had recovered herself.

'Pleasure. Is this the sherry? Shall I help myself?'

'Do. Did you find everything you needed upstairs?'

'Yes, thanks. Sorry I was so long. I was trying to ring my . . .' What was he? Boyfriend? Husband? Fiancé, strictly speaking. None of these things summed Will up. He was her lover, her second self. 'I rang my man,' she said awkwardly.

'I don't know anything about your family, or your home.'

Suddenly, and completely without expecting to, Caz told her. Told her about Will, and the baby. And then told her about her parents, and her brothers, and eventually even about her sister and everything. And she started to tell her about her silly misgivings, and why she hadn't gone to Italy, and wondered things out loud that she hadn't suggested even to herself. 'I almost feel I've run away. I don't know why on earth I should.'

'Why you should feel that? Or why you should run away?'

'Either.'

'How was he, when you rang?'

'I didn't get through. Still, he'll be home by the end of the week.'

'Come on. It's ready. We'll keep the curtains open so we can look out on the garden, like you said. Can you light those candles?'

The meal was amazingly good. Caz was impressed, being almost incapable of boiling an egg herself. As she mopped up the last of the sauce on her plate, she asked Ann about her work.

'Hang on, let me get the pudding first,' she replied.

'What, pudding too? This is brilliant.'

Ann came back from the kitchen with a fruit tart and a bowl of whipped cream. The pastry looked as if it would almost melt to the touch.

'I have a problem with my violin,' she said straight away. 'I just can't face it. I'll do anything rather than pick up my fiddle. It's as if there's a black hole in my life, and I don't dare go near it. I'd rather clean drains. I'd rather change other people's children's nappies – believe me, I can't think of anything worse than that. I'd rather do anything than face the music. I can sit down and play the piano, no problem. I could get a job tomorrow as an accompanist; you know, playing the piano for the local ballet school, that sort of grotty job.'

'Why don't you?'

'I'm not a pianist. Why do something at which I'm always going to be second rate?' She shook her head. 'I'll invent anything rather than practise my violin. And it's quite hard now. It was easy when Alan and Theo were around. I was genuinely fairly busy. I could fool myself that I had to do this and that and the other: cook a cake for Theo's tea; go and pick up some music for Alan. Of course, I didn't really have to do it. Other women have husbands and children, and still manage to get on with their lives.'

'Show me one.'

'What?'

'Show me a woman in a seriously competitive profession, who married at – how old were you when you married? – early twenty-something, with a successful husband and a happy child, who has got to the top of her profession. And stayed married. Show me one.'

'Well . . .' Ann considered. 'Maybe. Maybe you're right. But I still wish I could play my violin.'

'It's funny,' Caz said. 'It sounds just like being a writer. Perhaps that's why I've run away. I'm frightened—'

'You're frightened of becoming like me.'

'Yes,' Caz replied, looking straight at her and being almost brutal in her honesty. 'Yes, I am.' Then she smiled. 'There are times when I've had what you'd call "writer's block", and I've found myself thinking just the same as you: that I'd rather be shovelling sewage than have this for a job. Why sewage?

I wonderd. There must be things worse than that. DIY, for instance.' They both laughed. 'And yet, even at the time, I found myself thinking, Being a musician would be easier than this. At least you can play scales whether you feel like it or not.'

'Yes. I just don't, that's all. And you can't play Bruch's violin concerto if you seriously don't feel like it. Oh, you could play the notes . . .'

'Yes.'

They fell silent. One of the candles sputtered on the table, and went out. The candles had been stuck in bottles, which Caz could remember doing when she was a student. Something about Cambridge seemed to maintain some of the innocence of one's undergraduate days: the notion that only the important things were worth while; that one could stick candles in bottles, and put posters on the walls, and never have to grow up into the kind of adult who had to have candlesticks and framed pictures.

'Isn't there . . . ?' Caz started.

'Isn't there what?'

'I don't know. Isn't there some easier way of getting started again? I mean, obviously you're not going to audition for – I don't know what the big shots are – Covent Garden at the end of this week. But couldn't you . . . This is going to sound very patronising. I may be pitching this wrong, but couldn't you join some university orchestra to start with, and then the Cambridge Philharmonic or something, and sort of trick yourself into thinking you're just mucking around on your violin, just for a laugh, just temporarily?'

'It's funny you should say that. There's an audition for CUMS this week – Cambridge University Music Society – for the Christmas Oratorio. I saw it advertised as I went through the Porters' Lodge. And I thought, Oh! If only I were a first-year undergraduate.'

'Would it be too humiliating to play for them?'

Ann said nothing for a while. 'It's a lovely piece of music,' she mused at last. Caz held her breath. 'But the audition is Wednesday afternoon.'

'So?'

'There's no Evensong on Wednesdays. Theo sometimes comes home for tea.'

Caz scented victory. 'Come on,' she said. 'That's no reason, and you know it. Suppose he doesn't? You can't spend the whole of the rest of the week doing nothing, the whole of your life doing nothing, in case Theo comes to tea. What kind of mother d'you want to be? I say this, of course, not having been any kind of mother myself yet. I'll probably be just the same. But why can't I take Theo out for tea? I'd love it. He owes me a tea, in fact.'

Ann said nothing.

'That's settled then,' Caz said.

Ann smiled. 'Wouldn't it be awful if I didn't get in?'

'Yes,' Caz said. 'Actually it would.'

20 ∫

'Stay with me to-night; you must see me die' –

W.A. Mozart

Looking back afterwards, Caz couldn't remember how they got on to the subject of Alan's death. But in the end, she found the answer to her question when she had almost stopped wanting to know, and certainly stopped trying to find out. They had a jug of coffee between them, and were sitting cross-legged on the sitting-room floor, and Caz was just thinking it was time to go up to bed, when Ann told her about it. It had been an evening just like this, almost exactly two years previously.

'The anniversary's just coming up. The end of this week,' Ann said. 'Sunday night. It's all very well for Frank to say it was Whistler, but nothing could ever be proved. Whistler!' she said with a shake of her head. 'His name's Harold. Harry Bush. Why should he have such a cheerful name, when he's done so much? The boys used to call him Salieri, apparently, some years ago. Then the head master said it was unkind, and they were stopped.'

She sighed. 'But I don't hate him. Why should I? I think they should lock him up, yes. I think he's a menace to society, and he might be violent again. I'm sure he will be. But it's not up to me to put him away. He can't do any more to hurt me. Not now. He's hardly likely to attack me or Theo: he won't get the chance, I'll see to that. And if the police don't want to do it, if the rest of society can't be bothered, I'm not going to waste my life on that kind of thing. You see people eaten up with it, don't you? Revenge. The real victims of murder. The ones who don't just lose their loved ones, but lose their lives being bitter about it afterwards. I'd rather even play my violin than campaign for Whistler to be put away!'

'But I don't understand. Why didn't the police do it?' Caz asked.

'It's rather complicated. They arrested him and kept him in for a couple of days or so. But then it turned out that he'd been interviewed without an "appropriate adult" present, so it was all invalid. Because he's disabled, you see.'

'And that was it?'

'That was the first thing. Then they said he hadn't confessed anything anyway: normally, they can get him to own up pretty quickly, so they started to wonder whether he'd really done it. I knew he had, Theo knew he had, but the police didn't. And there wasn't enough evidence for a conviction. Take the fingerprints, for instance; or any forensic evidence. Useless. Because Whistler had been in our house before.'

'Oh?'

'Oh, yes. He'd been hanging around for years. He adored the choir. He went to Evensong several times a week. And he used to come round here. Goodness knows how he knew where we lived, but he did. I used to take pity on him, chat to him for a while, that sort of thing. He even helped me with odd jobs. You know, the garden. We planted that tree together.' She stood up, walked towards the window, and looked out into the darkness.

'You can't see it in this light, but there's a little Korean fir which I bought for Theo for Christmas when he was five. I asked him what he wanted, and he said, "A Christmas tree." I told him we'd be getting a Christmas tree anyway, that we got one every year, and that Alan would go to the market sometime before Christmas Eve and buy a tree for the sitting room. I said, "What do you want, for you?" He simply repeated, "A Christmas tree." So that was what I got him. A beautiful tiny fir with soft, bluey-coloured needles, barely eighteen inches high, to grow with him. The catalogue said it would have fir cones within a year or two. And it did. Lovely little purple cones like spongy flowers. That summer we talked about where to plant it, he and I, and we decided to put it there, where we could hang white lights on it at Christmas time, and see them from the house. Perhaps we will one day, when Theo and the tree are both six feet high.

'The day that we were due to plant it, Saturday morning, Whistler came round. He turned up a lot in those days. Peeled spuds for me. Cleaned the car. Sat around drinking cups of tea for hours. That morning he realised we were working in the garden, and asked if he could help. So I gave him the spade, and asked him to dig a hole there, and I held the baby sapling while he massacred my lawn. He made a terrible mess, dropping turf and spilling earth on the grass. By the time he'd finished, it looked like a JCB had been let loose in the garden. It would have been much easier to do it myself, really. I was looking forward to my morning with Theo, and I would have done it how I wanted, rather than having to explain it to Whistler. Still.' She shrugged.

Then, suddenly, she laughed. 'And, oh! He was smelly! If ever you had Whistler round, you had to put up with him smelling like a public lavatory: far worse than an animal could ever smell. All in all, we would have preferred to do without him. But I felt it was right, to include him like that. It was companionable. I can remember thinking, This is what life should be like. He's helping us, as much as he knows how; and we're helping him, giving him something to do, and somewhere to belong.' She sighed. 'It seems such a long time ago.' She turned back from the window again, and came and sat down.

'He used to do all sorts of odd jobs for me. Now that I think about it, he only ever offered to do things which gave him free access to the house, coming in and out with buckets of water, for instance, or in the porch to get the bicycle oil. So I suppose there was a motive to it all, even then. He was never altruistic in anything.' She looked at Caz, almost as if she were giving evidence. 'This was all before he pinched my rings.'

'Your rings?'

'You know how you leave them on the sink when you wash up? Perhaps you don't. I used to take off my wedding ring and engagement ring, and put them by the sink. One day Whistler was doing something to my bicycle, I can't remember what, and I was upstairs. As I say, he used to pop in and out, to get his tea, or wash his hands, or what have you. I mean, he was a friend. He came to Theo's third birthday party; he would have meals with us occasionally, if Alan was out – he avoided Alan, generally. So we treated him as we would any friend, and I left him to finish what he was doing while I went up to change. He called up the stairs to say goodbye, and I called goodbye back, and came down a minute later to get my rings, and they'd gone. There was no question about what had happened to them. Five minutes earlier, they'd been there, and now they weren't.

'And suddenly, it made sense of things we hadn't been able to understand before. Little things, and not so little, I suppose. A camera which went missing from a drawer in the kitchen. Twenty pounds housekeeping money which I'd thought I had, and then couldn't find. Things over the years. We had a jar we used to put loose change in, and one day Theo asked me what we were saving up for, and I said, "Oh, I don't know, we'll take Daddy out for a meal on his birthday." So Theo put in a whole five-pound note which his grandfather had given him for Christmas, which he'd kept for months; it was a fortune to him, and he put it in for Alan's birthday treat, and three days later it wasn't there any more. D'you know, when I think about that, it makes me so angry. To steal from a little child. Far worse, really, than taking my rings.'

'So what happened?'

'About the rings? I was beside myself. The engagement ring had been Alan's grandmother's. Even so, I didn't go to the police straight away. I rang Alan at college, and asked him what I should do. He said he'd try to find out where Whistler lived, and ask him for them back. He didn't manage to find his address, but it didn't matter: Whistler turned up for Evensong thirty minutes later, as innocent as anything, butter not melting and all that. Alan left his organ scholar in charge for five minutes, and went and appealed to him. Suggested Whistler must have slipped them in his pocket by mistake, you know, very tactful. Said they were of great sentimental value, and had been treasured in his family for generations, all that. Promised him we wouldn't take it any further.'

'And he gave them back?'

'He denied all knowledge. Never seen them. Alan wasn't even

angry. He said the poor bloke didn't know he'd taken them. We felt really sorry for him then. He was even more daft than we'd realised, and didn't know what he was doing half the time. We rang the police, but I didn't have any hope of seeing my rings again. If he didn't know he'd taken them, he wouldn't know where they were or anything. I was desperately upset.

'The police came round the same day and took a description. I asked them if they knew where to find Whistler. They said, Oh yes, they knew all about him; he did this kind of thing all the time. I was astonished. I asked them why they didn't lock him up, and they said he was always doing time, but it never made the slightest difference. I said, "D'you mean he's been in prison recently?" And it turned out he'd been inside several times since we'd known him, and we'd never even noticed. You know, he said he'd been on holiday, or to his auntie's.'

'And?'

'And they came back the next morning with the rings. They'd turned a little nasty, and put on a bit of pressure, and he'd handed them over straight away. Alan said he could have sworn that Harold – Whistler – didn't know anything about them. He even seemed quite upset for us. So it was all a brilliant act. Or he really didn't know, at the point when Alan asked him. It wasn't until it became necessary to know . . . That's what makes a successful liar, isn't it? You convince yourself: then it's easy to convince others. He took us in for years.'

'What happened after that?'

'We didn't let him in the house again. Funnily enough, the police didn't prosecute, I don't know why. I didn't think about it at the time. I'd got my rings back, and that was what I cared about. Anyway, as I say, we never let him back in the house. But there were things even then that I didn't know about him, that I know now. I've told Theo he's not to let Whistler come anywhere near him.'

'But he's always hanging about the choir, isn't he? Are the other children safe?'

'Probably not, entirely. But what can you do? Terrify the children with stories of what might happen to them? The choristers have been given general guidelines, which are now quite strict. They're not allowed to talk to anyone other than members of school staff, and known parents of other choristers. They're no longer allowed to go to Chapel and back without a member of staff. It's a nuisance, and it's not very pleasant if they have to ignore a tourist who is trying to speak to them, but not as bad as one of them being molested, or worse.'

'Worse?'

'Well, who knows? As the police said to me, euphemistically, "He has a very nasty infectious disease."'

'But this is awful.'

'Perhaps. Or perhaps not. Innocent, under British law, until proven guilty. It's not against the law to have infectious diseases. Besides, perhaps it wasn't him after all.'

'You said you were certain.'

'I am. But I could be wrong.'

'I don't understand why they couldn't take finger-prints.'

'The point, as I understand it, is that he had once had legitimate access to our house. So the defence counsel would make mincemeat of it in seconds. His prints could have been on anything in the house, including the murder weapon, without his having done anything illegal at all.'

'The murder weapon?'

'That fire extinguisher. Well, not that very one, but one identical. I replaced it,' she added, with a certain irony. 'The police took the other one away. It was annoying. They're quite hard to get hold of, those big, carbon dioxide ones.'

'What legitimate reason could he have had for touching the fire extinguisher?'

'Goodness knows. I asked them to fingerprint it just for my peace of mind, but I don't think they even did that. As a piece of evidence against Harold, it was useless.'

'So what happened exactly?'

'Nothing really. The file is still open. I don't know why they kept the fire extinguisher.'

'No, I mean what happened the night Alan died?'

'Oh.' Ann picked up the coffee jug as if to pour them both some more coffee, then felt the side of it and realised it was barely lukewarm. Caz wondered whether she would get up to make some more, and Caz would never hear the answer to her question. But no, instead she picked up the wine bottle and began to pour into Caz's glass. 'You have some,' Caz said, but at that point the wine ran out.

'It's all right. Really.' Ann picked up her nearly empty glass and drank what remained in it. Then she sat, staring into the dribble of wine at the bottom of the glass, and the way the tears ran down the sides. 'The night Alan died,' she said, 'he came home late. He quite often came home late. Would eat in college, you know, and work in his room. I didn't like it much. I used to get quite lonely. I couldn't go out, you see, because Theo would be asleep in bed. I'm not sure that I particularly wanted to anyway. Did I?' She looked up, thinking about it. 'I don't know; I've not thought about it much. I took to watching television quite a lot, which I'd never done before. I don't know why I didn't read; I think because I felt lonely, and I liked the sound of the television. I'm sounding rather sorry for myself, aren't I? I didn't resent it in a big way. I'm just remembering now what it was really like. The work had to be done, and he worked better in college than he would have done here. It's the perpetual dilemma, isn't it? If you want to do well, you have to put the hours in, and it seems you have to put them in most when your children are tiniest. Your work needs your energy just when your family, your marriage, your home, need it most too. Perhaps it was simpler when men poured all their energy into one thing, and women into the other, and together you had a success. If your husband did great things, you yourself basked in reflected glory.'

'Bollocks.'

'Probably. Anyway, Alan was around far more than some, and brilliant when he was around. On the days when he could get home early it was great. Such a laugh. He was bathing Tippy one time, and the two of them made such a mess. I heard this two-part aria coming from the bathroom, right? And Tippy was too young to be able to sing a line of music on his own. At least I thought he was. And I went into the bathroom to see what was going on, and the two of them were standing there, completely naked – Alan was out of the bath, but naked – and dripping with bubble bath. They were singing quite seriously. Then Alan said, "I've done it. I couldn't do the last two bars, and now I've worked out how to end it. Or Theo has." You see, even then, he was working.'

Ann was smiling incredulously at the memory of it. Caz wondered whether this was how it would be, always: spending her life reliving happy scenes. Or would the brightness of those images fade, so that in her sixties, in her seventies, Ann would be clutching at ever-dimmer mental film clips of Alan, covered in bubble bath, naked in the bathroom?

'That night,' she went on, 'he didn't come home early. Though it wasn't as late as he could sometimes be. About eleven, I think. I must have just dropped off. That was another thing. I like to go to sleep quite early, whereas Alan could work half the night. But I hate sleeping on my own. I used to sleep quite badly when I was single, and it wasn't until I lived with Alan that I ever got a good night. So I used to try and wait up for him. But it made me so tired. That night I must have just fallen asleep. I don't know if Whistler followed Alan home, but I doubt it. He was probably in the street, and saw him coming. He may have knocked, and I didn't hear him. He didn't often call late at night, but he'd done it once or twice, if he wanted to borrow some money. That's where he was clever: he would borrow a fiver, and he'd always pay it back. But he'd pinch twenty quid, and you'd never see it again. He's not nearly as daft as he makes out.'

'You said you didn't let him in the house any more.'

'No, but he used to call at the door. He may even have got into the house. It's possible. I never used to lock the back door if Alan was still out. He used to bring his bicycle round to the back of the house, through the side gate, and come in by the kitchen. He always had his keys on him, but I never locked the porch door. So Whistler might have come round the back, and been snooping around, and Alan surprised him. It's possible. In a way, I think that's the most likely. We'll never know.'

'When did you wake up?'

'Almost immediately. I wasn't properly asleep. I still don't know what it was that woke me up. It's funny: you'd think it would be the clearest night of your life, etched in your memory for ever, but it isn't. It's a kind of blur, a muddle, a bit like a nightmare. I'm not sure how much is genuine memory, and how much was simply me trying to reconstruct it for the police afterwards. Anyway, I went downstairs. I was calling, "Alan. Alan!"' Caz shivered. Ann had said it as if she were actually doing it, there and then, calling down the stairs, expecting him to answer any moment. 'I was looking forward to seeing him. I always loved seeing him at the end of the day, but I would be disappointed, sometimes, if he didn't come upstairs to see me when he got in. I can remember feeling a little irritated, that night, that he hadn't come up to see me yet, and thinking, No, I mustn't mind. He's very tired.' Ann looked up at the dark night outside.

Caz waited. Eventually Ann turned and looked at her, almost surprised, as if she had forgotten Caz was there. 'I went into the kitchen. He was stretched out on the floor. His head was sort of near the back door. I had these half-thoughts: Is he drunk? Has he tripped? But I knew they were absurd. You know, when you're first told shocking news, your daughter's died in a car crash or something, your first reaction is supposed to be incredulity. You've got the wrong daughter. She's only fainted. That sort of thing. But I knew straight away. He was white, you see. And there was blood.' Ann's hand went up to her face, her mouth and nose, as if to indicate where the blood had been. Caz sat utterly still, as if she had been frozen.

'It's funny. We'd had a row that day. Something stupid, I can't even remember what. And you'd think that you'd really mind, wouldn't you? That the day he walked out of your life was one when you had a quarrel, rather than one when he bought you red roses. But I don't mind that at all. It was just like any other quarrel: we would have made it up.' Her face looked haggard, naked, as if her grief had scraped it bare. She seemed to be waiting on the threshold, considering whether to go on, into the memory, or back out of it again and leave it undisturbed for another time. She braced herself.

'I picked up the phone. I knew the panic would start soon, and I knew I had to get through to the ambulance first. I dialled the number, and they asked me which emergency service I wanted, and that threw me. I knew I wanted an ambulance, but when they asked me, it was as if they were questioning my judgement, as if they were saying, You'd rather have an ambulance, for a dead man, than the police, would you? I was kind of sobbing by then; not screaming exactly, but beginning to go, and Tippy must have heard me, because he appeared. He was in his little towelling dressing-gown, the one I bought him for Christmas the year before, and I thought, That's it. That's your childhood over. I hope you liked it, because that seven years was all there was. Then I handed him the phone and said, "Tell them an ambulance, and give them our address," and then I ran out through the back door. I had no idea what I was doing. I must have heard something without knowing I had, because when I reached the street Whistler was just bicycling away. There was no one else in the road.'

'How did you know it was him?'

'I just knew. I'd know that bicycle anywhere, and the way he rides it, and everything. He's sort of heavy, and hunched up. You can't miss him, honestly. I know: he could have just been passing. It's possible.' She said it as if it were familiar ground. 'But afterwards, I thought I remembered hearing his bicycle disturbing the gravel. You know, when I was in the kitchen, deciding to ring for an ambulance.

'Besides,' she said, and she stared at Caz, as if she had just seen something. 'Besides . . .'

'What?'

'I've just remembered. I've been over it all those times, for the police, and I've only just remembered.' She stopped. Her hand went up to her temple, as if she couldn't quite believe it. 'He was whistling. As he bicycled off. He was whistling.' Then she started to whistle, breathily, through her teeth. 'That's how he whistles. It's like a bit of a dream coming back. What was it? Something from the Messiah.' Ann whistled four familiar notes. *'All we like sheep.'*

Caz heard the rest of tune in her head. *Have gone a-stra-a-a-y.*

'I went back into the kitchen,' Ann continued slowly, as if in a daze. She looked pale, worn out by the process of remembering. 'I'd only left Theo for a few seconds, but it was too long. He'd got through, given them all the information, but they wanted me, of course. They wanted to check the details all over again: so unnecessary, because Theo is far more reliable than most adults. I wanted to scream at them. There he was, seven years old and the head of his family, and they wouldn't even believe he knew his own address. I finished the conversation, and hung up, and we looked at Alan, and I made the worst mistake of my life.'

She was completely dry-eyed. Oh, cry, Caz thought, Please cry.

'Theo said, "He's dead, isn't he?" And I said, "Yes, Theo, Daddy's dead." I don't know why I said that. We hardly ever used to call him Daddy.'

'That wasn't a mistake.'

'No,' Ann said. 'No, it wasn't. When I was a student,' she went on, 'at the Royal College, a madman went into a school in Scotland and shot all the little children.'

'I remember,' Caz said. 'I was ten.'

'And we watched it on the news, and none of us really understood it, because we hadn't got children of our own, but we saw one of the reporters being interviewed, a seasoned old hack, and he said that as he walked down the road towards the school, several streets away, he could hear women wailing. Why didn't I do that? I come from Ireland, for goodness' sake, where they still have wakes. I ought to know. I saw him lying there, and I wanted to throw myself on him, and keen and howl into the night, and hug him till it hurt. And I thought, I mustn't. They'll want to know how he was killed. They won't want anything disturbed. Oh, Caz,' she said, and suddenly burst into terrible, racking sobs. 'Oh! We could have hugged him into the next world. He could have gone in the arms of the two people he loved more than the world, even more than the music he made. And we just sat, politely, on the kitchen floor, hardly daring to hold his little finger. He was warm. His little finger was still warm, and we never even gave him a cuddle. I could have given Theo a memory of his father to treasure all his life, and I chose to give the police forensic evidence instead.'

Caz put her arms around her, and held her, and felt the tears streaming down her face.

'It's all right,' she said, as if to a child.

'No,' Ann said, bitterly. 'No, it's not all right. We should have lain on his warm body, the three of us together, in a last embrace till the ambulance came.'

She wiped her eyes, and took a deep breath. The tears took no notice, and continued to pour effortlessly down her face. 'Then they took him away, and the next time we saw him he was cold, and it was in a hospital bed, and he wasn't Alan any more, he was just a corpse. Grey, and plastic, and dead like a body in a morgue. It would have been horrid to have touched him then. And there would have been people watching. But when he was lying there in the kitchen, he was still Alan. It wasn't too late to love him. While we were waiting for the ambulance to come and end our lives together. I shall regret it all my life.'

Caz shifted her weight on the floor, and in doing so, kicked the empty bottle, which rolled on its side, stopping when it reached the coffee jug. The two women held each other, the tears falling into each other's hair and running on to their lips.

'Oh!' Ann cried angrily, as the sobs began to subside. 'Oh, why did I have to get it wrong? Why don't they teach it at school? "How to cope when your husband dies." Hold him tight, and scream and shout, and to hell with the polite guests at the funeral service. Isn't it funny how you pray, in moments of crisis? I don't believe there's anyone up there, but I prayed over and over again, "Please don't let him die. Please, please don't let him die." What did I think I was doing? If there's no one up there when you're doing the shopping in Sainsbury's, why should He be there just because you need Him one night when the person you love is growing cold on your kitchen floor?'

'I can remember doing that too. As a child,' Caz said.

Ann shuddered, as if her grief were giving her a last shake before leaving her alone for the moment. Then she wiped her face, and sighed. 'It's late. Shall we leave these till the morning?'

'Yes,' Caz said, standing up and pulling her to her feet. 'Thank you for telling me about it.'

'Thank you for listening. I don't often talk about it.'

'You should. I kept my grief a secret much too long, and it ate up half my life.'

They went out into the hallway to go to bed. Suddenly, spontaneously, Caz turned and hugged her. She felt her hair, soft under her fingers again, and realised that it was newly washed. She had noticed the extra gloss on it earlier in the evening. She felt the tickly warmth of Ann's woollen jumper.

'Goodnight,' she said.

'Goodnight,' Ann replied.

21 ∫

'They think that because I am small and young that there can be nothing great and old in me. But they shall soon find out.'

W.A. Mozart

Theo had moved to the choir school when he was seven. His life changed.

It sounded odd to say that. It sounded as though one should say, 'His life changed when his father died,' and of course it did. After Alan, nothing would be the same again. But when he went to the choir school his life became very different. And different in a way that was much better.

One day he went and knocked at the headmaster's door. Mr Marshall was a large man with rather frightening eyebrows. Most of the other children thought he was frightening all over, but Theo found that Mr Marshall didn't shout at him, and spoke as if he wasn't stupid, and he found both of those characteristics a relief, in a teacher anyway.

So after lunch one Wednesday, Theo went through the dining hall into the headmaster's house and looked around him. He had only been there once before, when he was quite young. It was strange, in a way, that he hadn't been to the headmaster's house more often with Alan, because he and Mr Marshall had worked together and spent quite a lot of time together. But there it was: he hadn't.

He found himself in a hall with interesting tiles on the floor. They were patterned, red and yellow, but the pattern was not quite symmetrical, and Theo was just wondering why not – had the tiler run out of yellow, or did he think it was more interesting like that? – when he heard a tiny splat, and noticed a little circle of spit had appeared on the tile near his right foot. He looked up the staircase to the landing above. There was no one there. He looked down at the spit again, and then heard a suppressed giggle. This time, when he looked up, he saw a mass of curly red hair, and the face of little Lucy Marshall, whose head was so small she could get it through the bars of the banisters. It wasn't the banisters, in fact, because she was on the landing rather more than halfway up the stairs, but the bars and the distances between them were the same.

'Hello,' he said.

'Hello. If you spit from here, you can get it into the right square. You can decide which square you want it to go in, and it does.'

'Every time?' Theo asked, impressed.

'No,' she admitted. 'Not every time. But sometimes. If you're lucky. Do you want to see my daddy?'

'Yes. Is he in?'

'I think so,' Lucy said. 'I'll take you. You can hold my hand if you like.'

When they got to Mr Marshall's door and Theo knocked, he was still holding Lucy's hand. When Mr Marshall opened the door, Theo said, 'Please may I talk to you, sir? It's not particularly private,' he added, as Mr Hall, the maths teacher, stood up as if he ought to leave.

'It's all right, I've got to go anyway,' Mr Hall explained. 'Hello, Theo. Coping all right?'

'Yes, thank you, sir.'

'Good. Good, good. Hello, Lucy,' he said as he left.

'Hello, Clive,' she said, being cheeky on purpose, Theo thought, and not looking at Mr Hall.

'Well, Theo, what can I do for you? Is this the first time you've been up here?'

'Yes, sir.'

'Your daddy and I used to spend hours up here, sometimes.'

'Is your daddy dead?' Lucy asked.

'Yes,' Theo replied, conscious of how different he was from every other child he knew. A number of his friends didn't live with their fathers, but they all had fathers somewhere: weekend fathers, holiday fathers, some of them had two fathers, other people's fathers.

'D'you mind?' Lucy said. 'I'd mind, I think.'

'Yes,' Theo said, setting his mouth, and keeping his eyes wide open, determined not to blink.

'Lucy,' Mr Marshall said, 'please could you go and ask Mummy if we could have a cup of coffee, and a glass of squash and some biscuits.'

'Two glasses of squash,' Lucy corrected.

'One glass of squash,' her father repeated. 'And please stay with her while she makes it. And Lucy?'

'Yes?' she said, turning at the door.

'If you can't find Mummy, go and ask in the kitchens, please.'

'I'm not allowed in the kitchens. Too dangerous.'

'You're allowed at the door.'

Lucy left. Mr Marshall went and stood at the window, looking out across the Tarmac and the football field at the front of the house. 'Your father used to look out of this window,' he said, not turning round to look at Theo. 'By the way, there's a box of Kleenex on the piano, if you should want any. He used to tease me,' he continued so quickly that Theo wondered whether he had really mentioned the Kleenex, 'and tell me I reminded him of God after he gave the tablets to Moses on the mountain, looking down and seeing the children of Israel dancing round the golden calf. I gaze on all these ant-sized people being naughty, but there doesn't seem much I can do about it. Whereas he would look down on everyone, from his organ-loft in Chapel, and see them all being as good as gold.'

For the first time, he turned and looked at Theo. Theo had dried his eyes, and blown his nose without making any sound, and put the Kleenex in the bin. He had just finished when Mr Marshall turned round.

Mr Marshall smiled. 'You're looking at my new toy,' he said. 'I haven't tried it yet. It was just installed this morning, and I've been busy ever since, so I haven't been able to play with it.'

'What is it?' Theo asked.

'It's a Tannoy system. One of the parents works with PA

equipment, and offered to put one in for me. It's a bit of a gimmick, really. He said he got the idea from an old John Cleese film, about a head master. Ooh, careful! Don't do that!'

Across the playground, in front of Mr Marshall's study, boomed the words, 'Careful! Don't do that!'

Theo and Mr Marshall looked at each other, and then looked out of the window. Richard Ashley, the head boy, stood frozen in his tracks. He looked one way, and then another, and then up at the sky.

Theo had let go of the button. He was always being told off for that sort of thing. Even Ann got cross with him for pressing buttons. 'How many times do I have to tell you,' she would say, 'not to touch things which don't belong to you?' Once he had pressed a button in a ship, and Alan had been furious. Crosser even than the captain. He realised Mr Marshall was shaking. He couldn't remember that he had ever, before, made an adult so angry that he shook.

For a second or two nothing happened while Theo braced himself for the telling off. Then he glanced up at Mr Marshall. The headmaster held his hand over his mouth. 'Oh dear,' he said. 'I've never seen Richard so alarmed.' With astonishment, Theo realised that he was laughing. He stared at him for a minute, then started to smile. It was true: Richard had looked rather funny. He was supposed to be the best boy in the school, the most responsible, the best behaved, and he had just been walking to his classroom when a voice had come out of the sky and told him not to.

'Perhaps he thought it really was God, sir,' Theo suggested.

'Perhaps,' Mr Marshall said. 'Let's try again.' Mr Marshall put his hand on the button, and said, 'You may go to your classroom now, Richard.' Richard started looking around again, and Mr Marshall couldn't resist adding, 'Don't think we didn't see you picking your nose.' This time he looked up towards the head-master's study. 'Quick! Duck!' Mr Marshall said, and he and Theo crouched down so that the two of them were just looking over the windowsill. 'Isn't it tempting,' Mr Marshall said as they watched Richard rubbing his nose with his fingers, to try to make out he hadn't been picking it, 'to put your finger on the button and say' – and here he put on a deep, God-like voice – 'Richard

Ashley, this is your call to the mission field! Pack your toothbrush and go to Mongolia.'

As Theo laughed, he realised how long it was since he had been so happy.

'I think it's your turn again,' Mr Marshall continued. 'Oh, he's gone in; hard luck. There's Miss Henrietta. Go on. But remember to take your finger off the button afterwards, otherwise she'll hear us talking. It's difficult to reach it crouched down like this, isn't it?'

'What on earth are you two up to?' Mrs Marshall had come in with a tray of things, and was staring at her husband and Theo hiding under the window, peeking over the sill.

'Shhh,' Mr Marshall said, as if Miss Henrietta would be able to hear them. 'It's Theo's turn.'

'Miss Henrietta,' Theo said in a very deep voice, trying to keep his finger on the button, 'this is God talking to you. Your stockings are falling down.'

Theo couldn't ever remember laughing as much as he did then, when Miss Henrietta started, and looked around her, and then actually looked up at the sky, she really did, as if God had been talking to her in Theo's false deep voice, and had spoken out of the sky. Then she looked at her tights, but not very seriously, as if she knew they weren't falling down, then she looked, very slowly, up towards Mr Marshall's study, as if she were pretending to be cross but wasn't really, then it seemed as if she was about to shake her fist, but Theo and Mr Marshall sank down below the window again, and Theo held his sides and laughed and laughed, while Mr Marshall said, 'Miss Henrietta, this is God talking to you,' and then looked up at the sky, just as she had. Then they both laughed again.

Mrs Marshall stood at the window, smiling and shaking her head, perhaps at Miss Henrietta, who could presumably see Mrs Marshall.

'You'll be committed one of these days,' she said to Mr Marshall. 'Hello, Theo. How are you? Getting on all right?'

'Yes, thank you.'

'Good. There's a man from the Inspectorate coming at two,' she reminded her husband, as she turned to go.

'Oh, Lord. Well, let's hope he's late. If not, he'll just have to wait a few minutes. I think they're usually early. Put the clock in the drawing room slow, and show him in there.'

'It messes up the chiming if you do that.'

'So it does.'

Mrs Marshall went out.

'Come and sit down,' Mr Marshall said, putting the tray on a table between his two armchairs, and helping himself to the cup of coffee and one of the biscuits. 'Have some biscuits; squash. You know,' he went on, 'if you're homesick, and you can't get through to your mother on the telephone, you can always come and see Mrs Marshall or me. Or Miss Henrietta. Loads of the children do. You each think you're the only one to get homesick, because you're all so brave you don't talk about it, but nearly everyone feels the same. I felt terrible when I first went away to school. And in those days there were rules about how often you could ring home, and not going home for the first few weekends of term, and that sort of rot. Awful. Your mother's a wonderful person. I think you're very brave, both of you.'

'Why?'

'Being so cheerful, when it must hurt so much inside. I'm sure you know this, but I'll say it anyway. It's always all right to talk about your father. And it's always all right to cry. You might want to choose who you talk to about him, and you might want to choose who you cry in front of. Not because there's anything wrong with either of those things, ever; but because most boys and girls of your age haven't lost someone they love, in the way you have, so they might not know what to do if you cry. Some very silly ones might even tease you about it. I don't think they would, but they might. If you don't mind that, that's fine. But if you do, then you come and find me, or Miss Henrietta, or Mrs Marshall, or your mother, and you can talk as much as you like about your father, and you can cry as much as you like. And we won't ever think you less brave, or less grown up, for doing so. Or Mrs Havent,' he said, after a moment's pause. 'She seems strict, but she has to be, to run this place. She's very kind, underneath.'

Mr Marshall picked up his digestive biscuit, and held it suspended over his coffee for a moment, and glanced at Theo with a sudden naughty smile. 'I'll tell you what: I won't tell on you, if you don't tell on me. We can dip our biscuits in our drinks and no one will ever know.' And he did. He dipped his biscuit in his coffee, and Theo watched the chocolate melt and go glossy. His wouldn't do that because his drink was only squash.

'It's like going to the doctor, really,' Mr Marshall continued. 'If you've got something which hurts, and the doctor gives you medicine to make it hurt a little less, then you're not being less brave if you take the medicine. You're just being sensible. Tears are God's medicine to make it hurt a little less. So is laughter. Your father was such a wonderful man, it would be odd if you didn't want to cry every so often. Goodness me, I'm beginning to do it myself. What an ass I am. Where are those Kleenex? I was very fond of your father too, you see. He was amazing, you know that, don't you? Oh dear.'

Mr Marshall got up and went to the piano, and brought the box of Kleenex back with him and set it on the floor between himself and Theo. He took one, and wiped the corners of his eyes. He really was crying, though Theo wouldn't have realised if he hadn't told him. The corners of his eyes were wet. He blew his nose. 'There we are,' he said. 'And you know,' he went on, 'you can cry with your mother, too. If you make her cry, don't worry, because it's good for her as well.'

Theo nodded, and took another Kleenex. It didn't matter if Mr Marshall saw him use it now, because the headmaster had used one himself.

'Now then, d'you think I ought to go and see this inspector? And you'd better go to maths, or whatever you've got, hadn't you?' Mr Marshall go up and walked over to the window again. 'Look at us; what a mess,' he said, and put his finger on the Tannoy button. 'Right! We're going to have one and a half minutes of being smart. Could all the boys tuck their shirts in, and all the girls, um, tie your hair back or something? And all of you pull your socks up. And go to your classes. And don't be late.' He took his finger off the Tannoy button.

'And we just hope the inspector likes us. Otherwise we'll have to close down. Off you go. Come and see me again, any time.' Mr Marshall put his hand in Theo's hair, and ruffled it in the way that's awful if it's done by an adult you don't like. 'I loved your father too,' he said, just before he opened the door. Outside, in the narrow corridor which was lined with books, stood a man with his hands in his pockets. He had been reading the spines of the books, and he looked very bored.

'So sorry,' Mr Marshall said in a suddenly smart voice. 'Do come in.' Then he spoke normally again. 'Goodbye, Theo,' he said. 'Please come and see me again.'

When Theo turned at the end of the corridor, he saw the door closing on the two men, who were talking in low voices. He knew Mr Marshall would use Alan's death as a reason for having kept the inspector waiting.

He didn't mind. He'd forgotten to ask Mr Marshall whatever it was he'd been to see him about. And the headmaster had never asked him. Now he had to think of a reason for having kept his teacher waiting. He wondered whether 'I was seeing Mr Marshall' would be good enough. He'd have to try it and see.

22 ∫

'Nothing is so hateful as revenge; to be humane and kind, to pardon without selfishness – that is the action of the loftiest spirits.'

Die Entführung, No 21

Ann really did work for her audition. Part of her said she didn't want to be accepted by CUMS anyway: it would be such a drag to work with amateurs, and have to go to the rehearsal once a week, and make a date in her diary for the performance, which would be such a commitment. But another part of her recognised what a dreadful humiliation it would be to be turned down: the choral scholars would know about it, naturally, because most of them were involved in CUMS. So then of course the choristers, Theo's school friends, would know, and the staff at the school. And Ann herself would know. For ever and ever she would know that her standard of playing had sunk so low that she couldn't even compete with undergraduates who had left school with Grade VIII violin.

They wouldn't turn her down; she knew that really. But even so, she didn't want to get near even to risking it.

So she practised.

'Would you like me to leave the house?' Caz asked.

'No,' Ann replied. 'No, not at all.' She seemed to be urging her to stay. 'That is, unless you have to?'

'It's all right,' she replied. 'I've got my computer here. I'll go and get on upstairs.'

'You must have Alan's study. I mean, his old study, you know. I think it's the best room. It's right up in the attic, and runs the whole length and width of the house, and in the winter you can see the very tips of the Chapel, and Great St Mary's. It's a cosy, friendly room. It's where his boxes of books are. Rummage around, won't you? I'll clear it out one day. Or else I won't: I might leave it for Theo.'

'Thank you. I'll find it.'

Ann didn't offer to show it to her. She already seemed different somehow, as if the thought of playing the violin had turned her mind towards professional things, given her something more important to do than being polite to a guest. Even though Caz had only just met her, it made her heart leap with a kind of hopeful joy, to think that Ann might turn back to her music again. Before she had even got up the stairs to her own room, Caz heard some workmanlike scales, boring, repetitive, but scales none the less.

She picked up her computer, and went up the second flight of stairs to find the attic. It was just as Ann had described it. It wasn't at all morbid, as a dead man's room might be expected to be. On the contrary, it almost seemed to have a life of its own. One window looked out over the front of the house, east, towards Cambridge, and through this window at the moment the sun poured as if it had money to throw away. She looked through it to see whether she could see the tips of the Chapel roof, and was surprised to find how much foliage there still was on the trees. Red and orange and green and brown danced and turned in the sunlight.

The window on the other side of the room looked out over Ann's garden, and Caz judged that, from about teatime onwards, that side of the room would bask in gold. Alan had certainly chosen the best room in the house: presumably he had also had an excellent set of rooms in college. Then Caz checked herself. Other people must be free to manage their relationships the way they wanted. Ann didn't need a study in order to practise the violin. Though perhaps, if she had had a room like this, dedicated solely to her practice, with an antique wooden music stand in the middle of the room, violin music ranged in shelves around the walls, and pictures of great violinists hanging from the picture rail, perhaps then she would have practised. And perhaps if she had a family depending on her for the bread they must eat, that would have made her practise too. Or perhaps then she would have given the violin up altogether and become a civil servant, out of fear that otherwise her family would starve. It was pointless to judge the way other people ordered their lives. And it was untruthful to see it as Alan's fault: Ann had acquiesced readily enough; if she had been savagely determined to be a violinist, no matter what, she would have done it. But Ann Fitzwilliam was not savage at all. Any music she played would be inspired by her personality; vigorous, yes, when it needed to be, but always generous and kind.

She turned on her machine, stood staring out of the window for a minute or two, then turned back into the room. It spawned manuscript paper, and music, on every shelf. She moved down the bookshelves, reading a paragraph here and a page there, recognising the trend: the time-wasting before the work. She pulled herself together, and turned from the shelves. As she did so, her eye fell on shelf after shelf of CDs arranged alphabetically by composer. Albinoni: the beautiful *Adagio* and its evocative triplets, which always made her think, irreverently, of Coward, and how potent cheap music could be. Allegri. Allegri's *Miserere*, the most exquisite work ever written for the human voice. Caz remembered it, the uncanny, unnatural sound of a single child, like a needle, threading his voice through the impossibly high top C before tripping down again, always managing to sound as if he was echoing from far away, from heaven almost. On impulse, she put it into Alan's machine and turned it on, picturing the dark chapel, lit by candles in the early evening on Ash Wednesday in Rome all those years ago.

She knew the story well enough. Gregorio Allegri's *Miserere*, or Psalm 51, jealously guarded by the Vatican for 140 years. No one allowed to make copies. The music never permitted a performance outside the Sistine Chapel. Even those who sang it not allowed to keep or copy their music, All this on pain of excommunication.

Then one day in 1770, Ash Wednesday, the young Wolfgang was visiting the Italian capital with his father. He went to hear the famous *Miserere*. Then went home and copied out all nine parts, note-perfect. So the story had gone down in musical history as yet another example of the incomprehensible magic of the child and the man.

There it was again, the sublime pin-prick of sound of a lone boy in the distance. The structure of the piece was highly repetetive, and yet one never bored of that miraculous, otherworldly sound. It would be an interesting exercise, Caz thought, to see how often the average musician would need to listen to it to be able to do what the fourteen year old had done after one hearing. As far as she could tell, the succession of chords was similar each time. And of course it was repeated again and again. A gifted musician, with a good memory for chord-sequences . . .

Caz opened her eyes wide. She jumped up, and programmed the machine to the beginning of the track again. '*Hamlet*,' she said out loud. 'Rosencranz and Guildenstern are dead!' She didn't need to listen to it again, to hear the musical clue, but now she wanted to, to luxuriate in what she had just realised. It was a good twenty years before his death, but it was the beginning of the explanation.

'"Rosencranz and Guildenstern are dead?"' Ann repeated, confused.

'Yes,' Caz said. 'There were no copyright laws, in Shakespeare's day, right?'

'Nor in Mozart's,' Ann pointed out.

'Indeed. Nor in Mozart's. Plays were carefully guarded. The theatre's prompt copy was kept under lock and key. Actors only had their own speeches and cues. But that didn't stop plays being pirated. In the case of *Hamlet*, one of the actors, either Rosencranz or Guildenstern, memorised it as best he could, and sold it. We know it was one of those two, because he didn't cover his tracks well: the further you get from their scenes, the more inaccurate it is!'

'So why "Rosencranz and Guildenstern are dead"?'

'That was what struck me. We're so impressed with the fourteen year old memorising nine parts of a complex piece of music, that we miss the other remarkable thing. We all know Mozart could achieve extraordinary musical feats. We don't need the example of Allegri's *Miserere* to tell us that. The remarkable puzzle is, *why had nobody else done it before*?'

'Well, nobody else could,' Ann started to say.

'Wrong. Not many people could have done it at one hearing, at the age of fourteen. But what about the third counter-tenor, or the second bass, or any one of the men who were singing it every year? Why didn't they go home and write out their own parts, and cobble something together?'

'Why should they?'

'Why should Mozart? Just to prove he could do it? But to prove it musically? Or socially and politically? As soon as Mozart had copied it, everyone else started doing it. The taboo was gone. Mozart wasn't afraid of Rome. Nor of anything, or anyone anyone else; to Leopold's despair. Why didn't his son get preferment? Because he wouldn't kow-tow to anyone. This is the eighteenth century. Class mattered. But not to Mozart. He believed himself superior to the smallminded aristocrats he worked for.' Ann looked unconvinced. 'Don't you see? It's the clue. The clue to his character, his life, his failure to become rich and recognised. His confidence and arrogance and independence. His freemasonry, his anarchic passion for brotherhood and equality. And perhaps even the clue to his death.'

Ann baulked at this. 'That seems to be pushing it a bit.'

'Nonsense,' Caz said energetically, wondering whether it was. 'I've been thinking and thinking what enemies Mozart might have made who would have hated him enough to kill him. Loads of people disliked him. But who *hated* him?'

Ann entered into the game. 'The Vatican? No wait: that chap who sacked him . . . the archduke?'

'I love you!' Caz said, laughing. 'Archbishop, actually; but yes! That pompous, petty philistine whose social class Mozart later lampooned in *The Marriage of Figaro* in the stupid, immoral would-be adulterer, the count; while he, Mozart, was the superior and intelligent, but socially disadvantaged Figaro. Now, if you were the archbishop, and you employed a composer much as you might buy a Ferrari or a race horse, and your own ex-composer, servant, pilloried you and the rest of your class in a public opera for everyone to laugh at . . . Don't you think you might employ a hit-man, or perhaps a poisoner?'

Ann laughed. She was only half-convinced.
'More likely than Salieri, anyway,' Caz finished up.
'Yes. I think I agree with you there.'
It was triumph of a sort. It would have to do.

23

Caz was on a rollercoaster. Her book had taken shape overnight, and now she couldn't stop. She had sketched a plan by the time she stopped at teatime, and now knew where the whole book was going. And Ann had practised her violin for half the afternoon.

When they had tea together, Ann suggested ringing the school to let them know Caz was taking Theo out to tea.

'Strictly speaking, he owes me one,' Caz reminded her. 'Perhaps he should take me out.'

'If he organises it, it'll be a miracle. Anyway, you can sort that out between you. Either way, there's no need for Mrs Havent to tell you off again. This time it will be official.'

As soon as Ann had made the telephone call, informing the secretary that Miss Sanderson would pick Theo up for his exeat the next day, she put the receiver down, and said, a propos of nothing, 'I do worry though.'

'About Theo?'

'Yes.'

'I'm sure you do. Anybody would.'

'No, it's not that. It's not just that he's lost his father. I'm sure these things are always devastating. But he doesn't talk about it. It worries me. He used to be such an open child. At least, he was once we had explained to him why he should be open. After we found out how unhappy he was at his first school. I don't know how to describe it: "victimised"? "Bullied" seems too strong a word. No one was being deliberately unkind. No one was kicking him, or calling him names, or anything like that. It was a perfectly caring, lovely, normal school. But I honestly believe, if he had stayed there, he would have been a wreck by now. Theo is one of the gentlest people I know, and yet, two weeks before he left that school, I saw him kick another boy in the stomach. I couldn't believe my eyes. He was red all over, and shaking with rage, and he deliberately kicked another child. I was so shocked I didn't even tell him off. I did later, but not there and then. He was simply going insane with frustration and thwarted mental energy. And confusion. He has a natural confidence in his own abilities, you see, and that didn't fit with the view they had of him. He never got his homework done, he was always behind with his work, so there was a feeling that he was near the bottom of the class. And yet he knows, in himself, that he's clever. So he didn't know which to believe. He was having a five-year-old identity crisis, and turning into the kind of boy who could kick another child in the stomach. That's what would have happened if he'd stayed there much longer. Or else . . .' she wondered. 'Perhaps not. Perhaps I'd have been educating at him at home by now, and he'd have become a rather academic social misfit; an eccentric.'

'So did he go straight to the choir school?'

'Yes, but not straight into the choir. He was too young for that. That came after Alan's death. He changed as soon as he went to that school. He loved it. He used to say, in his prayers at night, "Thank you for school. Thank you that I look forward to it. Thank you for sending me there."'

'His prayers?'

'Yes.'

'I didn't realise . . .'

'No, I'm not really. I don't. At least, I don't think I do. I'm not bothered one way or the other. But Theo asked if he could say prayers every night. He must have read about it somewhere, I don't know. He didn't seem to expect me to say them too, so that was all right, but he seemed to like me to listen sometimes.

'Anyway, after he moved schools, we realised just how awful it had been for him. It was as if it was safe for him to acknowledge it, now he was out of it. So I talked to him about it. I told him that he must always tell us when things were bad. We said it was important for him to be in touch with his emotions, to realise what they were, to talk about them freely. Even the bad emotions. Otherwise, I said, they can get driven underground, and do a lot more damage.

'Alan was a bit like that. He was very intellectual: he lived much of his life on a cerebral plane. Which is good, in some ways. He wouldn't have messed about for years not doing his violin practice just because he didn't feel like it. He didn't give his emotions the time of day.' She smiled. 'But then, you know, they've got to come out somewhere. Usually they came out in his music. Usually.' Suddenly, Ann seemed to shake herself, invisibly, almost as if she'd gone down a wrong path because she hadn't been looking where she was going. She looked at the clock. 'I must go to the shops before they shut,' she said, and sat, doing nothing.

Eventually she continued, as if she hadn't stopped at all: 'Anyway, that was what I said to Tippy. You have to learn to control your emotions, one day. But first you've got to know that they're there. And that means, as a child, simply talking about them. Telling your father that you hate him, if that's how you feel. Saying you've fantasised about murdering your teacher. For a young child, there should be no "No-Go" areas. Parents must be completely safe. They are the fuse between you and the world, the safety valve. My mother used to call herself my "dustbin". I'd come home from school, and she'd sit me on her knee, and say, "I'm your dustbin. You can dump it all on me."

'The extraordinary thing was how Theo changed. By nature, he's like Alan. If he had gone to a conventional public school of twenty years ago, he would have come out never knowing he had an emotion in his body, I'm sure. Apart from with women, perhaps. He adores girls, even now. But from that moment on, he talked about his emotions as freely as I do. We had that one conversation about it, and he learnt the lesson as easily as if it had been how gravity works, or what a pentatonic scale is. No – a better analogy would be how to do something. Alan explained the rules of chess to him when he was five or six. Weeks later he asked Alan for a game, and Alan got ready to explain the rules again. He didn't need to repeat a single one. I suppose Theo had been playing chess in his mind ever since, practising how to do it. I had a tutor at college who used to tell me how to practise the violin in my head. He told me about someone who'd been in prison for several years, without a piano, and had practised all these pieces in his head, so that when he came out he could play them.

'And Theo was like that with his emotions. We talked about it just once, and after that he knew how to do it. I had to remind him occasionally. You know, "Are you angry with me?" that sort of thing. But he had grasped the point, and he did it.

'But that was before Alan died. After that, he shut up like a clam. Worse than ever before. He'll talk to me about some things, but he can't talk about Alan's death. Perhaps it was too much of a shock, I don't know.'

'It sounds fairly normal to me,' Caz said. 'We adults tend to think it's like leaving a splinter in: we must get it out, no matter how painful it is. But perhaps we're wrong. Maybe it's more like a scab. Perhaps he knows what he's doing, and the best way to heal it is to leave it alone. Has he seen anyone? A psychologist?'

'He doesn't want to,' Ann said. 'You can't force someone to see a therapist if they don't want to go. And when I mentioned it, he seemed . . .' She paused for a moment, and then shivered. She looked up. Caz was reminded of the moment with Theo, down by the river, when he'd turned his face from her. 'He seemed scared. I dropped the subject, and never mentioned it again.' She stood up. 'I must go shopping if we're to have anything to eat at all. There's a concert tonight, in the Senate House. Would you like to go?'

'Sounds good. What's the music?'

'All modern. Well, post-1950 at any rate.'

'Yuk,' said Caz. 'You'll have to educate me. I can't understand anything later than Elgar.'

'Oh, come, come. Britten? Walton?'

'Fair enough. I'll come. Would you like me to do the shopping?'

'No, thanks,' Ann said. 'The shops'll be shutting, and I know where to go. Another day would be lovely, but not today.'

'That's what you said about the wine,' Caz pointed out.

'So it is,' Ann replied.

24

The next day, at half past three, Caz turned up at the school gate again to take Theo out to tea. This time she waited for him. She waited while all the other children appeared, then she waited while they were all met by affectionate and enthusiastic adults, then she waited while they all disappeared again, in their Range Rovers with cattle-bars – necessary, Caz presumed, for ploughing a path through the difficult terrain of wobbling cyclists and playing children and other urban hazards – and still Theo was not there. Caz ventured down the school drive towards the main door, hoping she wouldn't bump into matron. It must be something to do with our memories of school, she mused, that we should have this Pavlovian fear of the staff even when they are no more than fellow adults, like ourselves.

She had just got to the front of the school when he appeared, a lone figure, struggling with a large and heavy carrier bag, which he was looking inside and fiddling with, so he didn't even see her.

'Hello,' she said.

'Oh, hello!' he replied, surprised, as if he hadn't expected her for hours yet.

'Didn't you know, you shouldn't keep a lady waiting?'

'Oh!' he said. 'Who?'

'Me, you daftie.'

'Oh, I see. Have you been waiting?'

'Well, since I was told to meet you at three thirty, and it's now gone ten to four, I conclude that the reason I've been standing here for what seems like hours, getting extremely bored and cold while everyone else comes and goes, means that, yes, I have been waiting.'

'Gosh, sorry,' he said, and smiled his face into dimples, causing Caz to hope that he would learn social skills like consideration and punctuality, before he learnt the value of his smile. 'Anyway,' he said, 'I'm taking you out for tea.'

'Good. Let's hope it makes up for making me wait so long. Where are we going?'

'Going? Oh, I hadn't thought of that. Let's go to Grantchester. That's fun for tea.'

'Have you got some money this time?'

'No, I've got the tea. Here in this bag. Look, I asked the kitchens to give it to me, and they did.'

'Great,' Caz said, and meant it. 'How are we going to get to Grantchester?'

'Um. Walk?'

'I suspect it's a lot further than we think. It's a good few miles.'

'Punt?'

'In October?'

'Why not?' he asked.

'Scudamore's are closed for the winter, one. Two, we'd freeze. Three, we'd just about get there when you've got to be back in bed.'

'Oh dear,' he said, and Caz felt a sudden panic, that he thought his tea was going to fail.

'It's okay, we'll go somewhere else. The Fen, or by the Mill Pond, or something.'

'I know!' he said. 'I've got it! We'll go to the Rifle Range! It's just round the corner.'

'It sounds rather dangerous,' Caz said doubtfully.

'Oh, it isn't. At least, not from rifles. There are cows and things, and horses which might eat our sandwiches, but no rifles. The army hardly ever uses it, and when they do they shut it off, so you can't go in. They're quite responsible really.'

'Come on then. Off we go.'

It was just round the corner. They turned up Grange Road, and walked for a few yards, and there they were, within minutes, in the heart of the countryside, heading towards the open fields and farms, going along a lane through meadows where horses looked quizzically over hedges.

'Here we are,' he said, when they'd walked for about ten minutes. 'Here we can play Pooh Sticks.'

'Do you still play Pooh Sticks?' Caz said, delighted.

'Why, when did I before?'

'No, I mean do children still play Pooh Sticks nowadays?'

'Why shouldn't we?'

'Why indeed? We still sing "Ring a' Ring a' Roses," after all.'

And they both chose a stick, and leant over the tiny bridge, and dropped their sticks the mere arm's-length that it was into the tiny stream which trickled over brambles and branches and pebbles as if it were playing at being a stream.

'Oh, no!' Caz said, dismayed. 'Mine's got stuck on a leaf already.'

'Never mind,' Theo said. 'You can have mine.'

'Thank you,' she said. 'I suppose that means I've won, then.'

'Yes, I suppose it does. But we'd better check. Look!' he said, stepping over to the other side of the bridge.

'What? What have you found?'

'There's Eeyore, floating on his back!'

'Where? Where? Show me!'

'Only teasing!'

And Caz, who had genuinely been fooled for a split second, at least into believing something was there, if not Eeyore, hugged him for sheer delight, so that he said, 'Hey, mind the tea!'

'Tea? I'd forgotten tea. I think we should have it beside the brook, don't you?'

'Yeah, come on!'

They found a log, which was slightly less damp than the ground, and sat on it, on the edges of their coats, under the prickly branches of a hawthorn and the flapping leaves of a sycamore, and Theo opened his plastic bag.

'Squash,' he said. 'Take a swig. I nearly didn't think of drinks, but Polly suggested it.'

'Who?'

'Polly. Our cook. She's really nice, you know, young and things, not big and fat like cooks are supposed to be.'

'So you mean, you didn't think of a drink at all,' Caz pointed out.

'Yes. Yes, I didn't. Now, there's Marmite and cucumber, or peanut-butter and marmalade. Which would you like to start with?'

'Crikey. I suppose the Marmite . . .'

'Though I think they're all squashed up, really, so I don't suppose it makes much difference.'

'Right, well, I'll have one of them then. A conglomerate.'

'Here you are.'

'Thank you.'

The bread was white sliced, pressed till it was a thin, bendy wad, but the cucumber was still crunchy and the Marmite nearly hid the taste of margarine. It could be worse, Caz thought. It could be raw fish in Japan, or sheep's eyeballs in Kashmir. They sat there companionably, shivering in unison while they watched the brook swirling round a twig which was caught in the water, ever changing and ever the same, like looking into the embers of a fire. But much colder. After a while, Theo got them each a second sandwich, but this time Caz's luck had run out, and it was peanut-butter and marmalade. He watched her eat it.

'If you don't like the marmalade,' he said, 'you can scrape it off with a twig.'

'I might just do that.'

'Seconds is good,' Theo said. 'Seconds is Battenburg cake. Though I think,' he said, looking into his carrier bag, 'that all the bits have come apart from each other.'

'Terrif,' she said.

'I thought they only said that in comics.'

'They do. I'm only really a character in a comic.'

Theo laughed. It was then that Caz noticed that he was shivering so much he couldn't drink out of the squash bottle without spilling it.

'You're not cold, by any chance, are you?' she asked him, vaguely wondering whether, in loco parentis, she ought to take some authoritative action.

'Um. I don't know. Am I?' He noticed his hand shaking, as if for the first time. 'I seem to be shivering. Aren't picnics supposed to be like this?'

'Of course they are. Autumn picnics are. Snuggle up and I'll put my arm around you. I'll tell you what: I've got the key to your house. When we've finished our picnic, let's go and make ourselves a cup of tea in your kitchen. It's not very far.'

'Are you supposed to have the key to our house?'

'No. I'm burglaring it.'

The moment the words were out of her mouth, she could have kicked herself. It was a glance, a look, no more; a slight tension in the small body. But something had come between them. He glared out across the water, and his face went very still.

'I'm sorry,' she said. 'It was a silly joke. Will you forgive me?'

He said nothing.

'Please?' she said.

'What?' he said.

'You know what. I just said a stupid thing, and I'm sorry.'

'It doesn't matter.'

'It does matter. It was tactless, which is why I've said sorry. We can't be friends again unless you forgive me. I didn't mean to say a stupid thing. Ann was telling me yesterday how you, we, any of us, must say when we feel bad things. If you feel something bad towards me, tell me. But don't pretend you don't feel it.'

''S all right,' he said, but this time he looked at her, so she knew it was.

A gust of leaves fell about them, and Caz hugged him closer. She wanted to talk to him, but didn't know what to say. The afternoon was getting darker, and the birds were changing their tunes to the sounds of early evening. Then she remembered something Will had told her about his grief, when he was a child.

'Are you angry with Alan?' she said. 'For dying like that?'

'It wasn't his fault,' he said simply.

'No. But that might not stop you feeling cross with him. You can feel cross with a car for not starting.'

'I can't drive,' he replied. Then he said, 'Or not entirely, anyway.'

Caz went back over the conversation in her mind, while they lapsed into silence again. 'Come on,' she said. Then, as she pulled him to his feet, 'Ann told me all about it. How it happened.'

'How what happened?'
'How Alan was killed.'

It happens occasionally in our lives that we do little things, supposedly trivial things, which subsequently turn out to have the most enormous significance. We strike a match and put it to a piece of twisted paper to see what will happen, and it turns out that we lit the touch paper connected to all the dynamite under the bridge. The bridge is blown, the war is won or lost, and we thought all we were doing was burning an inch of paper.

It seemed to Caz in that moment, and even more in the days to come, that she had lit the touch paper without even realising she was striking a match. Theo sat down on the log as if he'd been smacked across the face. He recoiled when she tried to touch him. He stared, unseeing, across the brook at the field opposite. And as she looked at his face, she realised it had turned, not white, but green. It couldn't just be the light from the trees. His face was actually green.

He was shivering still, even more violently than before. 'Please,' he said. 'Please.' And she began to realise that this was not anger or grief, but a vast, overwhelming, monumental tidal wave of fear. 'Please don't go to the police.'

Caz was stunned. 'Why on earth should I go to the police? Hey, look.' She sat down next to him and tried again. 'We're friends, right? I know we don't know each other very well, but so far we're friends. We're also cold. I'm going to take you to your house, and put the kettle on, and on the way there I want you to ask yourself whether you can tell me what you're frightened of. Now come on, up you get. Oof, what a lump.'

Caz didn't ask him to say anything till they got to his house. She spoke to him most of the way, explaining she had the key because Ann had invited her to stay, and telling him that she and Ann were becoming good friends too. She emphasised this, particularly, in the hope that it would help him to trust her. She was careful not to phrase anything in the form of a question. When they got to the house, she put the kettle on, and made a pot of tea, and put plenty of sugar and milk in Theo's cup without even asking him, and when he had his hands around it, and had clearly warmed up a bit and got over his initial shock, she reached her hand over the table and put it gently on his, and said,

'Now then. Please will you tell me what you're frightened of? I don't know if you know me well enough to trust me yet, but I promise to try and be your friend. To help as much as I can.'

'If I tell you, do you promise not to tell? Not to go to the police?'

Caz took a deep breath.

'I'm sorry, Tippy,' she began. She tried to imagine anything the boy might tell her, that she would want to report. Had he witnessed something? Why would he not want anyone to know? 'You see, I might feel I have to report something. It might be in your interest.'

'And if it isn't, do you promise not to?'

'Well, yes,' she said quickly, without even stopping to think. 'Yes, I can promise you that.'

He was frowning, as if he was considering something. In the end he looked her straight in the eye.

'I killed Alan,' he said.

LIMERICK COUNTY LIBRARY

25 ∫

Thinking about it, as she waited for her audition, Ann shook her head and frowned. She wasn't imagining it. Theo had changed since Alan's death, and he had changed in a way which seemed, to Ann, to be sad. He had become distant, and strange, and fearful. When he first went to the choir school he was sunny and confident. It had lasted only as long as Alan's life. After that fateful evening in October, two years ago, her son had withdrawn more than ever before, so that now, from time to time, he would have fits of depression so severe that one would say, if he were an adult, that he tended towards the suicidal. Perhaps, as Caz said, this was natural in a bereaved child. Yet it almost seemed to Ann – though this was surely absurd – it almost seemed as if he were hiding something, as if he feared something so dreadful that he couldn't even talk to his mother about it.

'Next,' she heard from the Keynes Room. She stood up and cradled her violin. 'Hello, Mrs Wedderburn! How nice to see you. Were you wanting to use the room? We're auditioning for the CUMS orchestra, but I think we've nearly finished. In fact, if there's no one else out there, we have finished.'

Tom Rally, one of Alan's basses, was smiling at her from under his mop of curly black hair.

'No, I wanted to audition actually. I'm very out of practice, but . . .'

'Gosh! I say. What, for CUMS? Goodness. Come on in. Boys, this is Mrs Wedderburn. You know, Alan Wedderburn. Um . . .'

'His widow,' Ann said for him.

'She, er, she very kindly said she might play in CUMS for us. Which is great. Of course.'

'I've come to audition,' Ann said. 'Like the others. You don't have to be a member of the university, do you?' she added, suddenly worried. Perhaps all her practice had been a waste of time.

'No, no, of course not,' Tom said, rather wildly. 'But, I say, you don't need to audition, you know.'

'I don't mind,' Ann said. In the chorus of protests which followed, she gracefully gave in. They did not want to audition her. She wasn't sure whether it was embarrassment on their part, or respect for her, or a tribute to Alan. Whatever prompted the sentiment, Ann was glad of it. She had assumed the worst: that the undergraduates would be arrogant, scornful of their elders, and full of their own success.

'Rehearsals on Monday nights,' Tom said. 'Eight p.m. First one next week. I'm conducting, I'm afraid. Unless you'd like to do it!' He laughed nervously. 'I'm afraid we've already got a leader.'

'Don't worry,' she said. 'I'll fit in.'

'See you Monday, then,' he said, and shook her hand.

As she walked away, she wasn't sure whether she was relieved or disappointed that she hadn't had to play. One more year, she thought grimly, and there won't be an undergraduate left in the university who's heard of Alan Wedderburn. He'll just be the name on a few carol books and arrangements.

26

Caz looked across the table at the angelic little choirboy opposite her, and for a moment felt almost delirious, heady, as if she had just jumped out of an aeroplane and not yet opened her parachute. You killed your father, she thought. There, there.

'D'you mean . . .' she began. She was casting around at random. She had to say something. Theo must know that Whistler had killed his father. How could he think that he himself was responsible? 'You mean, you caused his death, somehow. You made him come home earlier than he would have done, or later. And if you hadn't he'd still be alive? Is that what you mean?'

'No.' He looked puzzled as if he couldn't understand her being so dull. 'I mean I killed him. He was . . . he was murdered, right?'

'Yes,' Caz agreed. 'Apparently.'

'Well, I murdered him.'

Caz breathed steadily. She realised she'd tightened her grip on his hand, and very slowly, imperceptibly she hoped, she released it again. She wanted to say, I don't believe you, but she knew it wasn't true. Here was a child who knew the meaning of the words he spoke. Suddenly, instead of seeing the charming and intelligent boy who had simply seemed unusual, she saw someone who was so different he would never fit in with his peers; so unconventional he seemed almost to be part of outer space, a planet which hadn't been charted, an unknown country full of beauty and fascination, but which might be savage and dangerous too. She hardly knew this child. What was he capable of? In her heart, she felt a growing sense of horror.

Then, suddenly, her intellect revolted. Of course he couldn't have killed his father! As if she had been held down under murky water, she now sprang back up to the surface and burst into the real world again. The air was clear and clean, and she took a deep breath. He was a sweet and innocent child, disturbed by a terrible grief. He was barely seven when his father died, and Ann had said he was one of the gentlest children there was.

She watched him taking another sip of his tea, and let go of his hand altogether so that he could use both hands on the cup. I must keep this conversation going, she thought, but what on earth do I say? 'Why?' she said in the end. 'Why did you kill him?' Go on, prove it then, was what she was trying to convey.

He hardened his face. 'I hated him.'

That's it, she thought. I'm out of my depth. She cut them both a slice of cake, and put the lid of the tin back on. She wasn't hungry, but she wanted to have something to do.

'Why?'

He just shrugged. Fair enough. Plenty of grown men hate their fathers, but would be hard pushed to tell you why. He looked down at the table, ignoring his piece of cake, and his long, curled lashes seem to stroke his cheek. He is expectionally good-looking, she thought; almost beautiful. The words Dorian Gray sprang involuntarily to mind. Ann had told her how Alan had died. How were these two accounts compatible?

Thinking over Ann's account, she saw a faint ray of hope. How stupid she'd been not to see it before. Ann had asked him to get the ambulance, leaving him with a responsibility which was an intolerable burden. She didn't blame the boy's mother; she probably would have done the same. But for thirty seconds or so, he was left alone with his freshly killed father, believing himself to be wholly responsible for getting him back to life. He had failed.

'Listen,' she said. 'We often blame ourselves for all sorts of things that aren't our fault. Children especially, I don't know why. Couples bust up, and scream at each other, and get divorces, and it's entirely their own fault; and yet, time and time again, the children blame themselves. They feel that, if only they'd been easier to live with, less of a responsibility, their parents wouldn't have split up. It's not true. And it does the children a lot of damage. Feelings of guilt are very dangerous.'

'Even if you're guilty?' he asked.

'Well, that's different. I'm not sure, even then, that it helps much.'

'My granny says that nobody feels guilty for anything they do wrong any more. She says that's half the trouble.'

'That's as may be,' she said, feeling he was getting the better of the conversation. 'But you're not guilty of anything.' Immediately, she regretted it.

He said nothing.

'Look,' she continued urgently, 'when Ann left you on the telephone, to get the ambulance, and she ran out of the house' – she leant forward and took him gently by the shoulders – 'your father was already dead. Nothing could have made any difference. It wasn't your fault if you didn't get the ambulance.'

'I did get the ambulance.'

'Well then, it wasn't your fault they didn't get here any quicker.'

'No. It was their fault. They had to have everything told them twice. I told them everything, and then they made Ann repeat it.'

'That's because they have to be sure. If a child has told them, they feel they have to check.'

'That's their fault,' he pointed out. 'Besides, like you said, he was already dead.'

'He was. So why do you feel guilty?' she asked him gently.

'I didn't say I did feel guilty,' he corrected her. 'That was you.'

'Fair enough.'

'I said I killed him.'

'But *how*?' she cried, desperately trying to save him from what he had just said.

'How?' he repeated, as if puzzled by the question.

'How . . . ? Why do you think . . . ?' She stopped. She looked at him hard. This boy is intelligent, she said to herself. Nobody could deny that. He knows the difference between murder and ringing for an ambulance. I have to believe him. Otherwise I'm calling him a liar or a fool. 'How did you kill your father?'

There was a long silence. Caz heard the grandfather clock ticking comfortably in the hall. The goldfish tank, by the fridge, bubbled gently and continuously, in a way that should have been restful, though actually Caz found it was getting on her nerves. A fly buzzed somewhere near the larder, and she thought, rather crossly, it's surely too late in the year for flies. Neither of them had eaten their cake.

'He came home from college,' Theo said slowly, 'and I heard him. It was quite late, and I was in bed. I was reading. I was reading in the light from the landing, because my light had been put out. It comes in from the landing, and it reaches the head of my bed, so you can read in it. I was reading *The Way Things Work*. It's an interesting book, but it's a bit too big. It takes up the whole pillow and more, and gets a bit stuck under your chest. I was reading about cogs and wheels; how clocks work, that sort of thing. I heard him come in, and put his bicycle round by the back. Through the side gate, you know. And he came in. So I closed my book up, because I knew where I was so I knew I'd be able to find it again, and I put my dressing-gown on, and I went downstairs. And then . . .'

He stopped, and looked up at her. She was completely still, and felt a kind of chill deep within her. She hardly dared breathe. Perhaps he doesn't know what killed Alan, though, she thought. He'll get stuck now. I mustn't look at that fire extinguisher. She could just see it out of the corner of her eye, a long red blur by the open door to the hall, and had to use all her mental energy not to look at it.

As if perfectly reading her thoughts, he turned round and looked straight at it. 'You see that fire extinguisher?' he said. 'I was really cross, and I picked it up and hit him with it. He was sitting on this chair. And it hit him on the back of the head, and he got up, and went towards the back door, and fell down.

'I wasn't sure what had happened, so I dropped it, and went to find Ann. I'd just gone out into the hall, when I heard her coming down the stairs. She was calling. "Alan! Alan!"' Caz didn't move. The boy continued. 'It was dark where I was –

I was in shadow under the stairs in the hall – so she didn't see me. I wasn't sure what to do, so I didn't do anything for a while. Then I heard her calling the ambulance, so I came in. She asked me to hold the telephone, and she ran out of the house. I'm not sure why. While she was gone, they answered the telephone, so I said we needed a doctor. I hadn't realised we'd need the police. I didn't know it was murder. I gave them our address, and they said could they talk to my mummy or daddy. I said they couldn't talk to my father, but I'd try and get my mother. Then Ann came back in, and took over the telephone, and said it all over again. She was a bit annoyed with them, I think. Then we sat on the floor next to Alan and waited.

'He was dead already, but I didn't know that then. He didn't feel dead, but he looked a bit funny.'

Caz's eyes were hurting. She realised she hadn't blinked for a long time. She did so then, and looked down. She felt the dampness on her face, and wanted to wipe it away, but she didn't. Emphatically, she told herself that she did not feel sick. It fitted. It all fitted so hideously well. But it couldn't be true. Please, can it not be true! He must have some reason for having to make it up. He was an unusual child. So bright, and . . . different from other children. She looked back at his clear, blue eyes, and couldn't believe anything evil could come out of them.

'I didn't mean to kill him,' he said.

'What . . .' Caz started to say. She took a deep breath. Then she cleared her throat and started again. 'What did you mean to do?'

'I meant to hurt him.'

'Why?'

'He and Ann had had a quarrel that afternoon. He was unkind to her. I wanted to hurt him.'

Then Caz stood up, very carefully, very deliberately, and heard her chair tipping over and falling behind her with a startling crash. 'Come on,' she said. 'It's time I took you back to school.' She glanced at the clock, and realised he would only just be back in time.

'Are you going to tell the police?' he said.

'I promised, didn't I?' she replied, and realised it felt like a lifetime ago.

They walked back to the school in silence. Every so often, Caz felt like saying something, remarking on a tree, dressed in lovely reds and yellows, or a cat, dashing across the road in front of them, or the sound of a distant evening bird, but they all seemed such trivial things to mention. Finally, when she got to the gates of the school, she stopped, not offering to walk him up the long drive.

'See you soon,' she said. He nodded. 'Thank you for telling me.' He still said nothing, but merely gazed at her, solemnly and silently. She realised he hadn't shed a tear. She made a mental note to ask Ann why he hadn't wanted to see a psychologist. With a shock, she realised she had no idea whether she could tell Ann all that he had burdened her with. Surely, somebody should know what was going on in his mind? But how far did her promise extend? She felt stupid for making it. He had, after all, been too clever for her. If what he said was true, she could not go to the police. She must at least tell his mother. With a feeling of relief, Caz told herself she could tell his mother without betraying his confidence.

She put out her hand to shake his. 'Our friendship's important now,' she said. 'When you tell people secrets, your friendship becomes very special.'

'You mustn't tell Ann,' he said. 'That's very important.'

She hugged herself. 'Right,' she said. 'You'd better hurry, or you'll be late. Thank you for tea.'

'That's all right,' he said, and waved goodbye.

She watched him go down the drive, between the chestnut trees, in the nearly dark evening, till the only thing she could see any more was the white of his socks. She watched while even those disappeared, as the drive took a slight bend. And then she watched, for what seemed like a very long time, till a tiny figure re-emerged in the light in front of the school, under the Dead Slow sign. He looked impossibly small. She heard a little gasp, and found she had pulled her hands up to her face.

'It can't be true,' she said, muttering to herself. 'It can't. He's so innocent. It isn't true.' She was aware, in the pitiless scheme of things, that she could wish and wish as intensely as she liked, and it wouldn't make the slightest bit of difference.

He is in danger, she thought, with sudden clarity. He is frightened of something. She had to get help for him. But the only thing she had was the secret he had given her, and she was not allowed to use it.

27

Caz walked back to the house very slowly. She tried to remember his account as accurately as she could. Was it conceivable that a boy so young could have made something up so convincingly? Yes, of course it was. She thought back to her childhood, and stories she made up at a far younger age than this. But she was a writer, even then. Was Theo that kind of child? She doubted it. What she had noticed of him on their brief acquaintance was that he was almost fanatical about the truth. Not in a moral way. She didn't mean he was too good to tell a lie; she doubted if anyone were that. But it wasn't the way his mind worked. He had to have every detail correct.

Was it possible that he could have swung a fire extinguisher at a father he was cross with, and hit him an unlucky blow that killed him? It must be medically possible. Was it psychologically possible? Why not?

He had said, 'I didn't mean to kill him.' And of course a court would take that into account. But what on earth would happen to him? Taken into care, or what? It didn't bear thinking of. But of course, nothing would happen, because she couldn't tell anyone else about it.

She turned the corner into Ann's short drive, and noticed with dismay that the lights were on. Ann's bicycle was outside the front door, not put away yet. How could Caz face her? What could she say about their time together? 'Your son was quite charming, gave me a lovely tea, and told me he killed his father.'

She would have to summon up all the positive things she could remember about the afternoon, and tell her those: We sat in the feezing cold shivering our butts off eating peanut butter and marmalade squashed together with marzipan. That kind of thing. Then she would ring Will, and get the pressing weight of her secret off her chest. And then she would go out for the evening, or plead a slight illness and go to bed. Perhaps she would even go home to London tonight, and come back and finish her business in Cambridge another time.

She gritted her teeth and went round to the back door.

Ann was singing loudly in the kitchen, messing around with pots and pans and chopping boards, with a large glass of wine on the table. 'Hello,' she said cheerfully. 'Tonight's a celebration. I've bought champagne, and fillet steak, and all sorts of wicked things. You've got a direction for your new book, and I'm a violinist again. I say, are you all right?'

'Fine. Absolutely fine.'

'You look a bit pale. I'm assuming you're free this evening. Are you?'

'Of course. What else would I be doing? It sounds really great.' Caz smiled as best she could.

'You're not all right. Sit down. You've probably been over-doing it.'

'I just feel a little funny, that is all. I wish I weren't pregnant. I could do with a really big brandy.'

'I'll make you a strong cup of tea. Listen, we don't have to eat this stuff. It'll keep. Do you want to go and lie down?'

'Perhaps just for five minutes.'

'Go up to your room, and I'll bring you some tea with sugar in.' Even as she climbed the stairs, Caz heard Ann singing again, though more softly this time. The audition had obviously gone well. Caz felt some relief that she wasn't free to spoil it.

She took her telephone out of her bag, and lay down. She dialled the number, and closed her eyes. Thank goodness she could talk to someone about it. She would feel fine after talking to Will.

She rang his mobile. 'I'm sorry I'm not available at the moment. Please leave a message after the tone.' Damn and double damn. It was almost a physical pain, this sharp and sudden longing to go home. But she could hardly plead illness, and then jump on a train for London. She could hear Ann coming up the stairs with a cup of tea. She must cheer up, before Ann asked how she got on that afternoon.

Ann knocked on the door. 'Here we are. Have a little sleep. I won't cook anything till you come down, and then only if you fancy it. I used to get exhausted during my pregnancies.' Then, as Caz looked at her, she said, 'I lost a couple, you know.

'I wish I had them now. More to remember Alan by. Though I suppose it would be harder to cope. Theo's a pretty full-time job.'

'I'll come down soon,' Caz said, closing her eyes and letting her head sink on to the pillow.

When she woke up, it was gone eight o'clock. She sat up on the bed and rubbed her eyes. Without bothering to put her shoes on, she went to the door to go downstairs. She opened the door and listened. She didn't recognise the piece. It was lovely. Slowly, barefoot, she crept down the stairs, and when she got to the bottom just sat there listening. For the first time, she understood what they meant when they said the violin is the closest instrument to the human voice. It *is* a voice. It was alive, pleading, giving, imploring, taking. It would be impossible for any other instrument to talk like this. A flute can play tunes, can dance and joke, but can't move the human heart. A trumpet can rouse, a saxophone tease. A piano can impress and dazzle. But this! Only a cello, among the other instruments, could do this. And even a cello, though more melancholy, she had never remembered as being so haunting. She sat on the stairs, with the tears pouring down her face, and thought, What a gift! If I could move, like this, with my writing, I could change the world. Or change a few lives in it, at any rate. She hoped it would never end, and yet she looked forward to the end, because that was the way the music was going.

When it finished she didn't move. When Ann came out into the hall, to go into the kitchen, Caz was still sitting there, her face wet with tears, and her soul exhausted and quite content.

Ann smiled. 'I hope I didn't wake you.'

'What was the music?' Caz asked.

'Oh, that? Pastiche, really. It's called Praeludium and Allegro. It's Kreisler, pretending to be Pugnani. Frightfully corny stuff. What would you like to do?' she went on. 'Would you like

fillet steak and champagne, or shall I cook us a simple ome-
lette?'

'I'd like the celebration, please,' Caz said. 'I'm feeling much
better now.'

28

The moment Theo said, 'I hated him,' he knew, at last, that it wasn't true. He was so relieved, he kept nursing it all the way back to school. I didn't hate him, I didn't hate him, he kept telling himself. For two years, he had wondered whether that was why his father had died. Simply because he, Theo, had wanted it. An accident was one thing. To kill your father by mistake was terrible; it was one of those things that are so bad you never want anyone to find out, ever, as long as you live. But to kill him on purpose, because you wanted him to die, because you fed a secret hatred against him and wanted him to leave your life for ever: surely even God couldn't forgive that.

And now he knew that he hadn't wanted it.

Now, though, someone had found out. Part of it, at any rate. Not all of it, not most of it, not the worst of the truth. But she had discovered part of his dreadful secret.

He liked Caz. He hadn't wanted to tell her. He had had to make a quick decision. If he hadn't told her, she might have discovered the other for herself. And that prospect terrified him, hung over his dreams like a storm cloud, swung above his head like that sword in the Greek myth, that someone would one day find out. To tell her the other part seemed better. It must be. Now, at least, she wouldn't be able to tell anyone else. That is, if she was trustworthy.

He had an idea they didn't send children to prison. He had never heard of a child being in prison. He had also heard that, under the age of ten, you can't be accused of murder. That gave him another ten months to decide whether to tell the police. If he told them before he was ten, he wouldn't be a murderer. He wondered whether, somehow, without giving himself away, he could find out what happened to children who kill people before they're ten. Perhaps nothing happens to them at all.

Still, he didn't want anyone to know. It was probably cowardly, but he curled up inside at the thought of everyone hearing what he had done. Mr Marshall . . . he wouldn't joke with Theo any more, hiding under the windowsill, if he knew that about him. Miss Henrietta . . . she wouldn't smile at him in her lovely way when she came to tuck him up in bed. Amschel . . . would he be allowed to sing the psalms, the canticles, *Messiah*, if Amschel knew? Would he ever be allowed to stand, poised, in front of a discreet microphone and a congregation of several millions, and herald in Christmas for the little old lady alone by her radio, the busy mother surrounded by wrapping paper, and the preoccupied clergyman preparing his midnight sermon? Surely if he, Theo, were ever asked to sing that pure and perfect E, that Mary was that mother mild, the millions would rise in protest, and turn off their radios, and say, this boy is a murderer; he can't sing in Christmas for us.

Caz had promised she wouldn't tell. But adults are strange about promises, and you can never be sure. Theo thought back to a wedding the choir had sung for in the summer. At the beginning of the service the couple had stood in the middle of the congregation and said the vows, off by heart, looking at each other.

'For richer for poorer, for better for worse, in sickness and in health, till death us do part. And thereto I plight thee my troth.'

Then the choir had sung Byrd's Five Part Mass, and then the huge west doors had been swung open on to the afternoon sunshine and the largest lawn in England, and Amschel had played Widor's Toccata louder than Theo had ever heard it before, and Theo had mused on the lovely sounds of the words he had heard in the service. And thereto I plight thee my troth.

At the reception afterwards, Theo had approached the chaplain.

'Sir?' he said.

'Yes?' Mr Wright answered, taking a passing glass of orange juice.

'What does "thereto I plight thee my troth" mean?'

'"I promise." Why?'

'I liked the words.' He thought for a moment. 'But, sir, does everyone say that when they get married?'

'No.' Theo's confusion began to clear: he knew some people must have promised something different. 'Most people nowadays say, "This is my solemn vow."'

'What does that mean, sir?'

'Exactly the same. Have one of these little cocktail sausages. Oh, you weren't quick enough; here, have mine.'

'Thanks. So you mean everyone, when they get married, promises to stay with their partner till they die?'

'Yes.'

'But . . .' Theo couldn't find the words. 'I thought, if you've promised, you have to keep your promise?'

'That's right. You do.'

'How come some people don't, then, sir?'

'That, Theo, is one of the great unanswerables. That, and who made God, and how can we get that waiter to come this way again. Seriously, I don't understand either. But it's one of the reasons there isn't a Mrs Wright yet.'

'Why?'

'Because I'm not sure I could keep a promise like that.' Then Mr Wright looked at him and said, seriously, 'But, Theo we all fail. Don't criticise other people for breaking their promises until you've kept every one of yours.'

'Yes, sir. Do you want me to pass you one of these, sir?'

'Do I look that hungry? I am, actually: I missed lunch.'

'Why, sir?'

'Oh, something cropped up. Nothing special.' There was a burst of clapping from the other end of the courtyard, and the bride and groom bore down on the cake, brandishing a sword. 'A school mate of mine explained it to me once. He made the promise believing he would keep it, so that was all right. Then he realised he couldn't, so that was all right too. I think that's how the argument went, anyhow.'

'And that *is* all right, is it, sir?'

'I think it's a load of rubbish myself, but he's still a very good friend of mine. Take my advice: don't get married for a while. And grab that plate, and we'll share it.'

So Theo knew that adults don't always keep their promises. Caz seemed like the sort of person who would, but you can never tell. It was a risk he had had to take.

When he went to bed that night, Theo tried to pray. He hadn't prayed for a long time. He used to pray at home, with Ann, but she never joined in. But now that someone else knew a little bit, at any rate, of the awful truth about him, he felt that God did too, and he felt too ashamed to pray. He tried to remember some of the words from Evensong, the bit where you say how bad you've been.

He curled up in his school bed, and stretched his arms between his thighs, and held his feet. They were cold. 'Almighty God, our heavenly father,' he began. The words tasted like sawdust. He was no more wicked now than he had been before he had told Caz. But now he knew how wicked he was. God would not want to hear from him.

Comfortless, and alone, unconfessed and unforgiven, wishing he could still long for his father's arms around him, he stumbled into sleep.

29

Caz woke with a nasty feeling about something. It was like waking with a hangover and not being able to remember the drink. Something horrid had happened. What was it? She hoped it was a dream.

She sat up and rubbed her eyes and remembered the meal she had had with Ann. It had been pleasant, but subdued. Though the food had been delicious, the evening had not been as enjoyable as that first one together, when, although they hardly knew one another, they had felt able to tell each other anything. Last night, Caz had felt uncomfortably restrained. And now, of course, she remembered why. She ran her mind back, again and again, over Theo's conversation with her. She tried to replay it word for word, like testing a painful limb, or feeling a wobbly tooth with a tongue, as if she had to; as if she had to make it hurt just to be sure how bad it was.

Now, of course, in the light of day, as it were, she could see that the whole thing was absurd. Boys of seven do not kill their fathers. They simply don't. Certainly not boys whom one has got to know, and become fond of, who give you their Pooh sticks when yours become stuck, and peanut-butter and marmalade sandwiches squashed together with Battenburg cake.

She got out of bed, wearily, and dressed. It took her a long time. She kept stopping, halfway through cleaning her face or brushing her teeth, and trying to think of it from a new angle. No matter how much she disliked the idea, there was something about it which rang true. Some part of her had been horrified, convinced, swept up in it.

She had no idea what action she ought to take now. Someone

ought to know. Someone who knew something about it. A professional: a psychologist.

She must do something. And she felt, perhaps irrationally, that she must move fairly quickly. Now that he had told her, for all she knew the situation might have become unstable. He might do something stupid. If so, she must keep him safe, somehow. On the other hand, she had only to make one false move, and she might make it worse. Suppose she told the wrong person, and Theo felt his trust had been betrayed. What might he do then?

She went down for breakfast with a heavy heart.

Ann was practising already. The door to the sitting room was shut, so Caz was not worried about disturbing her. She stopped briefly outside the door. It was not music which Caz recognised. It seemed to be of great technical difficulty, but not, to Caz, particularly interesting or lovely. At one moment Ann stopped, and went back over something; Caz went on into the kitchen.

The kettle had boiled. Caz looked around for a teapot. She couldn't remember where Ann kept it. She looked in the cupboards above the kettle, and found the tins of tea and jars of coffee and coffee beans, and mint teas and strawberry leaf teas and teabags. She even found the coffee jar. But no teapot. She glanced around the work surfaces, under the cupboards and around the kettle. She looked on the table and in the sink. She couldn't even remember what Ann's teapot looked like. She started looking in the lower cupboards. She came across cheese graters and salad spinners and colanders and egg-poachers, and various gadgets whose use she couldn't even guess at. In one cupboard she found a pair of scales like the ones her grandmother had had, twenty years or more before. This was a smarter, cleaner, more beautiful and polished version, but it was the same idea: the dish on one side, and the graduated cast-iron weights on the other.

She took the scales out and stared at them for a while, even playing with them. They were perfectly balanced. A finger, lightly applied to one side, would make them swing up and down happily, adjusting themselves back to near stillness after thirty seconds or so. She turned back to the cupboard again and looked at the weights. There was a choice of metric or imperial, so she opted for imperial. She took them out of the cupboard and put them on the table, next to the scales. She even experimented with them, putting the 1 pound weight on one side, and the 8 ounce, 4 ounce, 2 ounce, and the two little 1 ounce weights on the other. They balanced perfectly. Then she put them all together on one side, and the large 2 pound weight on the other. Again a perfect balance. All she had left now was the tiny little 1/2 ounce weight. She had nowhere to put it. She felt rather sorry for it. In the end she added it to the 2 pound weight, and watched the scales swing slowly out of kilter.

For a while she did nothing. Then she lifted her eyes, slowly, and looked long and hard at the fire extinguisher which hung by the door. She came round the table towards it, and stared at it at closer range. It was large, for a domestic kitchen, and had 'Carbon Dioxide Extinguisher' written in white letters by the top. She tried lifting it down. It came off the holder easily, sliding into her hand as if it were intended to jump readily into the hands of a panicking cook, whose kitchen has just caught fire. Or even into the arms of a strong child. It was fairly heavy, fifteen inches long or so, not counting the handle, and perhaps five inches in diameter. She felt it in her hands for a moment, trying to compare it with the remembered feel of the weights she had just been handling. It was considerably heavier, surely. She walked over to the table and put it down on the disk of the scales. She started piling up the weights on the other side, dropping some of the smaller ones, and causing a bit of a clatter.

She listened. Something was wrong. What was it. Then she realised: the violin playing had stopped. In a sudden panic she grabbed up the extinguisher, causing the side with the weights to thump down with a crash, the weights rolling and tumbling over one another in their alarm. She dashed over to the doorway to put the extinguisher away. She tried to fix it back in the clip. It was one of those dratted things which was far easier to release than to put back again. Of course it was: the designers assumed that one would be in more of a hurry removing it from the wall than putting it back. Please go back in, please! she found herself saying to it, listening desperately for other tell tale sounds from the sitting room. She was shaking so much she couldn't get it to do anything, and she wasn't thinking clearly. Should she just leave it on the floor, by the wall, hoping Ann didn't notice, and then fiddle with it later when she was out, or something? Stop! Calm down. Read the instructions. 'To replace, lift the lever and press in.' She heard the drawing-room door opening. She lifted the lever and pressed in, and it went home like a dream. Still shaking, she returned to the table and began to pile the weights up again.

She heard Ann crossing the hall. She steadied her hands. Ann didn't come straight in, but seemed to go to the front door, and then come back. Then she opened the door and came in.

'Hello!' Caz said, rather too brightly. 'My granny used to have one of these. I haven't seen one for years.'

'Have you had breakfast?'

'Er, I started to. I boiled the kettle, I think. Then I got waylaid, admiring this. That's right,' Caz gathered herself: 'I was looking for a teapot. I couldn't find one anywhere, so I started looking in all the cupboards. That's when I found the scales.' She began to put the weights back in the cupboard.

'It's right in front of you.'

'What is?'

'The teapot. Under that cosy. On the table. I made a pot of tea because I wanted some, then I left it for you while I went to do some practice.'

Caz smiled, and shook her head. 'Didn't see it. Sorry.'

'Never mind. Let's have some breakfast. We need the light on. It's a bit gloomy, isn't it?' Ann walked over to the door. 'The switch is so inconvenient guests never see it, stuck behind this cupboard, the wrong side of the door. Now what would you like? Toast? I'd like some muesli, I think, and yoghurt. Crikey, whatever's the matter? Sit down. You look as if you've seen a ghost.'

'I'm all right. Really. I'll be fine when I've had some breakfast.'

'You're as white as a sheet. Have you rung Will? You ought to tell him you weren't well yesterday, too. He'll come and pick you up, won't he, when he gets back to England?'

'Yes, he would, actually,' Caz admitted, realising he'd come the moment he reached Heathrow, if she told him where she was. 'Yes, he will.'

'Why don't you give him a ring?'

'I did. I never seem to get him. I tried again last night.'

'Hasn't he got a mobile?'

'Yes, Caz said. 'It's permanently on the answerphone.'

'Why don't you try again? He's got my number, hasn't he?'

'No. I didn't give it to him. I . . .' How could she explain why she hadn't told Will where she was? It was so silly, so childish. 'I didn't want you to be disturbed.'

'Oh, don't be ridiculous. Ring him now. And if he's not there, leave my number. Go on, ring him now.'

'Okay. I'll just have a little breakfast first.'

'Good idea. Your colour's coming back a bit. It's what our old cleaning lady would have called "a funny turn".'

'Yes. Yes, I expect it is.'

Ann made her some toast, and put honey on it, and made her drink the sweet tea, and mashed up a banana with some fruit yoghurt, and within ten minutes Caz was feeling a bit better. She could understand why Alan had allowed his wife to stay at home giving him tea and sympathy, rather than pushing her on with her violin. She was very good at it.

They chatted around this and that, and Caz found herself hoping they hadn't lost the easy intimacy of the other night. But what could she do? She couldn't tell Ann what was bothering her, and she would probably never be able to talk to her freely again.

Eventually, Ann got up and began to clear the things away. Caz rose too, and thanked her, and excused herself, and said she would go and ring Will.

'Do you want to use the house telephone?' Ann said. 'It's cheaper.'

'No, it's fine, thanks,' Caz replied. She realised, guiltily, that she didn't want any possibility of being overheard.

She went up to her bedroom and dialled Will's number.

30

'Will! Oh, you're there! Oh, thank God you're there!'

'Darling, whatever's the matter? Hey, hey, calm down. I don't know whether to be thrilled you've rung me, or miffed that you don't ring until you're absolutely desperate. Have you been mugged, or what? Blow your nose, dry your eyes, and sit down, if you aren't already.'

'I am sitting down.'

'Good. Well, that's something, anyway.'

And she told him everything. Not in order, but all jumbled up, somehow including Ann and her violin, and Theo's letters, and his frightening absence of tears, and his hatred of his father, and Caz's own absurd performance with the fire extinguisher and the weights.

'Also—' she started.

'Hang on,' Will interrupted, and she heard him speak in Italian to someone else. 'Sorry,' he said, coming back to her. 'We were finishing a meeting. What were you saying?'

'It doesn't matter.' She had been on the point of telling him what she had noticed in the kitchen. No. It was only a detail. And now she thought further, it was only supposition after all.

'Fine,' he said. 'All right.'

'It's not all right. Not if this kid's killed his father.'

'No. If. But do you really think he has?'

'I don't know. I don't know what to think.'

'Okay. I think you're right: the one thing that's obvious is that he needs looking after. If his imagination is working overtime, somebody needs to help him to learn how to control it. If not, then he certainly needs help. To cope with his own guilt, if it was a genuine accident. And if it wasn't . . .'

'Oh, Will, it must have been! He's so sweet.'

'I'm sure. Anyway, if it wasn't, he'll need a lot more help. What we've got to do is work out how to get it for him. Look, my flight gets in mid-afternoon. Suppose I come up this evening, and we go out for dinner and plan a campaign? Would Ann put me up too, d'you think?'

'I'm sure she would. Oh, Will, thank you.' Not for the first time, Caz noticed his infallible instinct, which knew exactly how much independence she needed, had very cleverly given her a little bit more, and now, extraordinarily, knew he could take over like a primitive knight in shining armour and she wouldn't mind at all.

'Of course, there's one thing you're not considering. And, in a sense, it's the most obvious.'

'What's that?' she asked.

'Well, maybe he had a reason for saying what he did. And maybe it was a good reason.'

'Like what?'

'I don't know. But then, he doesn't want us to know, does he? You say he's a bright child?'

'Very. I mean, exceptionally, as far as I can tell.'

'And not particularly the sort who would make up a fantastic story?'

'I wouldn't have thought so, but I'm not sure.'

'So maybe he had to work quite hard to make it up. What was it that prompted it?'

'I can't remember. I said something, I think. Something about his father's death – I'm not sure.'

'And did he come out with this story straight away?'

'No. No, it was quite a long time later.'

'Right. So he had time to work out the details?'

'I suppose so.'

'Then we've got to discover why he would have needed to.'

Will was due to arrive at suppertime – about seven o'clock. Evensong was at five thirty. Caz decided it was time she kept her promise to Theo, to go and listen, or worship, or whatever the correct word was. She announced her intention to Ann at teatime, and issued a half-hearted invitation for her to join her, which, to Caz's relief, Ann declined. Caz vaguely wondered how someone like Ann, who, apart from her violin, had nothing to do all day except keep herself alive, had managed to fill her time till now. She never seemed idle. Was it really possible to make a full-time job out of shopping for oneself, keeping the house in order, and supporting one's son at school concerts and cricket matches?

Since the beginning of the week, however, since she'd decided to go for her audition, Ann seemed to have had a new purpose, a sense of urgency. Had she been like that as a student? Caz imagined her as ruthless, in her gentle, understated sort of way. Single-minded. Having nothing in her life apart from her violin and her career. So that, when she met Alan and put it all aside, she became like a bow with the string slackened, permanently relaxed and soft and gentle. Perhaps, after those unused years, it was possible to string the bow again and it would be as taut as it ever was.

'It's nearly five; you ought to go soon,' Ann said.

Caz nodded and went into the hall to get her jacket, keeping her eyes fixed straight ahead of her as she went through the kitchen doorway.

She stepped out into the October afternoon. The loveliest time of year, of all lovely times of year, in one of the loveliest cities in Europe. The trees along the road shook in the evening breeze. Rooks, going home to roost, cawed in the tall tree tops of the chestnuts which lined the drive of the choir school, as she walked past. Windows, lit up in the University Library, looked unblinking out on to the dark night, as those who had to read essays out to their tutors the next morning worked on into the evening, one day a week, far later than they were wont. Caz breathed in the cool night air, full of the smells of leaf and distant river, and walked on.

The Backs were aflame. The trees shook the red and yellow leaves out of their hair.

The lights in the Chapel shone through the west window as if it were an exquisite model on a table, the glass made of coloured tissue paper. She could imagine stretching out her finger, as a giant, and reaching across that vast lawn to poke through the delicate window, and spoil the model for ever. A few tiny figures trickled steadily towards the Chapel, their black gowns fluttering out behind them, tugged at by a playful breeze.

She followed them.

Just inside the vast north door she was accosted. 'Hello there. Nice to see you.'

Caz felt swamped with guilt. 'Frank! I should have dropped you a note. I enjoyed tea the other day so much. Will you forgive me?'

'Ahh, that's all right. I thought to myself, She's been busy, I thought,' he said cheerfully, making Caz feel worse. 'Lucky I saw you, though. You follow me. We don't want to put you down with hoi polloi. It's not *the* hoi polloi, you know. A lot of people get that wrong. I'll pop you in the MA stalls, seeing as it's only a weekday. Couldn't do it at the weekend. Nice this time of year. Not too many Japanese, if you know what I mean. Very nice, they are, but they don't know when to leave their cameras behind. There was one in here, in the summer, with his camcorder running, if you please. I had to ask him to leave. Most put out, he was. Couldn't understand what the problem was. I said, we can't have unauthorised recordings made of the choir, I said. What would that do to our contract with MFI? I said. He didn't understand a word.'

'Really?' Caz managed not to smile, as she coped with the image of a flat-pack do-it-yourself Missa Brevis.

'Of course, when he realised he couldn't put the experience into his little machine, he pushed off. Didn't seem to occur to him to just listen and enjoy it instead. Don't know why he doesn't just write to England for a film of everything, then he could stay at home in Tokyo and leave us all in peace. Here we are.'

Caz followed him up the steps to the MA stalls. 'I'll just find your place in the book,' he said. 'Lot of people come unstuck on that one.'

She thought she could probably survive the perils of the Book of Common Prayer, but she let him stretch over her to reach the enormous, leather-bound book which rested on the velvet cushion, and open it deftly and accurately at Evening Prayer, or Evenfong, as Caz childishly said to herself, reading the lovely old print with her modern eye.

The organ was playing quietly, meandering, not saying anything in particular, but wandering in and out between the tunes and melodies, the lines of music overlapping one another, as if they were not in any great hurry to get there, and would take you with them if you liked. How much it must cost to maintain this place! Caz thought irrelevantly, wondering how long it took to light all those candles every evening, and then put them all out again after the service was over.

She stood as the choir entered, row by row, the children first, followed by the men, with the choirmaster and the fellows behind. Two by two, the children slipped into their stalls, before nodding towards the east end. Caz watched them, looking for Theo's face. He was not there. I've got the wrong chapel, she thought, for an insane moment. He must have meant St John's College, not this one at all. Then she shook herself, and remembered picking him up from the school, and going round this very Chapel with him before.

Then she began to worry. What possible reason could a chorister have for missing Evensong? None, that she could think of. The choir took precedence over everything: sporting fixtures, extra homework, rehearsals for the school play. There was nothing in the timetable of a choir school that even compared with the importance of the choir. It was what paid for the children's education, after all. It was the reason for the school. Could he have lost his voice? Caz remembered, with guilt, the picnic of the day before.

The choir was singing the Introit. Caz was aware that it was as lovely as it ought to be, that its beauty was adequate, that it should be transporting her soul to wherever the saintly King Henry had intended when he founded the institution. But she was not concentrating on the transporting of her soul. She was hoping against hope that it was indeed a cold. A sore throat is nothing. He would be over it in a few days, and be more careful of his voice in future. Please, please, can it be no more than a voice lost on an idiotic October picnic.

Caz looked at her unwieldy Prayer Book, and realised she was completely lost. She turned on a few pages but could see nothing resembling what the choir was singing. She glanced up, hoping at least to look as though she knew where she was. Without even glancing at her, the don who stood in the stall next to hers uncrossed his arms and turned her book to the correct place.

Wash me thoroughly from mine iniquity, and cleanse me from my sin.

For I acknowledge my transgressions: and my sin is ever before me.

She wondered whether she could catch one of the other boys afterwards, and ask what had happened to Theo Wedderburn.

31

Will arrived at Ann's house at twenty to six. Ann was dismayed.

'You've just missed her,' she said. 'She thought you wouldn't
be here till seven, so she went to Evensong. She half promised
Theo some time ago, I think, that she'd go to Chapel, so she
thought she'd better get her visit in before she found herself
going back to London and unable to keep her promise. He's
quite a little evangelist, my son. He persuades everyone to go.'

'It doesn't matter,' Will said. 'She'll be back soon.'

'You could join her if you wanted. You could hear the other
half of the service from the ante-chapel, and catch her as she
comes out.'

'Don't worry. I'll unpack. I've brought a few things for her. I
bet she didn't have much of a change of clothes.'

'She's been wearing the same things every day, now you
mention it. I sort of wondered why.'

'She didn't pack anything, that's why,' Will laughed. 'She likes
to travel light. Shall I take these things upstairs?'

'Yes,' Ann said, and directed him to a room.

It was obviously Ann's room. It had a large double bed in the
middle, along the wall which faced the window. Will judged that
the window, which looked out across the road, must face east.
There were fresh sheets on the bed, and clean towels folded on
it, and on a table under the window Caz's computer and bag
sat side by side, as if to say, Who needs to pack more than us?
Behind the computer was a small vase of flowers. Will put his
case on the bed, unpacked Caz's clothes and shook them out so
that they wouldn't crease, and took out some more comfortable

clothes for himself, so he could shed the suit he had needed for his meeting that morning. The bedroom had a bathroom off it. He showered, shampooed, changed, and finally took a book out of his case.

Then he went back downstairs. Ann was in the sitting room. 'I had no idea what to get you,' he said, handing her the book. 'I thought wine or chocolates would be boring. This is Caz's last book. Have you got it?'

'No,' Ann said, delighted. 'I thought she wrote children's illustrated books.'

'She used to. This was supposed to be a new departure.'

'Thank you. What a lovely present. What would you like to drink?'

They sat, companionably, sipping their drinks and politely keeping the conversation above silence until they got to know each other better. Finally, Will said, 'Does Theo have any free time at the weekend? From what Caz told me, it sounds as if he's allowed out for either Saturday or Sunday afternoon. I noticed there's a fair on at the other side of Cambridge. It would be great if Caz and I could take him.'

'It's very kind,' Ann said, 'but don't you need some time together after you've been away? Wouldn't you rather just take Caz?'

'Definitely not. A child on these occasions is essential to the enjoyment of the event.'

'Well, that would be lovely. He likes to answer for himself, but as far as I'm concerned it would be lovely. We'll ring the school and leave a message for him. It's a good weekend to have asked him. There's no Evensong this Saturday, so he's allowed to stay out later.'

Then Will thanked her for giving up her bedroom for them, and did not say she shouldn't have. And Ann asked him what they would like to do for dinner, and Will said he had thought of going out, and would Ann join them? She tactfully said she was a bit busy that evening, if they would excuse her, but perhaps they could do something together the next night? Within twenty minutes of entering the room, Will was thoroughly content that he had got everything he wanted and could reasonably have expected, and more.

32

'I shall never forget his little animated countenance when lighted up with the glowing rays of genius: it is as impossible to describe as it would be to paint sun-beams . . .'

Michael Kelly, of Mozart

Theo was not well. Miss Henrietta had found him that morning, waiting for another boy to finish cleaning his teeth, shivering and shaking as if he had caught a dreadful chill. She asked him what the matter was, and he said he was fine. She felt his forehead and his temperature seemed normal, so she sent him down for breakfast. When she came down herself, twenty minutes later, she found him still sitting in front of an untouched bowl of cornflakes.

'Are you all right, Theo?'

'Mmm?' he half said, under his breath, without looking at her.

'Are you all right?'

The fourth time she asked the question, he turned, seeing her at last.

'What did you say?' he asked.

'Come on,' she said. 'You're coming up to the san with me to get your temperature taken.'

'I've got Choristers' Practice,' he said, looking at her and not moving.

'You should have thought of that before you sat here, making yourself late. There's the bell, you cottonhead. Everyone else has gone. Where are your books?'

'In my locker.'

'And you think you can get them and be in the music block before the bell stops ringing, do you?'

He smiled half-heartedly. 'If I were bionic I could. I'd have to go backwards in time, wouldn't I? It's already stopped ringing, you see,' he explained, as if to a younger child. Already his smile had faded. 'Do you think you can do that? Go backwards? On another planet perhaps? Do you think God can turn back time? And if so, do you think He can do things differently, if they've already happened? Or, once it's been done, do you think it's always and for ever too late to undo it? Perhaps if you went back in time you'd have to do it the same again.' He shivered. 'It would be awful.'

'Come on. Up you get. Off we go.'

Theo continued to shiver all the time she took his temperature. It was normal. Henrietta didn't tell him this. She shook the thermometer down before he could see it, and told him he was to go to bed while she went to tell his form teacher. When she came back, he was sitting bolt upright in his bed and his face was wet with tears.

She went over and sat beside him. 'What is it, Theo?' she said. 'What's the matter?'

He shook his head miserably, and said nothing.

'Has something upset you, or do you just feel rotten?' He nodded. 'Which?' Another nod. 'Can you tell me about it?' Shake. She sighed. Suddenly, with a conviction that took her completely by surprise, Henrietta found herself thinking it monstrous that a child of nine should live away from home. I will never allow it to happen to mine, she thought. Never.

She put her arms round the small body, and pulled him to her. 'Is it about your father?' He could contain himself no longer. He turned his face into her chest, and released himself to bitter, terrible sobs, crying loudly into her clean white shirt. She looked at the door, which was open on to the corridor, and thought, Please, can no one pass. The children should all be in lessons, but you can never be sure. And please, if there should be an adult out there, may he or she have the sensitivity not to look in. She put her hand on Theo's head, and rocked him to her as he wept.

*   *   *

At half past four, after the choristers had gone to Chapel, Theo went in search of Miss Henrietta. He padded along the corridor to her room in his bare feet, and knocked gently on her door.

'Hello,' she said. 'What are you doing?'

'Can I go to Evensong?'

'You're too late. It's gone half past four.'

'No, I don't mean to sing. I just mean to go.'

'I don't know,' Henrietta said, stumped. 'Wouldn't Amshall be cross? I mean, if you miss the practice but you're well enough to go?'

'I don't think so. You see, it's good for us just to listen. When Jamie lost his voice he still had to come to practices to listen, because Amshall said he'd be learning anyway, even if he wasn't singing.'

Henrietta was not sure. 'I'll tell you what. I'll ask in the staffroom, and if anyone's going to Evensong I'll see if they can take you.'

Sometime later, Mr Johnson, the Latin teacher, came up to the san. He was a strict teacher, but Theo liked him very much, mainly because he found Latin so interesting.

'Hello there,' Mr Johnson said. 'I'm going to Chapel in five minutes. If you can be dressed and down at the front of the school before I leave, you can come with me. If you're not there, I'll go without you. All right?'

Theo was at the front of the school within three and three-quarter minutes. He didn't realise that he then kept Mr Johnson waiting for nearly four more while he tied and retied his shoelaces: Mr Johnson had omitted to say, 'dressed and down *and ready to go'*.

He thought he wouldn't bother to tell Theo that his jumper was on back to front.

Theo had always had a sense that the reality he experienced in Chapel was far more real than the reality outside. He had heard someone talking to Alan, once, in their sitting room at home. A snatch of the conversation caught Theo's ear.

'But, Alan, bear in mind what "reality" meant to the medieval mind. Religion was *the* truth, and the rest of life a sort of transient waiting room. Existence is uncertain. Today you have five children. Tomorrow you may have two or three. But eternal life, and eternal death, are realities which last. So what a peasant in the Middle Ages, or a franklin or squire, saw and heard in the play, was more important, no, let's say more *real*, than going home to his pease pudding after the play was over.'

There was much that Theo didn't follow in this. But the idea of something being more real than reality itself was one which stuck, like a burr, in his mind.

It was his experience of Chapel. When he was here, looking up at these windows, listening to the music which must be a faint echo of the everlasting music which is surely playing somewhere else, he knew it was true. He didn't even know quite what it was that was true.

If he'd had to describe it, he would probably have called it Christianity: 'Christianity is real,' he would have said. After all, it was that which had inspired this building, this music. But he would have preferred not to describe it.

It didn't bother him at all that most of the choir, the fellows, the undergraduates who read the lessons and carried the candles, presumably Amschel, that most of them didn't 'believe'. He knew that some people didn't like Chapel because of that. A cousin of Ann's had come to Chapel with them once, and hated it. She said it was all meaningless and she preferred her little church in the country where all they had was somebody trying to bash out the melody on an out-of-tune piano, because at least there they meant it.

Theo couldn't understand why she minded. It didn't matter whether they believed, any more than it mattered whether the postman knew what was in the letter he brought you. After all, Theo thought, did all the people who built this building believe in God, or did they just put one stone on top of another because it was their job? Perhaps there was only one person, King Henry, who believed. It didn't matter: it didn't make the building any less beautiful.

So Theo was absolutely certain that this was the reallest thing there was.

But that was all he knew. For the first time, that day, as he sat next to Mr Johnson, and knelt when he knelt, and stood when he stood, he realised that, just because he knew it was true, didn't mean he was part of it.

Christianity was true. But he, Theo Wedderburn, was not a 'Christian'. It was there, but it was passing him by, like a mighty river: he sat helpless on the bank and couldn't swim. Mr Johnson was swimming in there, and the chaplain and the dean, he supposed. But he, Theo, was on the edge, for ever being left behind.

At the end of the service he sat, silent, his hands clasped between his knees, while Mr Johnson knelt down and prayed. At least, that was what Theo assumed he was doing. He'd never seen anyone pray before, other than out loud. Theo wondered what he was saying. Can you talk to God in the same way that you talk to other people? Theo didn't know. Nobody had ever taught him to pray. He wished Mr Johnson had turned to him, instead of turning to God, and told him how to pray. He wished he had the courage to ask him.

They said prayers in Chapel, of course: proper, written prayers, like the Lord's Prayer and the collects. But Mr Johnson wasn't saying those. He was saying his own, personal prayers.

Theo wanted to do that. To put his arms on the comfortable cushion on the lectern, and bury his face in his arms, and pray. He wasn't sure whether his arms would reach properly; perhaps he was too small.

Presumably he could pray where he was, staring up at the dark oak panelling, and the bleached white stone above it, and the coloured glass above that. What was he allowed to say? Anything?

Dear God, he started in his head. Then he heard a terrible voice. You can't pray, the voice said. You're far too wicked. Look what you did to your father. Theo stopped, stunned and terrified, as if he had heard the voice out loud. I didn't! he shouted in his head. I didn't, I didn't.

But of course he knew he had.

33 ∫

'I am excited as a child at the thought of seeing you again. If people could see into my heart, I should almost feel ashamed' –

W.A. Mozart, to Constanze.

Caz found she was approaching Ann's house just after ten to seven. Good, she thought rather frivolously, I've got time to 'freshen up', as my granny would have said. Wash my face, clean my teeth. She wondered whether she had some eye make-up, and possibly even some scent, at the bottom of her handbag somewhere. She certainly had a hairbrush. Hadn't she? Yes, she was sure she had a hairbrush. She had not, alas, got a change of clothes. She had asked Ann to lend her a dressing-gown earlier in the week, so she could put all her things in the washing machine one evening and dry them overnight. She had spare underwear and a different scarf, but those were the only changes she could make.

Then, when I'm ready, she thought, trying to keep her excitement under control, then I will see Will. Her face broke into a ridiculous smile as she tried to fit the keys Ann had lent her into the lock. She wondered what he would look like, how he would be dressed, whether he would be smiling. She would be calm and collected, sitting with Ann in the sitting room, sipping a glass of sherry. Will would ring the bell, and she wouldn't move. Ann would let him in, and Caz herself . . . perhaps she would even be playing the piano, quietly, gently, to show how nonchalant she was. She continued to fumble with the lock. Why couldn't people in Cambridge have normal, electronic locks?

She heard steps inside. Ann was coming to let her in, as she usually did. The door swung open, with Ann standing behind it so Caz couldn't see her, and she stepped in.

'Ahhhh!' she cried.

'Don't you like it?' Will asked.

'It's horrible,' she said. 'Shave it off.'

She didn't get a chance to speak any more.

A couple of hours later, as the waiter fussed around them with cups of coffee and chocolates, she said, 'Why on earth did you grow that thing?'

'I didn't. It grew itself when I wasn't watching.'

'Why didn't you shave?'

He looked sideways at her and raised his eyebrows. 'Why do you think?'

'I don't know,' she said, wanting him to tell her.

'You need to have a reason to shave, don't you? Just as you need to have a reason to get out of bed in the morning. It's quite a faff, all that messing about with a razor.' He took a drink of his cappuccino, and wiped the froth from his moustache with his napkin. Then he said very quietly, 'I have actually missed you, you know.'

She nodded. 'Sorry,' she said. 'I was just being silly. I think I was terrified actually. Perhaps I still am.'

'Of what?'

'I was frightened – don't smirk like that! – that I might somehow throw everything away for you. My work. My independence. Become like Ann, in fact.'

He raised his eyebrows. 'You could do worse.'

'Yes.' She thought for a moment. 'Yes, you're right. I could do worse. Have you not even been getting up in the morning then?'

'I have had work to do.'

Something in his serious face made her laugh out loud. 'It looks so horrible,' she said. 'And it's itchy on your lips.'

'Mmm, lovely,' he replied, chewing the bit which covered his top lip. 'As it happens,' he continued, scratching the part which grew under his chin, and then smoothing down the rest, around his cheeks, 'one or two people have told me how extremely irresistible it is.'

'You can't have grades of irresistibility,' she protested. 'You're either irresistible or you aren't.'

'That's what you think,' he said smugly.

She rose to the bait. 'All right, then: who?'

'Who what?'

'Who was finding you irresistible?'

'Ahh. Wouldn't you like to know?'

'Not particularly.'

'Several people,' he said, before he lost the momentum of her curiosity altogether.

'Like?'

'Like, well, like the architect I've been working with this week.'

'Male or female?' she enquired.

'Please!'

'It's equally flattering,' she pointed out.

'Female.'

'Did she try and get you into bed with her?' Caz asked, rather hoping she had.

He laughed. 'Yes, she did actually.'

'What? Tried, or succeeded?'

He pulled his napkin into a long cord, threw it behind her neck, pulled her face towards him, and kissed her quickly before he could embarrass the waiter.

'Euch! Your moustache tickles.'

'I love you too. Could we have the bill, please?' he called to the figure hovering behind the next table. 'Now,' he said, releasing her, folding up his napkin, and putting it on the table beside him, 'tomorrow I have some paperwork to do, which should take most of the morning. You may work up till lunchtime if you wish. Then we'll have a sandwich somewhere, and go to the Blake exhibition in the Fitzwilliam Museum: they've got some good stuff, which they usually keep in storage. Then in the evening we're both taking Ann out for supper. And on Saturday afternoon we're going to the fair.'

'What fair?'

'The Midsummer Fair.'

'But it's not midsummer,' she protested.

'No. The mid-autumn fair, which is held on Midsummer

Common, and hence known as the Midsummer Fair. And that's where we're going.'

'What on earth for?'

'I thought it would be fun.'

There was a pause while they finished their coffee, and the waiter brought the bill.

'And—' she started, and broke off.

'And what?'

'What am I going to do about Theo Wedderburn?'

'That,' he said, 'is just what I'm considering. I am on the case, as they say.'

'Are you going to be sickeningly male and strong and heroic, and go all Lord Peter Wimsey on me, and solve it all without even telling me what you're doing? And if so, can I reconsider that offer you made in the summer, on the grounds that I didn't know what I was letting myself in for?'

'Yes,' he said. 'And no. Now, shall we go?'

Ann heard them come in. She could remember how wonderful it used to be when she hadn't seen Alan for a while, when he'd been on tour, even if only for a few days. How hungry they would both be. How, sometimes, they would spin it out for hours, and sometimes have a wild five minutes. How she would always think it was worth being without him for the fun of his coming home.

She was glad for them. She spread herself, face down, on the narrow guest-room bed, and held on to the cold sheets, and thought there was not much to recommend living on one's own.

Except my violin, she thought. Except my violin.

She could hear them giggling as they went into her bedroom.

34

'A man who is in such a violent rage oversteps all order, all moderation; he forgets himself, and the music must do the same' –

W.A. Mozart

It had happened when Theo and Alan and Ann were on holiday in Portugal.

Theo had never been so far south. They usually went somewhere fairly ordinary in the summer: Cornwall, Yorkshire, Scotland; and at least every other year to Ireland, because Ann loved it so. But that year they went to Portugal. A friend of Alan's had offered them his villa, and it seemed too good an opportunity to miss.

Ann mused, rather morbidly, on the places that had been spoilt for her when they'd taken family holidays there. Portugal was not, of course, the first time it had happened. She considered. How often? Half a dozen times in all their married life? It was not too bad. But as soon as she said that to herself, she knew that it was too bad. It was half a dozen times too bad. It was unspeakable. Truly. So she never had spoken about it.

Perhaps that was the trouble. She knew she shouldn't take the blame for someone else: but perhaps, if she had been a different person, it wouldn't have happened. That did not make it her fault, any more than a child who is bullied is to blame. One has a right to be eccentric, to be slow, to be gifted even, without being bullied. A woman has the right to walk down a street in a mini-skirt at midnight, even to hitch a lift, without a judge telling her afterwards that she asked for it. After all, people have the right to be as irritating as they like to their families, without being murdered, for instance.

Nevertheless, she knew that, somehow, her personality as well as Alan's lay at the heart of it. She had never wanted to talk about it. She still didn't. She felt she had a right not to. But she had to acknowledge that, if she had been more open about it, it probably wouldn't have happened.

She had had a conversation with her sister, once, a year after Susie's wedding. Susie had married a fiercely intelligent, energetic GP whom Ann liked a lot. She thought Susie had chosen well. The two sisters did not normally confide much, and Ann couldn't now remember what had prompted these particular intimacies. They had been to see a film together, in London, and were having a glass of wine in a pub afterwards. Perhaps it was the subject of the film which had prompted the conversation. That was it: they had just been watching Julia Roberts in *Sleeping with the Enemy*. Ann had hated it so much she had wanted to walk out of the cinema, but Susie wouldn't let her. They had paid for their tickets, she said, and they were jolly well going to watch to the end. It was bound to work out all right anyway: those kind of films always did.

As they sat in the Slug and Lettuce afterwards, Susie suddenly said, 'Jamie hit me once.'

Ann was stunned. It wasn't so much that she couldn't imagine Jamie deliberately hurting anyone or anything, as that she couldn't imagine anyone lifting a finger to strike Susie. She was very different from Ann: tiny, dark-haired as Ann was but with her hair beautifully and expensively cut close to her head, efficient with the slightly frightening ruthlessness of those who make a lot of money.

'You?' she said, aghast.

'Well, who else?' Susie said, reasonably.

'What happened?' Ann asked, expecting her to relate what had led up to the quarrel.

'He smacked me round the face,' Susie said, 'and I said, "If you ever do that again, I'll tell Graham." Graham's his senior partner,' she explained.

'And did you?' Ann asked.

'He never did it again.'

'Oh.' It was so simple. She couldn't believe anything so simple could actually work. 'But would you have?'

'Yes. You can't go around hitting people,' Susie said, as if explaining to a child why you can't steal sweets off the counter.

'But he might have lost his job!' Ann protested, tying to think it through.

'Well, he had to weigh that up, then, didn't he?'

Ann was silent. She couldn't help acknowledging that Susie had found a solution. That was when she asked herself whether she had been fair to Alan.

But she had only been twenty-two. It was not the same. Susie was thirty when she married, Ann just twenty-one. And Alan had been nearly as old as Susie was now. It really wasn't the same. How are you supposed to know, when you are just twenty-two, what to do when something takes you so completely by surprise? She suspected, nevertheless, that Susie would have known even when she was twenty-two. Or perhaps she simply never would have got married till she knew what to do.

It had first happened when they had been married just over a year. Ann had no idea, to this day, why. She had no idea why it ever happened. It didn't seem to be linked to an argument they might have had, or not had – after all, they didn't argue that much. It just seemed to be linked to the fact that they were always on holiday.

On this occasion, they were going somewhere in the car. She was driving, and Alan was in the passenger seat. She usually did the driving. Alan was not fond of driving, and used to sit beside her, working, and sometimes singing things out to her. Quite often, he would tell her when to change down, or up, or use the brake.

'You don't need to indicate there,' he would say. 'You're in a lane.' 'You took that corner too soon. It's very dangerous: you couldn't see round the bend.' Or simply, 'Wrong gear.' Ann hated it. Alan was a good driver, she knew, whereas she simply got from A to B. She didn't care whether people said, 'What a good driver you are.' She'd never had an accident, not even a scraped bumper, but Alan said that was just because she was so slow and careful. She'd probably caused hundreds, he said. But when he started telling her how to drive, she would get flustered, and make mistakes, and she was convinced she was going to have an accident soon. Particularly when he said things like, 'You don't need to slow down here. You've got plenty of room.'

Once or twice she asked him not to make comments. So he said, 'Don't you want to improve?'

'Not particularly,' she said. 'I just want to get there.'

'Well, I'm sorry,' he said with a dangerous edge, 'but I don't want my wife smashing the car up and endangering our lives. Not to mention other people's.'

'Then please will you drive? Please, Alan,' she said.

But he answered, quite reasonably, 'Ann, I'm desperately trying to get this finished before we get there. When else can I arrange this piece? I'm earning a living for both of us, remember?' Which was true. He was.

So perhaps that was what they'd been arguing about. Or perhaps she'd lost the way. She often used to lose the way. And Alan, who had no sense of direction at all, and had to get to concert halls hours before the orchestra, would get in quite a panic, swearing and huffing and making it worse. On this occasion, of course, they hadn't been going to a concert hall. They were on holiday. They were always on holiday when it happened.

It was night, and they were on a country road.

Alan had hit her, across the face, presumably with the back of his hand. Ann couldn't remember what she did about controlling the car, but she could remember stopping, by the side of the road, and shaking. She had never been hit before in her life. Her parents had never hit her. She had no idea what to do. The man she'd married had turned into a monster, and she had no idea what had happened. She ran her tongue over her lip, and could feel it cut, and swelling up. Not much; just a little. Her nose was sore as well. She wasn't seriously hurt: no more than if she'd tripped on the stairs, or fallen off her bicycle. She stared at Alan.

He was apologising. His arm was round her, and he was stroking her face, and he was asking if she was all right. I'm still in love with him, she noticed, relieved.

He took over the driving. She sat there, for the rest of the journey, saying almost nothing, shivering, and pulling at the skin around her nails. It is all right, she thought. It is. Something awful, unspeakable, has happened, but we are all right.

And never, in her worst nightmares, did it occur to her that it would ever happen again.

Looking back on it now, she thought of Susie, and wondered again what she could have done. They were in the middle of the countryside, in the middle of the night. She could hardly have put Alan out of the car, and driven on to a police station. The next day, when she might have been able to do something about it, it was all over. Five minutes later it was all over. Alan seemed, if possible, even more shocked and horrified than she was. How could she have threatened to tell? Love is trusting. She knew he never intended to do it again.

But Alan would never have hit Susie twice. So she could see that, if she had been someone else, it wouldn't have happened.

She didn't know when the second time was. The other times were rather muddled up in her mind. Once, they had taken a house with a breathtaking view of Loch Ness, and Alan had hit her one evening in the kitchen; she could remember huddling in one corner. Once, Alan's mother had rung after he had kicked her, hard, on her leg. She hadn't wanted to answer the telephone, but Alan had made her, and as soon as she heard his mother's kind voice, she had burst into tears. She had felt bitterly ashamed of herself, but she thought, It's all right, Alan will explain what he did and she will know it wasn't my fault. But Alan took the receiver from her hand and said that Ann wasn't very well, and would be fine. She had listened, incredulous, to his explanation of her behaviour, and felt as if she had been made to look utterly ridiculous in his mother's eyes, and this betrayal, this letting her take the blame instead of telling his mother that it had been his fault, had seemed to Ann far worse than the hitting itself, because it was deliberate, because he never apologised for it.

Alan was always full of remorse. It was genuine. He would get very upset at what he'd done. Ann herself knew that, in some ways, it was better for her when it had happened. For one thing she knew it wouldn't happen again for a long time.

For another, it always heralded the end of the argument. But also, in a strange way, it gave her the upper hand. She didn't relish it, she didn't like having the advantage over Alan, and she honestly believed she never exploited it, but she knew that he would now be sorry, and subdued.

But what was worse, far worse, than being hit, was being threatened. It was never meant to be a threat, she knew that. It was meant to be a safety valve, a warning, a way of preventing it happening. 'If you go on like that,' Alan would say, 'you know what will happen.' And he meant, Please don't go on, because I might not be able to control my temper. But it felt like, You do as I say, or else. And that, Ann couldn't take at all. She had to have the right to be who she was, without being threatened with violence. At those moments, when he said that, Ann, quiet, gentle, submissive Ann, who always avoided quarrels, would dig in her heels, and not go away, and not be quiet, and absolutely refuse to do whatever it was he wanted, because she would not be intimidated.

Then she got pregnant. As soon as she knew, she said to him, 'You must never, ever hit me again; not now.' She believed doggedly in the idea that the reason Alan hit her was because he knew his grandfather had hit his grandmother. That feisty woman had put up with it for fifteen months, and then left with Alan's father, never to return. This black shard of family history had sunk deep into Alan's soul, she was sure, and poisoned their relationship with a problem that wasn't his fault alone. So Ann was determined that no child of hers would know that Alan had ever hit her. It was the only secret she kept from Theo, as he grew up. She wasn't sure whether she could have lied to him, if he'd asked her point blank, but she suspected that she might. So she said once there was a baby, even in the womb, Alan was never to hit her again.

By then, she had had her talk with Susie. She said to him, 'If you hit me again, I will go to the police.'

They went on holiday to the lovely little cottage in Brittany where they had spent their honeymoon. Ann had been looking forward to it for weeks. In the first twenty-four hours, Alan hit her across the back of the head. She went into the kitchen, and got the car keys, and went outside. Alan came and took them off her. What could she do? He was far stronger than she was. It had never occurred to her that he would bully her to that extent, would not let her take the car. She walked down the drive, and along the lane, and on for four kilometres, tired, because she was pregnant. She got to a little café, and asked if she could sit down. She had no money on her. She couldn't even buy herself a coffee to justify her use of the table. But they left her alone. They weren't busy, and didn't mind her sitting there.

Now what? she asked herself. What were the laws in France about hitting your wife? What attitude did the French police take? And how on earth was she to get to a police station? She sat there for an hour and a half, and then walked back again. Months, years later, she realised she could have asked for help. She could have told the man in the café what had happened, and asked if she could ring the police from there. She never even thought of it. She never wanted to go back to their honeymoon cottage again.

Then she said, 'Once the baby's born, you mustn't hit me. Certainly not if it's a boy.' She never wanted a child of hers to do to his wife what Alan had done to her. As soon as they had a son, it must stop.

The next time was another of the occasions that she could remember clearly. They were in a flat, by the seaside. Theo was under a year old. Alan was in the bath, so she felt safe even though he was cross with her, because she knew he couldn't reach her, until suddenly he rose up, furious, in the water, and she screamed in terror, 'Don't hit me! Don't hit me! Please don't hit me!' She had never before been frightened like that, but this time her baby, peacefully asleep on his blanket, was in the very next room, and she was frightened.

Alan explained afterwards that he thought it was that that made him do it. He didn't think he was going to hit her until that moment, and then it was as if she were willing him to. But that time, he didn't hit her hard. What hurt her that time was the fact that she finally took matters into her own hands and hit him back. She struck him, hard, with her fist against his arm, and her wrist was painful for a week. Then she felt real fear, because she thought she might not be able to play the violin. Alan understood this well. He laughed at her, but he took her seriously too, and kissed her wrist where it hurt.

'I bet the people in the flat below heard,' he said, later, after he had apologised and was holding her, gently, in bed. He seemed to understand how fragile she felt afterwards, and would never try to make love to her, but would put his arms around her, kindly and tenderly, as now. When he said that, she was embarrassed at the thought. The next morning, Alan said their neighbours looked at them oddly as they took Theo out in his carrycot to get some shopping.

And then she stopped being embarrassed, and was angry. 'If they heard me,' she said, 'why didn't they do something?'

'Like what?'

'Like interfere. Like bash on the door and make sure I was all right.'

'People don't like to, do they? Come between husband and wife, you know.'

'Well, they blooming well ought to.' She was furious. 'You ought to come between anybody and someone who's hurting them.'

'Calm down,' he said softly.

And then she said, and really meant it, that it was never to happen now Theo was old enough to understand what was going on. She knew it was already too late. She knew, instinctively, that you can absorb things, atmospheres between people, even asleep in the next room, even from the womb. Nevertheless, he had not been conscious of it, and he never was to be, she told Alan. Now it really must stop. He agreed. He would not do it again.

He did.

So she said, I need to talk to someone: I'm going to see the dean. Alan said, If you tell the dean that I've hit you, I will resign and leave Cambridge.

She looked at the house she loved, and considered the four-year-old son she had who already talked non-stop about when he would be old enough to join the choir, and remembered how much it had upset her brother when they had moved house when he was four, so much so that he still talked about it now, in his thirties, and she thought, What do I do now? If he resigns, it will hurt Theo and me more than it will hurt him. She knew that Alan had said it, not to threaten her or bully her, but because he honestly felt he would be so disgraced and humiliated that he would have to go. She felt more trapped and helpless than ever.

And part of her, outraged, thought about her own humiliation, and wondered how he could feel more ashamed that the dean should know, than that his own wife should know. That his reason for resigning would not be the action itself, but the fact that he had been found out.

And then it happened in Portugal.

It was the worst time yet.

And Portugal was the worst possible place it could have happened. Was there some part of Alan which knew this, which knew that, for him, it was safe? Ann didn't know.

She knew no Portuguese at all. They had no telephone, no car. The only people she had even said hello to were the couple who ran the little supermarket.

What could she do? Say, 'Wine, how much? Two bread, please. And where is the police? *Gendarme*? *Politzei*? Please help: my husband hit me.' And what did she want the police to do? Give him a warning, that was all. She recognised that he would welcome it as much as she would, that he hated hitting her, hated himself for doing it, that if she had gone to the police that very first time, she would have spared him so much. He had explained to her that once you've done something wrong and got away with it, it's much easier to do it again. Or rather, it's much harder not to.

He had been in a terrible mood ever since they had arrived. It was far too hot. The beach was crowded with people, and there was nothing to do except swim and then come out of the sea and burn, a smarting and painful red. They had hit a heatwave, and there seemed no way to cope with it. The house was too hot to sleep in, and the courtyard and balcony started to bake at ten o'clock in the morning and continued like that till eight or nine at night. Alan didn't even seem to want to work. Ann said nothing, for she dreaded spoiling anyone else's holiday, and hoped fervently that Theo would consider it exciting, playing with the local children, using that common language all children share, and being allowed out on his own to buy plums from the woman with the stall, and going down to the quay to fish.

Then it happened. Alan had been brooding for several days. She wasn't aware of anything that triggered it off, but he had not been well before they left England, and perhaps worry over that had been mounting. He hated being ill; became fanatically worried that he might not be able to work. She had been sitting at the table, writing in her diary, trying to keep cool before the electric fan. He asked her if she wanted a drink. She didn't quite hear, and asked him to repeat himself, then asked him not to finish the pineapple juice, if possible, because Theo loved it so, and within seconds he was angry, and a few seconds later he had hit her. It was her face again, and this time the blow came from behind and to one side. For the first time, she saw stars. She really did. Her vision went black, with pale blue and yellow and red stars, just like a Tintin cartoon.

The tears began to spring from her eyes, but they were not important. This time he had really hurt her. And this time she had had no warning, which was better because there hadn't been a build-up of fear, but this time she felt frightened afterwards, which was new.

Despite all this, her first thought was for Theo. She didn't know where he was. She thought he was upstairs on his bed. Had he heard? Did he know what was going on? If not, it was still all right. Just. Her diary had fallen on the floor, and she stared at it. She picked it up, and then went to the foot of the stairs. 'Theo?' she called.

'What are you doing?' Alan said.

'Leaving,' she said.

'You're not taking my child anywhere,' Alan said. 'He stays here.'

Alan was stronger than she was. Much stronger. She couldn't take Theo if Alan didn't want him to go. Nor did she want to make a tug of war out of him, either, and involve him in a struggle which would disturb and upset him. She recognised that Alan was as good a parent as she. Better, in some ways; more interesting. She would leave Theo behind. She walked through the small, stifling hall to the front door.

'Where are you going?'

'I don't know.'

'Are you coming back?'

'I don't know.'

She reached for the door. He reached it too, barring her way.

'Please let me out,' she said. She was still frightened, but very determined. She was shaking with the fear, but she would not let him bully her.

They stared at each other for a moment. She couldn't leave until he moved, but he couldn't stay there for ever. He couldn't make her live with him, against her will. One day, he would have to stop barring the door against her escape, and on that day, she would go.

And then he broke down. He wept, as she had never seen him weep before. His body crumpled, and he cried into his hands as if he had lost a child. She didn't know what to do. She didn't go to him. She simply stood there, watching, amazed at how broken he was.

'Don't you realise,' he said at last, 'how difficult it is to apologise? How ashamed, how despicable . . .' He wept afresh. 'I'm sorry. I'm so sorry. Please forgive me.'

She held on to him then, and he her, and they both cried together at the awfulness of it, not knowing what they should do. Ann thought, If Theo saw the blow, or heard it, he ought to be here now, part of this hug, knowing we've made it up. But he hadn't replied to her call. He hadn't known. It was better that he never did.

Theo lay on his bed, frozen still in the terrible heat. He hadn't seen. He had heard. He had heard what happened in the kitchen-dining room, though not what happened after that by the front door.

The next day, the whole of one side of Ann's face was red. After that it came up like a blotchy rash, and stayed like that for a week. He noticed her scratching it sometimes. She didn't have to explain it to anyone else because they didn't know anyone there. And Theo didn't ask.

He knew.

*　　*　　*

Ann realised with a shock, but dispassionately, objectively, that it would be possible to leave Alan. The thought had never crossed her mind before. Sometimes she had wished she had never come into his life, but for his sake, not hers: she simply felt in the way, a nuisance. But she had never before thought of leaving him. Now she considered it. It was a possibility.

Her life would be completely bleak, black, a meaningless and comfortless inferno worse than Don Giovanni's hell, but nevertheless it was a possibility. She thought, if she did it, she would just be counting off the years, for the rest of her life, till she could die. She would have nowhere to live. She would have nothing and no one to live for. She would not take Theo away from his father and his home and Cambridge and all he loved.

But she could leave if she wanted to.

Also, for the first time, appalled and frightened at the thought of it, she contemplated not loving Alan. That was worse. But that, too, was now possible. The good times, the wild, rose-flushed, breezy memories of spring and falling in love and Theo's birth and the whole photograph album of their married life together easily outweighed the painful times. But the painful times were very painful. If she dwelt on them, if Alan worked non-stop and brooded and was irritable, it was perhaps possible to imagine not loving him.

And this was serious. This was dangerous. The thought of leaving him was a choice, an option, which she would consider and then reject. But the thought of not loving him could destroy them all.

This time, she was going to do something. When they got back to England, she was going to do something.

And she did.

35

'Hide thy face from my sins, and blot out all my iniquities' –
Psalm 51

The fair was not as crowded as Caz had expected. Perhaps because it was October. Perhaps because it was the afternoon.

She had expected hordes of rough teenagers, with leathers and loud voices and big boots, and she had thought they would need to keep a close eye on Theo all the time, perhaps holding his hand, if that was acceptable, so he would not get separated from them in the crush. Instead, there were young children, parents in their twenties and thirties, a grandad with a toddler grandson. And it was a real, old-fashioned, grubby fair, where the candy floss and the prizes were the only things that looked new, and the stall-holders would give you back your change with that old trick of folding the middle notes over, to make them look double, so you were done, though you didn't realise it till ten minutes later when it would have been pointless to have gone back and complained.

Caz could remember going to a fair like this herself, as a child, with her brothers and her grandfather. Suddenly, out of nowhere, her grandfather had said, 'Look. Isn't that sad?' And she had looked, and there, on the ground, by the side of a caravan and nearly underneath it, on a filthy blanket and shivering with cold, was a dirty little child trying to get to sleep. It never would have occurred to Caz that it was sad. She had thought it was romantic to be a child who seldom or never went to school, to live with the fair and run away with the raggle-taggle gypsies oh.

She glanced about her now, half expecting to see the same sad child under the caravan.

'Well,' said Will, 'where shall we start?'

Theo had never been to a fair before, and didn't have any idea.

'What?' Will exclaimed when he heard this. 'Here is a child who has been to – how many performances of *Messiah* have you been to? – not to mention several Christmas Oratorios and a few masses in B minor thrown in, and you have never been to the fair? What is the world coming to? It's a disgrace. I must talk to your . . . to your mother about it.'

'The dodgems,' Caz said.

'The dodgems,' Will echoed. 'The lady says the dodgems; the dodgems it is. Do you fancy the dodgems, Theo? The correct answer to that is yes. That's the easy one. The difficult one is, do you want to team with me against Caz, or with Caz against me? She's a terrible driver, I must warn you.'

Theo looked from one to the other, and his natural chivalry inclined him to say, 'With Caz.'

'Dear oh dear,' Will said. 'What a frightful choice. What on earth induced you to say that?' He pulled out his wallet while they queued up and waited for the previous Dodgem drivers to finish.

'I don't think she'll win,' Theo said truthfully.

'Which is why you chose to help her. A gentleman as well as a scholar,' Will said, and Caz thought, What a strange mood he is in. She had never known him like this, so outgoing, so talkative. She wondered whether he was ill at ease with Theo, and realised she had never seen him with a child before, apart from his younger cousins. Like Theo, he too had been an only child.

They climbed into their dodgems, Theo choosing a bright yellow one for Caz and himself, while Will went for an aggressive black.

Caz was driving. Immediately, Will rammed them from behind, and Caz set her teeth and tried to turn the car.

'It won't go! It won't go!' she shrieked, as Will nudged them forward a couple more times.

'He's not very good at steering, is he?' Theo said, looking for the choke or the ignition to get their car going. It started with an unannounced leap, and Theo was thrown back in his seat while Caz went in hot pursuit of Will's retreating black car.

'Careful!' Theo shouted, grabbing the steering wheel just in time to swerve the car and miss a dodgem in front of them. Several cars hit them all at once, from different directions. 'Hey!' Theo shouted. They were nearing Will. 'Careful. Careful,' he said, taking the steering wheel to try to avert the collision. Caz was too strong for him.

'There!' she said triumphantly, bumping him twice.

'Right!' Will shouted, turning his machine towards them. He came alongside, their cars nose to tail, and grabbed their car by the side that was nearer Caz. She tried to unpeel his grip, but, just as she had been too strong for Theo, so he was too strong for her. 'Look after your passenger,' he said, quietly but clearly in her ear, and then he turned and sped off after the cars of strangers.

She turned and looked at Theo, abandoning the controls, so that their car was hit several times. He was staring ahead, silent, blank-faced, still. His face had gone unnaturally cold, and he looked strangely dangerous.

'What's the matter?' He said nothing. Oh, heck, she thought. 'Do you want a go?' Still nothing.

Then, at last, he said quite quietly, 'Why is everyone being so stupid?'

'It's a game,' she said. 'The idea is to bump into everyone.'

'Then why is it called dodgems?'

She shrugged. 'Dunno.' They were jerked forward again by another bump. 'I know,' she said, jumping out of the driving seat and risking being mown down, 'you drive. Quick, move! Before I get run over.' She jumped into the passenger seat, forcing him to move over. 'Let's rename it hittems!'

And then his mood lifted, instantly, even more quickly than it had descended. He laughed. 'Hittems!' he said, as if it were the silliest suggestion in the world. The car surged forward, and a new maniac driver was born.

When the cars slowed down and their go finally finished, they staggered to the side, jelly-legged. Theo was cheerful and happy, and Caz glanced sideways at him, wondering at the strange twists and turns of his mood.

'Now it's your turn to choose,' Will said to him.

'Or yours,' he pointed out.

'Or mine. Let's see. Big wheel. Little wheel with aeroplanes on it. Carousel with horses that bob up and down. Coconut-shy with superglue. Shooting gallery. Shocking pink candy floss.' He gave them a running commentary as they wandered around.

'Shooting gallery,' Theo said.

'Good choice.'

They stood in line for the shooting gallery. It seemed as if the odds were stacked fairly: it was possible to hit the ducks, but not too easy.

When it was their turn and Will had paid for him to have a go, Theo said, 'Is it an air gun?' Will had turned to Caz and didn't hear the question, so Theo repeated, 'Will?'

''Ere, mate,' the stall-holder said, 'I'll show you how to do it.' He came round behind Theo helpfully, and held the rifle round him. 'You look along 'ere, right, and when you can see the duck along the barrel and through that thing at the end . . .'

'I'm not ready,' Theo said. 'I'm not ready . . .'

The gun went off, missing the duck.

'I told you I wasn't ready.'

'Oh, bugger off then, do it yourself,' he muttered, going to take the next person's money. Theo stared at him, not upset or cross, but astonished that anyone could be so rude.

After a moment Caz said, 'Never mind, Theo. Have the rest of your go anyway.' Theo aimed carefully, and with his next three shots, he hit a duck each time. Caz said, extremely politely, to the man, 'Please could he have one more go, as his first one went wrong?'

'Bloody toffs,' he said, reloading the gun. 'Don't go thinking he can have a prize, though,' he growled ominously. Theo took careful aim, and brought down the fourth duck, the requirement for a prize. 'Oh, take the ruddy thing then,' he said angrily.

'No, thank you,' Theo said, though Caz could see his dignity was costing him dear.

'I will,' she said happily. 'I'll choose a prize for you.' She looked at the array: the enormous teddy and the goldfish in the bag and the toy accordion.

'Not those,' the man said. 'These 'ere are the prizes for four ducks.'

'How do you win this teddy?'

'Twenty-eight ducks, that is.'

'I'll have a go,' Will said, and shot down another four. He chose a water pistol, and handed it to Theo. 'Half yours, half mine,' he said. 'Happy fellow, wasn't he?'

They debated the big wheel.

'Is it safe?' Theo wanted to know.

'A lot safer than crossing the road, I should think,' Will said. 'There was a nasty accident some years ago, but that's the only one I've ever heard of.'

'What happened?' Theo asked.

'I think somebody got killed.'

The boy made a face. 'Why does anyone go on it, then?'

'Calculated risk,' Will said. 'You ride a bicycle, don't you? Go swimming? Get in a car? Any of those could kill you. Be far more likely to than that thing. I can pretty well guarantee that you will be all right. You might be sick, though.'

'Let's do something else,' Theo suggested.

He wanted to go in a huge cup and saucer which spun round, with other cups and saucers, on a large wheel.

'I don't think I will,' Caz said. 'I feel a bit queasy these days.'

'Come on,' Will said, going off with Theo. A minute later, after settling him in the giant cup with another child, who was chewing gum as if her life depended on it, he was back.

'Said he'd be fine on his own,' Will said, and then, strangely and uncharacteristically, he drew her hand through his arm. Caz felt very old fashioned, as if they were in a black and white film, with trilbies and suits and overcoats, and men who cared for women and brought them cups of tea when they were pregnant.

The cups started spinning, and they caught Theo's face in a silent shout of delight. 'I'm looking forward to ours,' he said. She said nothing. She didn't know whether she was looking forward to it or not. She knew nothing about babies, and felt frightened of the nappies and mess and smell of sick. She could see the responsibility clinging to her for years into the future. But she tightened her grip on his arm, and he responded in the same way.

'Your turn, now,' Theo said to Will when he rejoined them.

'Right,' Will said. 'My turn. Okay. What can I really show off at?' They set off again. 'I know,' he said. 'Now where did I see it?'

They walked around for about ten minutes, with Will constantly saying, 'I know I saw it somewhere. Where is it?' and Caz and Theo saying, 'What?' 'What is it?' 'Couldn't you choose something else?' Till eventually he said, 'That's it!' and Caz looked at it and felt as if they'd arrived at the fête in the Vicarage Garden.

'That? We walked all this way for that?' she said.

'Yes. Now I'm going to beat you both.'

'That's not fair,' Theo said. 'You're stronger.'

'Exactly,' Will said, and bought them three goes each.

It had a large sign, painted in red on a white background: 'Test You're Strength.'

'Caz,' Theo said, pulling her sleeve and indicating the sign.

'I know,' she said in a stage whisper, 'but don't tell them.'

'They ought to repaint it,' he objected.

'Yes, but *please* don't tell them. Not till we've finished our go, anyway.'

'Why not?'

'I don't know. I just think it might upset them.'

'Who wants to go first?' Will said.

'You go first,' Caz replied. 'You're the one who wants to show off.'

Will picked up the mallet and took an almighty swing at the target. The little red ball went racing up to the top, and the bell gave a tiny ting, as if it were just giving a suggestion of being rung. 'There,' Will said triumphantly. 'Beat that!'

'We don't stand a chance,' Caz said.

'Speak for yourself,' Will replied. 'Give Theo a go. He'll beat me.'

Will handed the mallet to Theo. It nearly swung to the ground with its own weight. Theo hoisted it up on to his shoulder, and let it fall on to the target. The little red ball went up about nine inches. 'Oops. That wasn't very good, was it?' he giggled.

'Caz's turn. She'll be far worse.'

Caz managed to raise the ball about a foot and a half. It was Will's turn again. He took the mallet, looked at the target, and then turned to say something to Theo. 'We used to do something like this at school,' he started. 'Ooh, that's not fair. It slipped.' The mallet dropped on to the target, and the ball went up nine inches or so again. 'Your go, Theo.'

'That looked like you did it on purpose,' Theo observed, picking the mallet up again.

'Why on earth would I do that?'

'Some grown-ups do. To make it look like you've won. I mean, like I've won. Like the child's won.'

'Why do they do that?'

'To make the child feel better, I suppose. Only you don't feel better, of course, because you haven't won properly.'

'And do I look like that kind of grown-up?' Will asked.

'No,' he admitted. 'That was no better than last time,' he complained, handing the mallet to Caz.

'Now come on, Caz,' Will urged. 'Make a proper effort this time.' The ball registered about two feet.

Will had one more go. This time he swung at it as if he wanted to kill it, and the bell proclaimed a loud hit. Caz clapped. 'Your last chance, Theo,' Will said, fingering the head of the mallet and giving it a quick glance. 'Give it a really good one.'

Theo tucked his lower lip under his teeth, and concentrated hard on the target. He swung the mallet heavily up on to his shoulder and rested it there. Then, with a loud grunt and a big effort, he brought it down again. Twelve inches.

'Give him your go, Caz,' Will suggested.

'Certainly not. Don't be so patronising. Besides, I want my go. Thank you, Theo.'

Caz took up her position, spread her feet out for further stability, rested the mallet on the ground, and then, with a great sweeping movement, swung it behind her shoulder, like bowling a cricket ball with two hands, to bring it down.

She started to swing.

To Will, it was as if the director had suddenly cried, 'Freeze frame', and she had been arrested, with the mallet just beginning to move behind her, and her eye on the target. There was a click, a jerk, a moment of telepathy between them, as if Caz had known something without being aware that she knew it, and now she had suddenly realised. Then, a split second later, the director said, 'Keep rolling,' and the movement continued.

But it had been disturbed. Something had gone wrong. Caz gave a little cry, and the mallet came down crooked, tipping the side of the target and barely moving the red ball.

'Oh, bother,' she said, avoiding Will's eye, and gave the mallet back to the boy who was taking the money.

'Ta,' he said, handing it on to the next people in the queue.

'It's a lot harder than it looks,' Caz said to them in a loud breezy voice. 'Come on. Where are we going now?'

'Tea,' Will said. 'I think there's a kind of tea tent. And it's starting to rain.'

They walked on for a few minutes in silence. Will seemed genuinely preoccupied with finding the tea tent. Caz and Theo both followed blindly, wrapped in their own thoughts. An outsider looking on would have seen an over-energetic young man with what appeared to be a tired family in tow.

'Come on,' he called to them, and Caz pulled herself together and caught up with him, putting her arm through his.

'Come on, Theo,' she called over her shoulder, putting her hand out behind her for him to hold on to. He didn't respond, and a moment later she turned around and saw him some way behind them, walking very slowly. Suddenly he stopped. Will turned round too, and they stood, waiting for him. He didn't move. Caz made a movement to go towards him, but Will restrained her.

'Wait,' he said quietly. 'Just for a moment.' They waited for what seemed like several minutes, during which time Theo just stared at the ground, then eventually Will said, 'Go on then. See if you can get him to come. Gently,' he added unnecessarily.

He watched Caz approach the boy. She spoke to him, and he took no notice, so she bent down a little to speak to him again. He still took no notice. She put her arm around him to try to encourage him to come, and he shook her off, angrily, almost roughly, but still without speaking to her or looking at her. His face was beginning to go red. Will walked slowly towards them, till he was almost next to Caz. This time Theo looked up, and stared at both of them as if he hadn't known they were there. And now his face went pale, white, and Will thought he looked as if he were trembling. He seemed almost out of control, almost what one might call, beside himself, and Will found himself thinking, Thank goodness he's young enough to learn how to control that temper, otherwise someone could get badly hurt.

Then he turned, and walked away from them, and stopped, right in the middle of a crowd of people pushing and shoving past him and treading on his feet. And then he just stood there, stock still.

Will was next to Caz. She saw, out of the corner of her eye, a barely perceptible shake of the head. She turned and looked at him. She had never seen him look so stunned, as if he had seen something he couldn't believe and didn't want to.

'He's worked it out,' he said at last. 'Good God, he's worked it out. I honestly never thought that would happen. He's worked it out.' He sighed heavily, as if he didn't know what to do now. 'That kid is too bright for anyone's good. Most of all his own.'

Caz said nothing for a moment. They both watched Theo's back, immobile in the busy crowd. 'Is that what you were doing then?' she asked.

'Of course it was,' he said, 'but I never thought he'd work it out.'

She turned to ask him something else, and found to her astonishment that he wasn't there any more. There was a small flurry in the crowd in front of her, and shouts of 'Hey!' 'Watch it!' and both of them had disappeared.

36

'Cast me not away from thy presence; and take not my holy
Spirit from me' –

Psalm 51

At that moment, Will felt there had been a purpose, after all,
in all the years he had spent in the cold and the mud of the
school rugby pitch. He knew how to keep his eye on the ball
and how to dodge through resisting opponents. He employed
all his latent skills now. Theo was not a fast runner, but the
crowds, now spotted with umbrellas, closed in around him as
if they were trying to hide him, and for one awful moment
Will thought the boy was lost. He stopped for a split second
and looked around, and somehow realised Theo had changed
direction and was over to his right. Then he caught up with him
easily. He wasn't really trying to run away, he was just trying to
run, as if to forget something.

Will caught him by the shoulder. Theo tried to shake off his
grasp, as he had Caz's, but Will was too strong for him.

'I know you're angry,' Will said. 'And I think I understand
why. But you're not my child and I can't let you go off on your
own. It's too dangerous. Sorry,' he added as an afterthought.

Theo stopped struggling.

'Now,' Will said after a moment, 'we've lost Caz. We'll go back
to where we last saw her, and if she's not there we'll go on to
the tea tent because that was the last thing we talked about. I
won't hold you as long as you promise to come with me. But
if you try and run again, I'll hold you all the time. I know it's

jolly irritating, but I'm not used to looking after children, and I'm worried about your safety because you're not mine.'

They walked on in a resentful silence. It was beginning to rain in earnest now, and Will, as a gesture of the friendship that he hoped would survive the present constraint, took his jacket off and put it around the boy's shoulders. Theo looked as if he might reject it, then he muttered, 'Thank you,' and pulled it around his shoulders.

Eventually they found the tea tent. It was dripping in all sorts of places, and beginning to fill up, but Will said, 'You try and get seats while I get drinks. Get three,' he said, hoping to goodness he could trust Theo not to run again.

He got three small packets of biscuits, three teas, and several packets of sugar, unsure whether Theo would drink tea but assuming he might like sugar in it if he did. When he emerged from the queue he saw the boy sitting on one chair with his hands planted firmly on another two, despite the efforts of a large woman with two daughters telling him he couldn't save them like that.

'Thank you,' Will said to him loudly. 'I'm sorry if you've had problems.' And he gave the woman a sharp look and sat down. 'I hope you like tea. The biscuits look very boring, but they're all they had.'

'Thank you.'

There was silence while they stirred their tea, and opened the biscuits, and started to drink.

'Now then, I'm going to say a few things which you may or may not believe,' Will began, wondering what on earth he was going to say. 'Whether you believe them is of course up to you, but I hope you do.' Stop stalling, William, he said to himself. 'First, Caz is very fond of you. I know she's only just met you, but she likes you very much. Second, you very generously confided in her the other day. That means you told her something private, which you didn't want her to pass on.' Now I'm lost, he thought. I have no idea where to go from here.

'And she did,' Theo pointed out. 'She told you.'

'She told me, yes. She told me because . . .' Help! She told me because she broke your confidence. She told me because she didn't think you'd ever know, but you're so bloody intelligent you worked it out. Well, at least Caz isn't here, he thought. That makes it slightly easier. And at that point she entered the tea tent. Will looked at her, and then went on talking to Theo, ignoring her. 'She told me because she was very concerned about you. She thought, if she'd been in your position, she'd need help.'

'What sort of help?'

'Someone to talk to.'

'I talked to her.'

'Yes, and that's what made her want to help you. But she didn't know what to do. She knew you didn't want your mother to know. She could guess that you might not want any of your friends or teachers to know. You told her you didn't want the police to know. But I didn't even know you, so she didn't think it would matter if she asked me for advice, as long as I didn't tell anyone. And I'm her best friend, so it was natural for her to tell me.'

'Are you?' Will wondered whether there was a hint of regret that Theo couldn't be her best friend himself.

'Yes. I'm going to marry her. And wives and husbands usually don't have any secrets from each other, so we're practising by not having any secrets between us now.' Theo nodded. Will breathed out slowly, and felt as if he had crossed Niagara on a tightrope.

'I see,' Theo said.

Now Will dared to turn round and smile at Caz, and offer her the chair. She smiled back, and sat down, but didn't attempt to enter the conversation.

There was a pause. Theo picked up his biscuit as if to dip it in his tea, then looked up at Will to see whether he was allowed to. Will smiled, and nodded.

'And that thing with the mallet?' Theo asked. 'Did you do that on purpose?'

Will looked him straight in the eye. 'Yes,' he said. 'I did. Caz didn't know, though.'

Nobody said anything for several minutes. Theo drank his tea, and ate his biscuits, and then, as if summoning up great courage, said, 'You don't believe me, do you?'

'No. No, I don't.' Caz stirred, and Will quietened her with his hand. 'That mallet,' he explained, 'weighs eleven pounds. I would have judged it to be about that anyway, but by a complete fluke, it was written on the head. Your mother's fire extinguisher has four point six kilograms written on it.' He kept going, quickly, hoping Theo wouldn't ask whether that was the only reason he'd been invited to the fair. Will didn't think he would be able to lie to him successfully. 'And, yes, you were right, I dropped the mallet on purpose. I wanted to measure how high the ball would go when all it had was its own weight behind it, without any additional momentum at all. Now' – he picked up his cup, cradling it in his hands, but keeping his eyes on Theo all the time –' you were two years younger than you are now when your father died. A fire extinguisher is a heck of a lot more difficult to manoeuvre than a mallet. A mallet is designed to be easy to lift, to use the weight of it. A fire extinguisher isn't. Even now, you don't have the strength to swing an eleven-pound mallet. So it seems to me extremely unlikely that, two years ago, aged only seven, you could have swung a four-and-a-half-kilogram fire extinguisher with enough force to have killed a man with it. Not just unlikely: impossible.'

Will paused. He didn't need to spell it out, he knew. But he wanted to. 'The only certainty about your father's attacker was that he used a four-and-a-half-kilogram fire extinguisher. *Ergo* . . . Do you do Latin?'

Theo nodded.

'*Ergo*, you did not kill your father. Not with your own hand anyway. Which leaves us with the problem of why you said you did.'

I have outmanoeuvred him at last, Will thought. I think I could beat him at chess.

37

For the first few days after getting back from Portugal, Ann did nothing.

She unpacked, she straightened the house, she checked Theo's uniform for the next term, she took him to Eaden Lilley's for new shoes, and to Robert Sayle for a new school jumper, where she was told she was lucky they had one in stock his size, Because you've left it very late, madam, next year you'd be better to do it in June or July, really you would.

She went to Sainsbury's and bought two trolleyloads, marvelling for the hundredth time how people with several children cope. She filled the freezer to the brim, and stocked the larder with fresh bottles of olive oil and tins of tomatoes and anchovies and ante-pasti and vanilla essence; she baked two cakes and managed to squeeze one of them on top of all the other things in the freezer, and she spent all the rest of her time with Theo because he only had just under a week till school began.

So she did nothing about her resolution.

But she didn't abandon it. She kept it safely in the back of her mind, ready, waiting, till she should have time to give to it.

She had changed. She knew she had. In the past, she and Alan had always made up quarrels very quickly: he because he was of a generous spirit and a passionate nature which flared up easily, but forgot and forgave even easier; she because, though she never forgot anything, she loved Alan dearly and hated quarrelling with anyone.

But this time she was different. He had said sorry, he had tried to make up for it as he always did, and he had probably forgotten. But there was something in Ann which said a bunch of roses and an apology would not do any more. Something had snapped. She still loved him. She just didn't want him any more. She didn't look forward to his coming home, as she pottered through the house and the hours and the pleasant chores. She had detached herself from him. Presumably the days and weeks would heal the place which hurt. But she had acquired a poisonous little store of memories. There was now a pretty cottage in Brittany which brought back images, not of their honeymoon, but of the car keys being confiscated from her while her head throbbed. Did Alan understand that the humiliation of that was worse even than the humiliation of being hit? Did he even remember? She doubted it, and half wished that she too had a short, forgiving memory.

She marvelled at the things Alan forgot. Moments when they had just started going out together, which were like diamonds to her. The time he took her for a picnic on Wimbledon Common and first kissed her, beside the pond. The champagne reception full of celebrities, after a student concert he had conducted at the Royal College, which he abandoned to take her out for supper. The time he sprayed the hospital bed with Bollinger when Theo was born, and the matronly nurse came tut-tutting in so he offered her a toothmugful as well. Ann would never forget these things, just as she would never forget seeing pale blue and yellow stars on a black background in an isolated house on the west coast of Portugal. The box of memories was precious. It meant that she would never want to live with anyone else, because no one else had first kissed her by the rippling little waves at Wimbledon. But it was dangerous too. The bad memories were there. And if she could stop loving Alan for a second, for a day, for a week or two in Portugal, presumably it was possible that she could stop loving him for ever.

Theo's first day of term was a Tuesday. Ann always got him ready well ahead of time, so they could walk to school. Alan was an early riser anyway, needing little sleep, and often working from six or six thirty in the morning. When he remembered, he would bring Ann a cup of tea sometime before seven.

The aim, each day, was for Theo to be ready for school by half past seven. Then there would be a whole luxurious half an hour for him to do one of his music practices. This was necessary in order to get through the rest of the day and be on time for bed. Everything with Theo took so long that the time between tea and bed was filled and overlapping with his other commitments: his second music practice and half an hour's homework absorbed the entire afternoon and evening even with a full-time monitor helping him do it. How would she ever have managed if they'd had another child? Sometimes the entire schedule would be thrown out by his needing the loo, and spending half an hour sitting on it despite Ann's reminder every so often that he was supposed to be in the middle of writing his description of a visit to the prehistoric caves.

It was a rare morning that went according to plan. But sometimes, once a week or fortnight, by a monumental effort on Ann's part, Theo would be ready by half past seven or soon afterwards, and she would tune up his cello or sit him down at the piano and try to get him started. There was still plenty of room for error. The stand would fall over, or the music fall off the piano desk, or the A string not be tuned to his satisfaction, or some imaginary distraction would fly past the window and he would be lost for ten minutes. Yet sometimes he would concentrate so magnificently that she could have left him for another hour and he would still be perfecting that slide up to fourth position that he needed for the second octave of the G major scale. And then the exhilaration she felt at having succeeded almost seemed to make all the other mornings worth it.

And always, every day, whether he succeeded in his practice, or, as was more often the case, she only just managed to get his tie done up before he went through the front door, when she came back from walking him to school Ann was absolutely finished. She felt exhausted and confused and worn out, as if she had spent a day in the company of thirty-five seven year olds, instead of a couple of hours in the company of one. Sometimes she went back to bed when she got in, and lay there, listening to Radio Four and feeling guilty. Sometimes she made a strong pot of coffee in the hope that it would wake her up. Once or twice she tried pampering herself with a hot, foamy, aromatic bath. Nothing worked. By nine thirty every morning she felt like a zombie.

Which, she told herself, was a major reason she no longer played her violin.

But this particular day, Tuesday, the 12th of September, the day Theo started school the term after he had moved to the choir school, she didn't feel tired or confused. This may have been because it was only the first day back in the routine. Or it may have been because she knew she had to do something. Now there was no reason to delay. It had to be today. Today or not at all.

She delivered him to the front of the school, kept half an eye on him while enquiring after the surfing in Cornwall or grouse in Scotland or how on earth did you survive the heatwave if you were in Knossos, you poor things, and then she went home. She cleared up the kitchen and made herself some toast and poured herself a coffee.

And then she thought.

There was no question of 'fault'. It wasn't Alan's 'fault', any more than it was hers. It was a problem they shared, which they had to solve. For years she had left it up to him to deal with, just as he dealt with the servicing of the car and the paying of the gas and electricity bills. Presumably, though, he found it so embarrassing that he would rather live with it than face it, but this was a stance that was alien to Ann. She couldn't understand people who didn't go to the doctor when they feared they had cancer, or didn't open their bank statements when they suspected they were overdrawn. So if he wouldn't deal with it, she must.

She recognised, also, that it would be all too easy to present herself as the victim. She knew this wasn't true. She was responsible as well. Being brutally honest with herself, she knew there was something in her that she could have changed if she had wanted to, if she hadn't had some little hard pebble of obstinacy within her which said she was as she was and she didn't want to be hit for it.

There was something unattractive about her, a pinched quality, a meanness of spirit which was as alien to Alan as his response to it was to her. He was generous. He would lend books he really treasured to people he knew were unreliable. He would spend time on students who were not worth it. He would cherish hopefuls who, he knew, would become hopeless. Ann would never have done this. She would turn her back on people and save up her time for the few she had decided to love.

She admitted it. She was a miserly person. Alan possessed a kindness and openness which she didn't have at all. It was understandable that he would feel occasionally disillusioned, that he would rebel against her sometimes.

He would have to find another way of doing it, that was all.

She thought hard about the next step. It was simply a question of telling someone. But who?

The obvious choice, a close girl friend, did not appeal at all. Alan was her closest friend. And what could a girl friend do? Ann did not want to talk to someone just to give herself some therapy. If that was all she wanted she could go to a gym or hire a psychologist. She didn't want to 'feel better': she wanted something to change.

She thought of going to talk to Alan's mother. Paradoxically, it was because she had always got on so well with her that she decided against it. She didn't want someone who might take her side. There were no sides. She and Alan were on the same side, fighting for their marriage against his uncontrollable rage. She did not want to be confirmed in her own self-righteousness. She must go to someone who would see it from his point of view.

Another man, then. One who might influence him, perhaps, but one whose loyalty to Alan was stronger than any chivalry towards herself. Most of his friends, musicians and colleagues, would be hopeless. Tim Marshall might be sympathetic, but it was hardly fair to involve him. A clergyman seemed the obvious choice, but did she know any? There was the dean, of course, but Alan had forbidden her to tell the dean. And Alan had to work with him. She couldn't tell the dean.

Which left John Wright, the chaplain. A single man, younger than Alan, perhaps even than Ann herself. She hadn't met him more than a handful of times. What would he know of the strains of marriage? He would probably think they were on the point of divorce if she confided in him. A man's man. She had an idea he had been something of a rugby player. Played full back, whatever that was. University blue, anyway. Even Alan spoke well of him,

Alan, who had no time for religion, and considered that most of the clergy had been put on the earth by a malicious-minded God chiefly to interfere with sacred music. He was the most unlikely confessor she could think of. And that, after all, was what she had wanted.

Ann put on her coat to set off for college before she could change her mind.

She mounted the polished, oak stairs, with the tread worn in the middle by five hundred years of students. She was breathing hard, and trembling. She had never been as bad as this when she performed. She gripped the warm, friendly banisters, and paused near the first landing. 'The Revd. R.J.A. Wright', she read above the door, in the white, hand-painted lettering which adorned every door frame. The oak was open. He was in. She wondered what the R. stood for. Even now, she was not sure she was doing the right thing. How would Alan react?

Then she remembered how she had reacted to the coloured stars she had seen in Portugal, and knew that, for once, what Alan thought was not the only thing that mattered. She, Ann, thought she ought to do something. This was the least hurtful thing she could think of.

She stood there for at least ten minutes, and might have gone on doing so, had she not heard a burst of laughter above her and realised two or three undergraduates were coming down the stairs. They stared at her, wondering what this middle-aged woman could be doing in their college.

She knocked boldly on the inner door, realising as she did so that she heard voices. Thank goodness! He was giving a tutorial. She would have to go away.

'Come in,' he called, and she opened the door, with the wonderfully easy idea that she could say she was looking for Alan and wondered whether John had seen him.

She entered. The dismay must have registered on her face as she saw that he was alone, speaking on the telephone. He waved her to a chair and said that he wouldn't be a minute.

He was about five minutes. He laughed and chatted down the line, and took his time to finish the conversation, and when he had, he turned, delighted, to her and put the kettle on. 'Mrs Wedderburn. How good to see you. What can I do for you, other than give you some coffee and a flapjack? Here we are. Gosh, I'm so sorry. My students must have finished them when I wasn't watching.'

'Please call me Ann,' she said, rather quietly, and then continued all in a rush: 'I hope you don't mind my coming to see you. I hardly know you, but I wanted to talk to someone. Alan hits me, you see. He doesn't mean to, and he doesn't do it often, and he doesn't hurt me seriously, but I didn't know who else to turn to. I'm sorry. It's all right, I've got a hankie. It's stupid and embarrassing of me.' She wiped her eyes savagely. She had no idea whether she should be horrified at what she had just said. It was up to him now.

John Wright sat down on the sofa opposite.

He nodded his head, slowly, as if he understood. 'Gosh,' he said eventually. 'Poor you. Well, let me make you a coffee anyway.' He jumped up, put the Nescafé into a couple of mugs, realised he had no milk and apologised for the second time, offered a scraping of sugar instead, and then sat down again.

'Have you any idea what I could do to help?' he asked.

'None,' she admitted, and smiled weakly. It was almost like losing some kind of virginity. She had told someone. It was done. She didn't know whether to feel tremendous relief, or horror.

'Well then,' he said, 'why don't we pray? Do you believe in God?'

'I don't know,' she said, astonished and rather alarmed by his suggestion. 'I don't think so.'

'Okay,' he said. 'Then I'll pray.'

So he did. Ann sat and watched, and listened, not feeling quite as uncomfortable as she had expected. Afterwards, looking back, she wondered whether his ingenuousness was quite as real as it seemed. For in those few moments of prayer he told her more about his attitude, and how he would approach the information she had given him, than he could have done in half an hour of explanation to her face, as it were. He established his absolute commitment to, and expectation of, the permanence of their relationship; that it was only to be expected they would have various struggles; and that there was tremendous hope for the two of them and their future together. All that, in what was probably less than a minute. It was clever. She had no idea whether it was deliberate or not, but it was very clever.

Then he said 'Amen', and looked up.

He smiled, and said nothing. Then he asked her if her coffee was all right. She realised she hadn't touched it, so she took a sip.

'Horrible, is it?'

'Bit hot.'

'Horrible, too, I expect. You probably drink delicious real coffee at home. And you probably take milk, too, I expect.'

She smiled. 'Yes, I do,' she admitted.

He smiled too then, and went on, as if it were as natural as the way she took her coffee: 'Do you want to tell me about it?'

'I don't know. There's nothing to tell really. It's not that bad. Once a year or so he gets cross with me and hits me. It doesn't really hurt, not much. Not physically, anyway. No more than falling off a bicycle. Do you think I'm making a fuss about nothing?'

'Not at all. I imagine it colours your whole relationship, doesn't it, at the back of your mind?'

She was relieved at his perception. 'I wasn't sure whether men . . . you know, whether it's like rape: you can't quite see why we mind.'

'I can imagine it would be galling to be frightened of the person I love. Will you tell him you've been to see me?'

'I suppose so. I don't want to have secrets from him. I never have.'

He got up and went and stood by the window for a moment, looking out. His room overlooked a back courtyard. Ann wondered whether he was watching the domestic staff scurrying to and fro to get the lunch: teenaged boys in white kitchen coats carrying large silver platters with domed lids. 'He'll mind, you know. That's something we men are never sure if you women understand – our pride. His pride will be badly hurt.' He looked back at her. 'Will he take it out on you?'

'No.' Alan? Of course he wouldn't. There was nothing resentful about Alan. 'Surely not,' she said.

He looked at her carefully, as if he didn't quite believe her, and then he said, 'I wonder whether I should talk to him.

Tell him you've been to see me, instead of you having to do that.' Inwardly, he shrank from the thought. Alan was a senior colleague. He was fair-minded and reasonable. But he was also tough, determined, and probably ten years older than John himself. John would hate to get on the wrong side of him.

'I'll try and see him today,' he continued, 'so you don't have to pretend anything when he comes home. And I suggest that, if it happens again, one or other of you comes to tell me. If he doesn't want it to be me, which is quite reasonable, he should choose a different third party instead. You must agree on somebody, acceptable to both of you. And agree that he or she will be told if it happens again. If Alan objects, you'll have to do it on your own. You say to him: "If it happens again, I'll go and tell John." Or someone else. But decide what to do, so that when it comes to it, you go through with it. And then tell him what you've decided.'

'It's funny . . .' She stopped, blushing furiously.

'What?'

'I'd been told you were very reactionary. A bit of a . . . well, a bit of a chauvinist, I suppose. Opposed to the ordination of women. Letting people keep the obedience vow in the marriage ceremony, and all that.'

'Really?' He raised his eyebrows, as interested as anyone in what was said behind his back. 'You believe all you hear? And you think I should tell people what they can and can't promise, when the law gives them the choice?' He considered. 'But I suppose I am reactionary, if you describe it like that. Come to that, I believe children should honour their parents. But that doesn't mean I like to see abused children. Relationships are two-way. So the responsibility is two-way. I'd better shut up: I suspect if I say any more, I'll annoy you. I'll start saying things like, "Perhaps men have more responsibility to their wives than vice versa." You may have noticed, I don't trust myself enough to put it into practice.'

He smiled. She stood up. She had expected the interview to take a long time, and be very awkward, but there seemed nothing left to say. He had known, immediately, what needed to be done. There was no need for her to stay.

'Thank you,' she said.

'I'll ring you after I've spoken to him, so that you'll know. Will you be in today? After lunch, say?'

'Yes. Yes, I think so.'

'I don't want to leave a message on your answerphone. Now listen,' he added, in a different tone.

'Yes?'

He paused, his hand still holding hers as he had taken it to shake goodbye. 'He's not going to like it. I mean, he is seriously not going to like it. It will feel like a threat, and it'll feel like you're taking control, which I suspect is not how you usually organise your relationship. And because he won't like it, you're not going to like it either. He may get very angry with you. Though I doubt if he'll hit you.' She frowned. Was he right? She had said, a minute ago, that Alan wouldn't mind. She wondered how long John was going to hold her hand. 'Bear in mind that you're doing it for both of you. It's going to help you both. And, at the end of the day, he may find it a huge relief that the responsibility's been taken away from him.'

He released her. 'Thank you,' she said. Now that she knew what to do, she also knew she would do it. It would be nerve-racking, but she knew where she was going, and nothing would stop her now.

'And, um . . .' He gave a nervous little shrug, like a fifteen year old daring to talk about something he oughtn't to. 'Er, I know nothing about such things, but if you can manage to make him feel a man, over the next few days, you'll be doing both of you a favour. You know. If you feel up to it. Sorry, mustn't interfere.'

He shepherded her to the door. She tried to picture herself aged seventeen again, when John Wright had probably been about twelve. She thanked him, and left.

He was quite right. She hadn't touched her coffee. The Copper Kettle was just over the road from the Porters' Lodge. It was years since she'd been there. Presumably it served decent coffee. She would treat herself.

As she came back down the old oak steps, which had witnessed so many broken hearts and drunken revels and hopeful dreams, and her own petrified uncertainty of less than an hour before, her heart sang. '*O sole mio*,' it sang, and then couldn't remember any more of the words.

She had done the right thing. She knew she had. They were turning a corner.

38 ∫

'Deliver me from my bloodguiltiness, O God, thou God of my salvation: *and* my tongue shall sing aloud of thy righteousness' –

Psalm 51

'Have we all finished?' Will said, standing up. 'What time have you got to be back at school?'

'Six o'clock.'

'It's five now. Let's get a cab, go to the warmest, driest, and favouritest tea shop you can think of, and buy you another tea. If my memory of prep school serves me right, no human being can survive on school high teas.'

Then he added, lightly, 'And then you can tell us what really happened.' I hope, he thought.

The crowds on Midsummer Common had mostly dispersed because of the rain. Will put his arms round both of them, and they marched, in a companionable line, through the mud, letting it splash up on their ankles. This is the kind of event, Caz thought, that makes it wonderful to have a bath and a glass of brandy to go home to. No brandy for Theo, sadly, but presumably he would get the bath.

She was troubled. Despite her relief at Will's conclusion, there was still something bothering her. She had noticed it in the kitchen when she was talking to Ann. She had nearly mentioned it over the telephone to Will. It hadn't seemed important after all. But now it meant there was a detail which didn't fit. If the boy had had nothing to do with his father's death – which made sense, of course it did: he was simply not that kind of child – then there was something in Ann's kitchen which didn't add up.

They had reached the entrance to the common. They went out on to the road and succeeded in hailing a taxi immediately.

Theo didn't know where to choose for tea, so Will consulted the driver. Large log fire, he said, hot buttered toast dripping with butter and honey, constantly refilled pots of tea, and plenty of privacy: any recommendations?

'Coach and Six, Trumpington,' the driver replied without a pause.

'That would be delightful. Thank you,' Will said.

It was nearly perfect. The long, low-ceilinged room, its dark oak relieved only by glittering horse brasses and photographs of the landlord in his younger days on impressive point-to-pointers, was almost empty apart from a roaring fire.

'Plonk yourselves there,' Will directed, 'and I'll get the nose bags.' He drifted to the bar. 'Pot of tea for two, Earl Grey. Hot chocolate for one – you know, large and frothy and lots of it. And the kind of tea that will keep a boy going for the rest of term.'

'Right you are, sir. I get the picture.' The barman winked at Theo, and disappeared.

'I think you can put your shoes and socks by the fire, if they're very wet,' Will said to him. 'I'll check that the landlord doesn't mind when they come back with the tea.'

By unspoken agreement Caz sat by the wall, out of the conversation, unobtrusive. When the waiter had laid out all the tea in front of them and melted away again, Will said quietly, 'Now, I want you to tell us everything. I realise you may not want to, but I honestly believe it will be better.' He looked at Theo, who was sitting politely with his hands in his lap, listening carefully. 'But first of all let me explain that enjoying your tea does not depend on your agreeing to tell us. I don't want to send any of this back. And nobody is to speak again till you start drinking your chocolate and eating an unreasonable amount of jam on one of those toasted muffins. Right.' He took his cup of tea, which Caz had poured, and offered her a muffin in exchange.

'If you get hurt,' he went on after Theo had started tucking in, 'particularly when you're a child, you may need help to get better again. Suppose you break a leg. A doctor can set it, and it will heal, probably perfectly. Even a friend might bind it up, and it would mend reasonably well. But if you don't go to anyone, it may set crooked and you could be lame for the rest of your life. Or you might have to get it broken again, to reset it, which will be far more painful and not as good as if it had been done properly at the time.'

'Are you a doctor?' Theo asked.

'No,' Will said. 'I'm not. Have another muffin. Try the apricot jam this time.'

There was a comfortable, easy sound of the three of them enjoying their tea. The fire crackled. All it needs is a clock ticking, Will thought, and it would be too good to be true.

He had said all he wanted to say, for the moment. There was no point in adding to it. Theo would either be convinced or he wouldn't.

The boy said nothing. At least he was enjoying his tea, Caz noticed with satisfaction. She feared for him. He was the kind of child who could take a secret to the grave.

After a bit more awkwardness, she began to ask Theo what pieces they were learning in Chapel at the moment, and tried to nod intelligently as if she knew the difference between the Howells and the Darke, and asked him about football, and got him to explain the scoring of rugby to her, and suddenly Will stood up and walked over to the window and stared out at the rain, which glared brashly in the light of the street lamp. Caz and Theo looked at him for a moment, then Caz tried to pick up the small talk again.

Will was back as abruptly as he had gone, tapping his teeth with his fist, and Caz wondered, slightly alarmed, why he looked so angry. Had she said something wrong? 'I didn't want to talk about this,' he said almost harshly, then stopped. He looked from one to the other, then he sat down and looked away. When he turned back to them both, his face was grim.

'My father walked out of my life when I was seven,' he said at last. 'And d'you know what I felt? For the next ten years or more?' He glared at them, as if daring them to answer. 'Mmm? I hated him. When he did that to us, when he left my mother alone, to cry like that, night after night when she thought I couldn't hear her, to get thin, and old, and poor, I hated him. I believed I could have forgiven him anything else, but not that.'

The door of the bar opened, and a man put his head in, and then went out again. Will gazed at where he had been for a moment, and then continued. 'Then I started to hate myself. I was letting her down too. I had made her come back to England, where she was cold all winter. I couldn't earn money, or stop her crying. I couldn't even pay for my own school fees, for goodness' sake. I was the one who was making her poor. I was as bad as my father. The two of us, between us, had ruined her life.' Caz was staring at him, open-mouthed. She had never heard him talk like this before. Not when he had told her about his childhood, nor when he had described the death of his own newborn baby. She had never realised he was vulnerable. Oh, Will, she thought. I never knew how much I loved you till this moment. She put her hand out to him, and he brushed it away.

'I never wanted to talk about it, ever,' he continued. 'I told Caz we would share everything about one another, but I never wanted her to know what I felt about my father. I was so ashamed.'

'Why?' Theo asked at length, in the unnatural quietness. I am not part of this, Caz thought. The two of them have something in common which I will never understand.

'Why?' Will asked. Then, for a moment, he couldn't say anything. He covered his eyes with his fingers. This time it was Theo who put his hand out towards him. Will took the boy's hand and put it against his cheek. Caz looked down at the table. It is frightening, she realised. Seeing a man cry is like losing the ground from under one's feet. 'Why?' Will repeated. 'Do you know whose fault it was that he left us?' Theo looked at him, and waited. 'We were in Italy. Wine, women and opera. I love my home country. Men drink a jug of *vino* and drive home, every night. My father was out buying my mother some flowers, and a neighbour drove over him.'

He hadn't intended it to come out like this. He had intended to say less, and more. He had meant to try and persuade the boy . . . He should have kept quiet.

Caz and Theo said nothing for a few minutes, and then Caz asked, 'What's the time?'

It was gone a quarter to six. 'I'll get a taxi,' Will said, as if relieved. While he was gone, Theo suddenly said, 'When you break your leg, the best person to go to isn't your friend but someone whose job is mending legs.'

'Yes,' Caz agreed, then added, 'you don't need to talk to us. It's just important you talk to somebody. Have you got someone in mind?'

'I don't know,' he replied.

'A doctor, perhaps? Have you got a school doctor you know well? Or like?'

'No. Not really,' he admitted.

'Or a teacher?'

'No.'

'Anyone?' She was losing hope. Will had made the telephone call, and came back to join them. They would have a job to get Theo to school by six, even if the taxi arrived immediately.

'I'm not sure,' he said. Caz held her breath, and didn't look at Will in case he spoilt it. 'No,' Theo said at last. 'I'm just not sure.'

They waited for several minutes, in silence, for the taxi. Just before it arrived, Caz tried once more. 'This person you had in mind,' she said. 'Is he or she kind?'

'Yes,' Theo said. 'He is kind.'

'Then go and see him. Tell him everything.'

Theo nodded. 'All right,' he said. 'I will.'

'Promise?' Caz said.

'Yes,' Theo said. And, he thought, This is a real promise, not like the wedding promises that adults don't keep.

'And go soon.'

'Do I have to tell you who it is?'

Caz smiled. She would spend the rest of her life longing to know what had really happened. 'No,' she said. 'You don't have to tell us who it is.'

39

Purge me with hyssop, and I shall be clean: wash me, and I shall be whiter than snow . . .

Psalm 51

There had been one more incident.

Ann put it down to a bad year. Alan had been under considerable strain. Old Jack Higgins, the headmaster for over twenty years, had left the choir school, and Tim Marshall had been appointed in his place. There had been controversy over his appointment, and such things take time to die down.

Tim had no experience of the private sector. He had been head of a Yorkshire comprehensive for five years, and before that, deputy head of a primary school. He had no more knowledge of college politics than he himself had picked up as an undergraduate at Oxford. And he was no musician. He had learnt the piano as a child, and could play the trombone well enough to join the senior orchestra, but that was it.

Alan thought his appointment was lunacy. Still, it was not Tim's fault he'd been given the job, and, provided he didn't make Alan's work more difficult than it had to be, Alan would try to be loyal.

But that was not how others saw it. It is perhaps impossible for anyone to take over a traditional institution, and not make enemies. If he changes nothing he is weak. If he changes anything he has made a mistake. If he changes everything he is a disaster.

Tim set out to change as little as possible. He had no desire to upset people, and he recognised that the school had run successfully for many centuries without his help. He saw himself as a tiny cog in its long history.

But of course, as with any new appointment, he changed a great deal without knowing he had.

There were restrictions on extra practices for a recording, because something now clashed with a rehearsal for the school play and Mr Marshall hadn't thought to tell so-and-so that such-and-such would be needed for this-and-that. Or a child would turn up late for a practice because prep had been disrupted because Mr Marshall hadn't done the exam practice week the way it had always been done: 'So Mr Harris kept us late for maths, sir, to catch up.'

After a few weeks of this, Alan blew a fuse. He went to see Tim. 'What the hell's going on?' he said as he walked into Tim's study without even shutting the door behind him. And before five minutes were up, 'Why don't the silly idiots tell you all these things they think you ought to know?'

He had come down on Tim's side.

Alan was not a man to cross. He got his own way in the end, as he always did, but he came home frayed and irritated by these encounters, which he thought unnecessary and time-wasting. Or that was the reason Ann gave herself, the next time it happened.

It was her birthday, and it was the first time it ever happened at home. And the last. Indeed, it was the last time it happened at all.

After she went to see John, something changed. Just as she changed in Portugal, so Alan changed when she went to see John. After they had recovered – and the first few days, the first week, were awful: Ann needed all her strength and courage to handle Alan's dreadful mood – she realised that they had indeed turned a corner, and things might be different from now on.

That was, until her birthday. Wednesday, the first of March. Ann, not particularly thinking of celebrating the day, had agreed that a friend of Theo's could come and stay for the night. She was, improbably, called Constance, and she was not at all as her name suggested, but a gutsy little tomboy with a gap between her front teeth as wide as the Wife of Bath's, Ann observed when she first saw her. She and Theo had become close friends, and Ann liked it when Constance came, though this wasn't often because her family lived the other side of Cambridge and always seemed frightfully busy, with a house full of guests and older children and stepchildren, and they were usually unable to drive her back and forth.

But tonight, Theo said, she was free to come. So Ann had happily agreed. Constance's mother was bringing her over at six, after they had both done their homework. Or rather, after Constance had done her homework, since there was seldom a day when Theo did both his music practices and his homework to his satisfaction. Then they were going to have high tea together and watch some video that she was bringing with her.

Just before half past five Alan came home, busy, excited, happy. 'Quick!' he said. 'Get ready. Have a bath, put your best dress on, or whatever. We're going out at seven. Tippy's going to stay with the Forsters. I've fixed it up.' It was so unlike him. Sometimes he would suggest they went to this or that, but it was almost always up to Ann to arrange it. He was simply too busy. Even when he did organise something, it was usually something he particularly wanted to do, rather than something he had arranged for Ann, and it was almost unheard of for him to arrange a baby-sitter.

Ann was completely thrown. She tried to think clearly. If she could book a baby-sitter, someone reliable, then Constance could still come, and the baby-sitter would have to put them to bed and cope with tea. Was it too late to put Constance off? Would her mother have left already? It had been such a business to organise, such a rarity, that Ann shrank from changing it. Would Constance ever be free to come again? Theo would be very disappointed. While she dithered, wondering what to do, Constance's mother was probably leaving the house, and it would soon be too late to change anything.

She tried to explain some of this to Alan. 'It's early baroque,' he said. 'Violin music, mostly,' and she realised that, though he had probably organised it because the tickets happened to be there, and he'd probably bumped into one of the Forsters and thought of asking them to have Theo, nevertheless he had managed to arrange something she would particularly like. 'And we're going to Dominique's afterwards, just the two of us. I've booked a table for half past nine.'

'Couldn't you have rung me from college?' she said. 'Just half an hour ago, and I could have rearranged Constance for another day.'

It was one of those conversations which got out of hand when you weren't looking, so that, afterwards, it's hard to tell at which moment you went wrong, whose exact fault it was, and when it had reached the point of no return. Everything that was said was no doubt reasonable. Alan had gone to some trouble, and thought she would be delighted with her surprise. And so she would have been, if she had still been a student, as she was when he remembered surprising her, before, in the days when she could abandon her plans or her evening's practice or her meeting with friends, and love it. She, on the other hand, would have looked forward to it all afternoon, and had time to wash her hair, and not eaten a large tea, in anticipation of Dominique's excellent cooking, if only he had had the consideration to telephone when he first knew about it. But he couldn't have telephoned when he first knew about it, because he only just had time to fix it up before giving an organ recital in another college, and he'd been on the go ever since till just ten minutes ago. But he had a secretary, hadn't he? Yes, but he had other things to think about than telephoning her all afternoon. The truth was, it would never have occurred to him to let her know.

It was an ugly few minutes. It couldn't have been much more than that, because Constance still hadn't arrived and she was due at six. Theo must be hearing all this, Ann thought, and it's ruining the one evening when he has succeeded in inviting his best friend to come and play. Bad enough that we had to spoil our own evening, but did we have to destroy his too? She turned to go and check on the fish fingers, which were Theo's choice for high tea, and which she had put under the grill.

'Come back here,' Alan said. 'I haven't finished.'

But Ann was weary. A year before, she would have come back without a word, feeling diminished, humiliated, treated like a servant or a dog, but seeing no point in antagonising, and feeling no particular desire to anger him. But this was the man who had made her see coloured stars on a black background and wear a rash on her face for a week, and she no longer felt any reason to do his bidding. The fish fingers needed seeing to. She was bored with the conversation. She hoped they would be able to salvage the evening, but the responsibility was not hers alone. She walked on out of the room.

There were tears in her eyes as she turned the food over. It would be ready in fifteen minutes, just when Theo had asked for it to be served.

'Mummy,' Theo said, 'Daddy's tearing your pictures.'

Ann felt a chill grip her body from the inside. It couldn't be true. Theo must have made a mistake. She put the fish fingers calmly back under the grill, turned on the heat under the peas, hung the oven glove back on its peg, and went heavily up the stairs.

Ann was strangely proud of her pictures. She had been gifted at art at school, and at one point, before it became obvious that she would be a musician, her art teacher had asked her whether she was interested in art college. Her real talent was portraiture. She could do the other things adequately, the landscapes, the still lives, but there was nothing remarkable about these. They looked like what they were supposed to look like, and that was all. But somehow, with portraits, she managed to catch something that eluded the other A-level art students. Her portraits had character.

After she left school she did no more art, until one day, on holiday with Alan, she picked up a pencil and drew a sketch of his face. And she produced an excellent line portrait. It was him: the eyes, the mouth. Anyone who saw it would have said, immediately, 'Alan Wedderburn'. She didn't resent the time spent sitting looking at Alan while he composed or read in front of her.

As soon as Theo was old enough to sit still, she drew him too. Gradually, over the last two or three years, she had produced several sketches. She decided to pick the best, and paint them properly. And she did. She spent many months sketching, water-colouring, learning to use oils, until she had two portraits of Theo and three of Alan. Then she framed them and gave them to Alan for Christmas. Her idea was to add to them every so often, as Theo got older. She felt they were the best present she had ever given Alan. They represented the three of them: her work, and her love for both of them, framed and hung on the landing. She loved guests seeing them too. She felt they made a statement about their family.

She also thought they were rather good. Alan had never said so, but Ann thought, as portraits, they were as good as she could ever do.

It was impossible that Alan could destroy these. It would be like tearing down the house. Worse, it would be like tearing down everything they had built together.

When Ann got to the landing and saw the frames empty, she breathed a sigh of relief. In his anger, he had removed them. When they had made up their quarrel they would put them back.

She went into their bedroom. Alan was not there. He must have gone up to his study in his anger. She glanced at the clock. It was five to six. One or other of them would have to stop being silly, ring a baby-sitting agency, and make sure the girl could come well before seven. She would hardly have time to dress, and would have to hurry if she was going to wash her hair. Constance's mother would be here soon. Ann would have to explain the slight change of plan. She went over to her dressing table, and saw, in the wastepaper basket beside it, her pictures torn into tiny pieces.

It was the end. So far as Ann was concerned, it was the end.

She cried as she could never remember crying before, howling into the bedclothes, not caring if Alan heard, or Theo heard, or even if Constance and her mother heard. She hoped they heard, and went away again. She could never do those pictures again. Why, oh why, hadn't he hit her, and at least the bruises would have gone away? Theo came and lay on the bed with her, and she held on to him as tightly as ever, and cried and cried into his soft hair. She vaguely heard the door bell go, but neither she nor Theo took any notice, and she simply cried some more. She didn't know whether Alan would show the child and her mother in, and if so how he would explain the sound of her howling from upstairs, or whether he would say she wasn't well and perhaps they'd better cancel it for today. She didn't care. She grieved that Theo's evening had gone wrong, she grieved for the wasted tickets and the terrible agony of Alan's kind gesture, which had gone so disastrously wrong, but nothing was of any importance compared with what he had now done. She wondered whether the fish fingers were burning, and whether Alan would think to cancel Dominique's. She wondered whether the Forsters were still waiting for Theo to come. And she didn't care about any of it. She just cried and cried again.

She never went downstairs that evening. In the end, she took off most of her clothes and got into bed, without washing her face or cleaning her teeth or anything. Theo stayed with her much of the time, but after a while Alan called him downstairs, presumably to give him something to eat, and she didn't see him again until he came in to say goodnight, after he was in his pyjamas.

The only definite thing she did, other than cry, was to take a used manila envelope out of her little bureau, in their bedroom, and put all the pieces of the pictures into it. She wondered whether they could be put back together again. She wondered whether she could copy them. And then she realised that, if anyone restored them, she would be the one doing all the work, not Alan, and the injustice of it, and the fact that he had no idea what he had done, and even if he had, would be too busy ever to bother to put it right again, made her cry and scream again.

At one point she looked at the wedding photograph of them which hung on the wall behind their dressing table. She wondered why Alan hadn't torn that up too. It occurred to her that the gesture now belonged to her. That she could smash the frame, and tear the photograph, and grind the glass into the carpet. But she had no desire to. The glass would then need sweeping up again. They would need to get another picture. It was all so *pointless*, she couldn't understand why Alan had done it.

Then she got back into bed, her face red and angry from the tears, and turned to the wall to sleep. She didn't know whether Alan would come to bed, or whether he would sleep in the guest room. She didn't care. She didn't care what he ever did again.

The next morning Ann got up as usual to get Theo ready

for school. Alan was not in the bed. Nor had he been in it.

She got Theo up and dressed, quietly, methodically, with no enthusiasm for that task or any other. She made no attempt to hurry him so he could do his music practice before breakfast. While she was giving him breakfast, Alan came down to refill his mug of tea.

'Good morning,' he said.

'Hello,' she replied, barely looking at him, and went back to buttering Theo's toast. She turned to Theo again, taking no notice of Alan any more. She had no desire to talk to him again. But nor had she any desire to be 'not on speaking terms' with him, in the kind of silly situation which demanded the writing of notes to someone one refused to talk to. She didn't want to be bothered with any of it, talking to him or not talking to him.

She walked Theo to school, and then went on to the college. Her stomach was a fist of fear. She had to stop herself running, and she shook as she entered the college gates. Every few seconds she glanced over her shoulder to make sure Alan was not behind on his bicycle. If she had seen him, she knew she would have run and hidden, thumping on John Wright's door and asking him to let her in. She was frightened of Alan as she had never been frightened of anyone or anything before. How could anyone be capable of such destruction and hatred? She didn't know, she didn't understand it, it was completely incomprehensible to her.

She reached John's staircase, and stood, leaning her back against the wall, her heart thumping in relief that she hadn't been seen. Then she ran up his stairs and knocked, almost falling in when he opened the door.

He was just putting on a jacket and gown, and she realised he must be on the point of going out.

'Sorry,' she said. 'Sorry. I'm so sorry to trouble you.'

'Sit down. What's happened?'

'Nothing.' She sat on the edge of the scruffy, comfortable armchair which seemed positioned to trip up anyone who entered the room. 'He didn't hit me. You're just going out. I'm sorry.' She jumped up again. 'I'll go away. He didn't hit me.'

He looked at his watch. 'Have you had breakfast?'

'Um.' Had she had breakfast? She had no idea. No. She had given Theo his breakfast, but she hadn't even had a cup of tea herself yet. 'No, I don't think I have.'

'Right. There's tea and coffee, and, oh dear, no milk, I'm afraid. If I've got time, I'll get the kitchen to bring you up a roll or something.' She shook her head, thinking of a member of the kitchen staff seeing her in this state, wondering what she was doing in John's rooms. 'Or, no, perhaps not a good idea. I've got a couple of pounds if you want to go and get something?'

'I think I'd rather just stay here.' She couldn't venture out into the college again, where she might bump into anyone she knew, including Alan himself. The idea filled her with horror.

'Right,' John said again. 'I'm giving a lecture at nine fifteen. I'll be back about half past ten, or a bit before. You can lock the door if you like. If you're interested in theology, you'll find plenty to read. I'll see you later.'

Five minutes later, there was a knock. 'It's John,' Ann heard through the thick inner door. 'I hope no one finds out there's an attractive woman having breakfast in my rooms.' He grinned, handing her a tray with rolls and butter and jam, a carton of milk, and a new copy of *The Times*.

'It's eighteen minutes past,' she said.

'I know,' he said, taking the stairs three at a time and reflecting that he seemed to have abandoned the principles laid down by his theological college for counselling frustrated housewives. Always leave the door open, he'd been told, and always let her know you can be overheard. Never see a woman on her own if there's no one else in the house. Their tutor had not thought it necessary to add, Do not lock another man's wife in your rooms with a tray of breakfast and a copy of *The Times*.

Alan was at a loss. He had been so relieved, so triumphant that he had managed not to hit her, that he naturally assumed she would be too. When the dreadful rage had filled him, and he recognised the beginning of the awful loss of control – the terrible sense that, unless he ran out of the house or escaped or Ann stopped doing whatever it was she was doing, then, yet again, he would hurt the person he loved more than anything else in the world – when it happened, this last time, he had thought of John Wright's kind but uncompromising face, and he had stopped. He had left the room, and run upstairs, and, instead of hitting Ann, he had simply torn something up.

Then he sat on their bed, thinking, I've done it! I have controlled myself. It's over. I will never hit Ann again.

And now this. It was nearly a month ago, and she was as cold towards him as if they were strangers. How could people build up such bitterness and harbour it? He couldn't understand it. It was weeks ago, and she was still punishing both of them. It seemed so fruitless.

He tried to understand it from her point of view. He tried not to think she was being unfair. He tried to fathom why she was so upset, still. He remembered how he had deflected his anger, and it still seemed to him that he had done the right thing. Her violin had been in its case, under the piano. He had contemplated taking it out, and smashing it up. Ann's most treasured possession. The ultimate symbol of Ann-ness, the target of all his fury.

He hadn't. It was a decent violin, worth something, but it wasn't that which had stopped him. Was it because it was Ann's one link back to her professional life? Was it because it had occurred to him, as he thought of it, that smashing her violin would signal the end of her career, as surely as if he had broken her fingers, as surely, in fact, as when he asked her to marry him and gave her a child?

Then he had seen the pictures. They were his. She had given them to him for Christmas, so he could do what he liked with them. He tore them up, and with each tear, he thought, Thank God I am not hitting Ann.

And then this.

When she went to see John again, he felt as if he was living with a permanent sneak at school. Was she going to bleat about his every failure to his colleagues in the college? John had been very good about it, but it was humiliating; embarrassing. He hated seeing John in college now.

He honestly wanted to make it up to her. He really did. But he had no idea how.

He loved Ann. He adored her, though he didn't often tell her because it made him feel awkward and gauche. He didn't like to admit how much he needed her. He knew he had failed her again and again, but he had no idea how to say sorry any more. He had a fear, when he was brave enough to own up to it, that, even if he apologised, she might not accept him any more.

At the beginning of April, Ann said, 'I've been in touch with Addenbrooke's. They have anger-management courses. There's a waiting list of about nine months, and you have to refer yourself. You can't be referred by someone else. You can go through your GP, or you can just ring them up at the hospital.'

'Oh?' Alan said, not knowing how to react. 'Why are you telling me this?'

'I think you should go,' she said. She had meant to say, 'I will only go on living with you on condition that you do,' but she couldn't bring herself to say it. She couldn't issue an ultimatum like that. He was Alan, after all. She didn't want to see him humiliated.

'I'm sorry, Ann, but I can't handle something like that.'

'I think you need it.' And I can't handle life with you if you don't go. No, not can't: I won't.

'I don't need it.'

'Alan, you can't control your anger. You need help.'

'Please, let me do this my way. I can control my anger, without help.'

'Then why don't you?'

'I will, from now on.'

'Will you? You'll never hit me again?'

'No. I will never hit you again.'

'And you'll never again destroy anything, pointlessly, like that.'

'No. I will never do it again. I might break the odd Woolworth's mug, perhaps.' He smiled. It was a joke now. He had promised.

And she believed him. She absolutely and utterly believed him. He would not hit her again, and she would never be frightened of him any more.

That night they made love for the first time since before her birthday.

40

'Create in me a clean heart, O God; and renew a right spirit within me' –

Psalm 51

'Will,' Caz said, as soon as they had dropped Theo off, late, at school.

'Mmm?' he said, moving close to her, and giving her a great, bear-like hug.

'There's still something that doesn't make sense.'

The taxi driver turned in his seat. 'Where now, sir?'

'Ah. Do you want to walk, or stay in the car?' he asked her.

'Oh, we might as well walk. It's so close.'

Immediately, she regretted her decision. It was still raining, she was tired, and the backs of her legs ached again.

Will paid the fare, tipped the driver, and they watched the car sweep round the drive and disappear down the avenue of huge horse chestnuts.

Caz put her arm through his. 'Are you all right?'

'Course I am,' he said, shortly.

'I just wanted to tell you—'

'I know,' he interrupted. 'I don't mind you, either. On a good day, at night.'

Suddenly, a mischievous gust shook the branches over their heads, and tipped a shower of raindrops down the back of their necks.

'Eurghh!' Caz cried, and Will took the opportunity to put his arm around her and pull her off balance towards himself.

'Don't,' she said. 'Matron will see us!'

'So?' he challenged. 'I'm sure I've met tougher matrons than her in my time.'

'I very much doubt it.'

They walked up beneath the chestnuts towards the main road, but said nothing until they reached it. Then, as he steered her over to the opposite pavement, he said, 'Now then, what's troubling that pretty little head?'

'Oh, shut up,' she said playfully. 'You patronising oaf!'

'Oh? That bad, eh. What is it that doesn't make sense to London's most intelligent, up-and-coming writer?'

'Never mind. You've probably spotted it.'

'Something to do with the fire extinguisher?'

'Yes.'

'Not the weight?'

'No.'

'Size?'

'No.'

'Date?'

'What do you mean?'

'The date it was installed.'

'Er. No.'

'Position?'

'Position?' she repeated.

'Position in the kitchen?'

'Yes.'

'Kitchen layout?'

'Yes.'

'Accessibility?'

'Damn. I knew you'd guessed it,' she said, quite put out.

'Schweet-heart,' he said, 'I'm an architect, remember?'

'Bother.'

'Never mind,' he consoled her. 'I'd still like you to show me what you mean. When we get in. I hadn't given it that much thought, to be honest.'

They reached the house. The lights were on. Will would have to wait before she could demonstrate the problem.

41

'Hide thy face from my sins, and blot out all mine iniquities.
  'Cast me not away from thy presence; and take not thy holy
spirit from me' –

Psalm 51

Theo had to wait till the next day. He thought he might have
to wait longer, but after Matins, in the vestry, when they were
disrobing and hanging up their surplices and cassocks, Mr Wright
came and hung his next to the men's cassocks, where the clergy
cassocks always went, and Theo managed to ask him, when
nobody seemed to be listening, 'Could I have a word with you,
please, sir?'

'What, now?'

'Well, I meant in private, sir, please.'

'Certainly, Theo; certainly. We'll meet up. Come with me, and
I'll get my diary. Now. Where are we? Some time this week?'

Theo's face fell. The chaplain looked at him. 'More urgent than
that? I see. What about today? You've got to be back in Chapel
at three fifteen. After Evensong?'

'We're supposed to be back at school, sir. We have tea,
and letter-writing, and the evening's entertainment. Which is
compulsory.'

'Looks a bit hopeless, doesn't it?'

'We usually finish lunch by one, though, sir.'

John Wright hesitated. College lunch was at one. On Sundays,
there was no college tea. The next meal was not until dinner
at seven thirty. And college meals were free. Instinctively,
he felt in his pocket and realised he had enough coins for

about three-quarters of a round of sandwiches, if he went out for lunch.

He looked at the hopeful young face, and smiled.

'One o'clock would be fine,' he said. 'I'll come and pick you up.'

Theo was actually waiting for him when he arrived.

They walked from school to college companionably, their hands in their pockets. After a while, John said, 'Are you allowed to put your hands in your pockets?'

'No.' Theo grinned, pulling them out quickly. John removed his hands too, grinning back, and noticing what an attractive smile the boy had. It seemed to fill his whole face with joy.

They walked on a bit further, and John said, 'Aren't you supposed to wear a cap, out of school?'

Theo stopped, worried. 'Shall I go back for it?'

'No, no. We're nearly there. I'll take the blame. Do you want to come up to my room?' he asked, as they walked between the autumn crocuses, towards the bridge, which sat, comfortable, beneath the protective five-hundred-year-old gaze of the stately Chapel. 'Or shall we walk by the river?'

'I don't mind,' Theo said politely, actually minding quite a lot. 'But I, er, wanted to talk to you in private, please, sir, if I can.'

They went up to John's rooms. He managed to find some rather old squash, and a few broken biscuits, and installed Theo on his battered sofa with a low table in front of him with his refreshment on it, and then told him to fire away.

Theo didn't seem to know how to start. He clasped his hands together, and gripped them between his knees, and looked at John. Eventually he said, 'In the Protestant Church, sir, do you have anything like the Catholics, you know, like confession?'

'You can make a confession if you want to. To me, if you wish.'

'And,' Theo stopped again, clearly wondering how to proceed, 'do you, like, do you tell anyone?'

'No. Certainly not. You can tell me anything you like, in absolute confidence, and it will go no further.'

'Even really bad things?'

'Anything I won't be shocked.' John tried to imagine what Theo would consider the worst sins. He could hardly offer adultery. 'Stealing, murder, anything. In fact, the law exempts me from telling anyone. Suppose you committed a murder. If you tell anyone else, they have to go to the police. I don't. Even the law recognises the secret of the confessional.'

'Oh.' Theo digested this. 'So what happens to other people if they don't tell?'

'They're breaking the law. I think you can be sent to prison.'

'Oh.' Theo stared at him, and said nothing.

'But that needn't bother us,' John reassured him. 'You can tell me anything. What did you want to say?'

'I killed my father,' Theo replied.

John had promised not to be shocked. He had quite often said that before, to boys who stammered and blushed before telling him what they did, alone at night, when the rest of the dormitory was still, or to girls who had tried things at parties that they didn't dare tell their mothers about, or even to contemporaries who had been away from home too long. From the ages of ten to thirty it was usually sex. Then it was usually money. After that, John didn't know what it was because he wasn't old enough to have heard those secrets yet. Under ten, it was usually lying and stealing, but those didn't seem to cause so much pain.

But he had never before taken the confession of someone who had killed. He swallowed almost imperceptibly. It never, for a moment, occurred to him not to believe the child. It would have seemed like the grossest of professional misconducts, as if he were to say, Well, *that* sin, of all sins, is too awful to be taken seriously. His Master would not have done it, and he tried not to either. But his Master would not have been shocked. There, he had let him down.

'By accident?' he said after the briefest of pauses.

'What do you mean?'

'Well, you said "killed him"; you didn't say whether you'd done it on purpose. So I suppose you didn't.'

'No. No, I suppose I didn't really. Does that make it not so bad? Sir . . .' The boy was close to tears. John went and sat next to him on the sofa, and put his arm around him. 'Mr Wright, sir, will God hate me always?'

'Theo, God doesn't hate you at all. Not now or ever. There.' He pulled the boy's head on to his shoulder, and held him as he sobbed, trying to remember whether he had ever suffered so much as a child. He thought not. He had heard one or two of the members of staff at the school say that Theo Wedderburn would suffer for being so bright, and had thought it a ridiculous thing to say. For being difficult, yes; for being eccentric, perhaps, in the wrong school. But no one should ever suffer for being bright. Losing a father, though, that was different.

'Don't you know who are the people who love God the most?' he said. Theo shook his head into the chaplain's jumper. 'The ones he's forgiven the most. And who are the ones he's forgiven the most? The ones who've done the most wrong. So don't you go thinking you're too bad for God to love. You and I are just the ones he does love. As much and more than the good people.'

Theo sat up, and looked at him through his wet eyelashes. 'Aren't you one of the good people?'

'Me?' John laughed. 'Why on earth did you think that?'

'Well, because you're the chaplain, you know.'

'Oh, Theo. Did anyone ever tell you Christianity's for the good people? If so, they told you wrong. Hospitals are for sick people: Jesus is for bad people. You and me.'

'What are the bad things you've done? Sir.'

'Oh, dear. I don't want to give you ideas.' What could he honestly tell Theo about his own sins, which might not be open to misinterpretation by a meticulous parent?

'Are you queer, sir?'

'What?'

'The other boys say you're queer.'

If Theo had asked him if he was gay, John would have started, and taken his arm from the boy's shoulders, and perhaps jumped up, covered in confusion, to be asked a question which, in his more lonely and depressed moments, he had occasionally asked himself. But queer was such a ludicrous, old-fashioned, quaint expression, John could hardly believe schoolboys still used it.

He kept his arm where it was, lying companionably over the boy's shoulders. 'No, Theo,' he said slowly. 'I don't think so, no.'

'You don't think so, sir. Don't you know?'

'Well, it's an odd question, isn't it, Theo? You're not asking me which sins I've committed, but which I'm capable of. If you asked me, "Are you an adulterer?" I would say no. By the grace of God, I've not committed adultery yet. But if you asked me, "Might you ever want to?" Well, then you ask for my dreams. I'd have to say yes. I might do anything. We're all capable of any sin, and we have to remember that. Now,' he said, before the conversation strayed further into realms he would not like repeated even to the other children, let alone relayed to the parents, 'why don't you tell me what happened? You told me you killed your father. I think you should tell me how.'

42

'The threefold knocking on the door of a lodge by a candidate for initiation was represented in stylised form . . . the "three knocks" occurs in the *Magic Flute* overture, between the two sections.' –

Katharine Thomson, *The Masonic Thread in Mozart*

Caz was longing for Ann to go out. Their relationship felt strained. At least, to Caz it did. Perhaps Ann hadn't noticed anything. Will was completely relaxed and in control. It amazed Caz that he was able to go on as before. She herself found she was now torn between the friendship she had begun with their hostess, and the new thoughts that plagued her: sometimes absurd, sometimes plausible, and always ugly.

Yet Will remained his usual charming self, covering, at break-fast, every topic from Drambuie marmalade to the royalties his great-grandfather's estate still received from *Hymns Ancient and Modern*. Caz had had no idea Will's great-grandfather had even been a clergyman, let alone one who wrote popular hymns.

Before lunch, Will said he would pop out and buy the Sunday papers. While he was gone, Ann asked Caz about her book. 'How's the archvillain, the archbishop? Is he still the most likely suspect?'

'Yes, and no,' she admitted. 'It was one of those lovely theories which are very exciting until you start looking into it properly.

He treated Mozart appallingly, but there's no evidence that he employed anyone to put arsenic in his tea. Naturally. Otherwise someone would have written a book on it before me.'

'You knew that already,' Ann pointed out.

'Yes. His main quarrel with Mozart seems to have been that he thought church music was for the worship of God.'

'Alan would have fought with him then.'

'Probably. But the idea did enable me to get started. Because, in another sense, my theory was right. You could say that he murdered him as surely as if he really had put arsenic in his tea.' Caz was forgetting her immediate concern, the more recent homicide, in her enthusiasm to explain the historic one. 'Mozart felt that the archbishop stifled his talent, denied him his freedom, refused to allow him to blossom or be recognised or even to earn a decent living. One evening, Mozart was offered a job which would have brought him in half a year's wages. Archbishop Colloredo had a party that night and wouldn't let him go. In a sense this was reasonable: the archbishop employed Mozart to play at his parties. But Mozart couldn't accept that kind of treatment. He couldn't accept any authority other the authority of merit. He would have been much happier if he could.'

'Sounds a bit like Theo,' Ann said with a smile.

'Yes, I think he was a bit. They both see through the silliness of it all. And unfortunately for them, they can't play the game. They're both out of step. So who poisoned him? *Noblesse Oblige*. If you want the privileges, you have to take the responsibilities. Colloredo failed to recognise, and support, the genius under his own roof. I think you could say that he, and his class really did kill the greatest composer who ever lived, in the prime of his creative life. Quite an indictment, that.'

Will had returned. As soon as Ann was comfortably surrounded by papers on the sitting room sofa, he said he would cook the lunch.

'I'll help,' Caz said, and followed him into the kitchen.

'Pasta?' he asked.

'I don't care,' she said. 'I just want to talk to you.'

'Grumpy!'

'I am, a bit. On edge. I can't handle it, Will. I really can't.'

'All right. Show me what you mean.'

First Caz listened carefully, to make sure Ann was out of earshot. Then she shut the kitchen door. Then she said, 'You be Alan. No, I'll be Alan. Then you'll see how difficult it is. I'm stronger than you, remember. I'm a man in my mid-thirties, five foot eleven, fit. You're not.'

'Who am I?'

'You're Whistler, of course. For the moment, anyway. Though we're going to have to re-cast, when you see it.'

'Never mind that,' he interrupted her. 'How do you know you're stronger than I am?'

'Something Ann said. I'm not sure . . . It's a bit of a guess, I suppose, but my theory doesn't hang on that anyway. Let's assume, then, for the sake of argument, that our strengths are comparable. I'm Alan. I've just come in.'

'Through the back door?'

'Of course. It was unlocked, remember. It was the way he always came in. Ann made a point of telling me she always left it unlocked. And we're assuming, for the moment, that Ann's version is the truth.'

'We have to assume that, to prove anything,' he pointed out.

'Exactly. If it's not the truth, well . . . That's another story. I come in by the back door, I'm tired, perhaps I flop down at this table.'

'Shhh!' he hissed. 'I thought *orecchietti al pesciolino rosso*,' he continued.

'What?' She screwed her face up, puzzled, then realised. 'Oh. I don't know, you're the expert. But I love that thing you do with tomatoes.'

'I just wondered if you could find everything,' Ann said, entering the room, still clutching one of the papers. 'You know, you two should be reading the papers, and I should be cooking this.'

'Not at all,' Caz said, sincerely. 'We hardly ever get a chance to cook anything. It's a treat.'

'You don't seem to have got very far.' Ann smiled.

'Will was looking for the *orecchiette*, whatever that is,' Caz explained. 'Why don't you just point out a packet of Sainsbury's pasta to us, and then go on reading, or play your violin, or something? I'll peel onions and clear up whatever mess Will makes.'

At that, Will really laughed. 'There's got to be a first for everything,' he said.

Then Ann opened a cupboard and showed him an impressive range of different colours, shapes and sizes of pasta, apologised for them not being fresh, and explained that she did have a pasta machine, if they could be bothered, but said it was quite a nuisance. 'It's more the sort of thing you do with prep-school boys when they come home for half-term,' she explained, 'than something you use to knock up a quick Sunday lunch.'

'Quite,' Will agreed. 'By the time I've finished,' he promised, 'you'll hardly know it's not fresh.'

'I hope that's true,' Caz said, after Ann had left them again. '*Al pesciolino rosso* indeed! She's a ruddy good cook and she'll spot Oxo cubes a mile off.'

'You have offended my deepest feelings of nationalistic pride,' Will said. 'I do, at least, know what to do with pasta.'

'You've never cooked any for me.'

'This is true. It will be a new experience for you.'

For a few minutes, they chopped and peeled in silence, as if they had nearly been caught by the headmistress when they were about to do something dreadful behind the bike sheds.

From the sitting room, Caz heard the flowing of a gentle piano piece, half familiar, haunting, Debussy perhaps. She would have loved to have gone and listened to it, but time was too short.

'Right,' she said, putting down her knife and wiping her hands on a tea towel. 'I'm Alan. You're Whistler. You ring the back door bell. Don't do it!' she said, alarmed, as Will went to the back door.

'There isn't one,' he said, 'so I don't. I knock, perhaps call, but I don't ring.'

'Fine. Stand there. In the doorway. In the porch, but not inside.' Caz stopped, and listened. The piano played on. Will stood dutifully to attention. 'Now then, you want to borrow a fiver. You are not allowed inside the house. The aim of the exercise is for you to kill me, with that fire extinguisher, without arousing my suspicions. No prolonged struggle. No loud noises. Nothing to wake the household or alarm the neighbourhood or even cause Alan to cry out for help or sock you on the jaw. Go for it.'

'Um,' Will said, standing just inside the porch. He tried to think himself into the part. He wanted a fiver. He knew Alan Wedderburn, but was a bit in awe of him. He had hoped to find Mrs Wedderburn here, because she was an easier touch, though she wouldn't let him in since he had given her rings to the police. He was taken aback to find her husband here instead of her. If he'd realised, he wouldn't have knocked.

'Hi,' he said.

Caz was sitting at the table. She looked up. 'Harold,' she said wearily, 'it's gone eleven. I'm going to bed. I can't ask you in, you know why. What do you want?'

'Can you lend me a fiver?'

Caz sighed. 'What for?'

'I've got no food for the cat. She's hungry. She's just had kittens.'

'Harold, it's ten past eleven at night. Where the heck are you going to buy cat food?' What a plonker Will is, Caz thought, determined not to giggle. Why on earth would Whistler want cat food? 'I'll give you a tin of tuna. How about that?'

'Haven't you got any money?'

'Yes, I have, actually. But I don't want to give you any. I'm very tired, I'm going to bed in a minute, and if you don't want the tuna, I'd be grateful if you'd leave, please.'

Caz turned back to the table.

It stood in the middle of the kitchen, taking up most of the floor space. It was the only possible position for it. If it had been placed anywhere else, it would have blocked access to work surfaces, cupboards and appliances, so presumably it had always been there. Caz sat at the table, in front of the back door but slightly to the side, so that if she looked up and turned her head, she could see Will's face, and have a natural conversation with him; but if she turned to the table, as now, her back was to him. Coming in, late at night, after a day's work, one might, of course, sit anywhere: it would depend where one hung one's coat, whether one helped oneself from the fridge, . . . and so on. However, Caz had sat in the most obvious place. Where you would collapse into a chair, after coming home through the back door.

Will hesitated for a second or two, no more. Then he reached inside the porch, grabbed a spade, and lifted it above Caz's head.

She turned, and screamed.

43 ∫

'The sacrifices of God *are* a broken spirit: a broken and a contrite heart, O God, thou wilt not despise' –

Psalm 51

'Well, sir, I don't know how to tell you, without . . .'

'Without telling me things about your parents that you don't think I ought to know?'

'Yes, sir.'

'Then, if it would help, let me tell you that a couple of times your mother came and told me something I don't think she ever told anyone else. She told me your father sometimes got very upset, and lost his temper, and very occasionally he hit her. She didn't want you to know, but I suspect you did?' Theo nodded. 'I thought you would. People we live with usually know either far more, or far less, about us than we suspect. Now, does that help you to go on?'

Theo nodded again. He looked at the carpet, and rubbed his toe in a hole in it. 'I used to get cross with him,' he said. 'And her, really. I didn't understand why she let him do it. I thought it was silly. She just used to stand there, and do and say nothing. If I'd behaved like that, she wouldn't have let me. Adults say they won't let you behave badly because they love you. They love you too much to let you grow up being naughty. So if she loved him, why did she let him behave like that?'

'Perhaps she didn't know how to stop him.'

'But she didn't say anything. She didn't say, "You mustn't behave like that."'

'Go on,' John prompted softly.

The boy looked at him for a moment, before deciding to continue. 'They had a quarrel. He was shouting at her, and he went out to work and slammed the door, and I said, "I don't think you should let him behave like that." So she said, "What do you think I should do, then?" And I said, "You must tell him to stop." Theo turned and looked at John. His large eyes were dry, but he looked frightened, as if what he was about to say was too big to think about. 'She said, "I don't think he'd take any notice." But, sir, if children don't take any notice, then adults say, "If you do that again, you'll get a smack." And that teaches them not to do it again. Or it's supposed to. Ann said it never worked with me.' He smiled, nervously, almost as if he thought he should finish there.

'So what did you do then?' John said gently.

'I said . . .' He stopped, swallowed, and started again. 'I said, "Well, you should hit him then." I wanted to say, "You should hit him back." She laughed a little, and said he was stronger than she was, so I said she should hit him with something. In some schools, the masters hit the boys with a stick, if they've been very naughty, and the boys are big. Or they used to.'

He bent forward and pulled some loose threads from the carpet. John got the impression that now he really had said all he wanted to say. 'Is that it? Is that what you did?'

'Yes.' He looked up again, as if to see how he would be judged, now he had confessed his crime. 'I didn't . . . I didn't know what would happen when she did.'

'But, Theo,' John said, 'your father was killed by a stranger. His death was nothing to do with what you said to Ann.'

Theo looked at him. Then he looked down, and John thought he saw a slight shake of the head.

'You're saying he wasn't killed by a stranger?' The boy nodded. 'You mean . . .' John hoped he was not hearing his own thoughts correctly. If what the boy thought was true, it didn't bear thinking of. 'You mean, you're saying you know how he died, and the police got it wrong?'

He nodded.

'All right.' Outwardly, John was very calm. 'Tell me what you know.'

'I heard him come in. I was worried, you see. What would happen if Ann did hit him? He might have hit her back. He might have hurt her. I was awake.'

'Are you sure? It was very late. Do you know what the time was?'

He nodded again. 'I can hear the clocks from my bedroom. All the Cambridge clocks. I hear them strike the hour. I heard them strike nine, ten, and eleven.' He continued: 'It was just after that that he came in. I heard the gate open, and I heard it bang to again, and I heard him put his bicycle away; it must have been a bit windy, because I heard the gate bang again. I thought I heard him come into the kitchen, but I can't hear that door very well from my room. Then I heard Ann get up and go downstairs. I heard something in the kitchen, something knocking: a stool against the table, probably. Then I heard voices. Alan was cross. Then there was nothing for a few minutes, then Ann started shouting. Screaming really. Then I went downstairs. He was on the floor and she'd hit him and she was telephoning for an ambulance. She gave me the telephone and ran outside.'

'Why did she do that?'

'I don't know. Then we waited for the ambulance. But he was already dead. She told me afterwards. It wasn't her fault, sir.' He was almost pleading. 'It was mine.'

John thought for a moment. He had to admit that he believed every detail of the boy's story. Except perhaps the one thing that he hadn't witnessed. Suddenly, he said, 'How many people live on this staircase with me?'

'What?'

'The names at the bottom of the stairs, painted in white in the doorway. How many?'

'Nine,' Theo said. 'No, sorry. Ten.'

John heard his own sharp intake of breath.

'It is ten, sir, isn't it?'

'No, Theo, it isn't.'

'Yes, it is. Because there's ten, and ten A.'

'That's eleven.'

'No, it isn't sir. You said how many people live on this staircase with you. You're number seven. Then there's one to ten A. That's ten.'

'I beg your pardon. So it is.' John rubbed his eyes with his fingers, and shook his head. He must phrase his questions more carefully. 'What order did we go out of Chapel this morning? The Dean and I, and the fellows?'

'I don't know, sir.' Thank goodness for that, John thought. Nobody's memory can be that accurate. 'You process out behind us. We can't see you.'

'Right,' John said, undefeated. 'You've made one mistake. You've reported one thing that you didn't witness. Do you know what it is?'

'What do you mean, sir?'

'You've told me one thing that you can't have seen. What's called an inference. You've come to a conclusion about something, and presented it as if it were fact. Do you know what it is?'

'No.'

'That your mother hit your father. You don't know that. You can't have seen it.'

'But, sir, I didn't see any of it. I heard it. I didn't see her going down the stairs, but I know she did.'

'And did you hear her hitting him?'

'Yes.'

'You didn't say that before.'

'No.'

'Why not?'

'Because . . . Because . . .' He looked into John's face, pleading with him not to make him say any more. 'I didn't want to.'

'Why not?'

'I didn't want to remember it.'

'All right. You heard words, but you presumably didn't hear what the words were.' Theo nodded. 'How did you know what the sound was? The sound of your mother hitting your father?'

'I didn't. Not until afterwards. Then I did.'

'I see.' John stood up and crossed his room aimlessly, and his eye caught the title of a book on his bookshelf, *Love, Sex and Power*, advertised in a brash orange script on a black background. He remembered the evening when he had broken up with the only serious girlfriend he had ever had, sitting in a friend's room, holding her hand and fighting back the tears and telling her and himself that it was all for the best, and his eyes had lit then on the spine of a book which proclaimed, *I'm OK, You're OK*, and he had pointed it out to her, and the two of them had laughed, in their pain, at the irony of it. They had shared a sense of humour; perhaps it would have worked out. Too late now: she was married to someone else, and John thought he remembered a card announcing their firstborn.

He turned back to see the face gazing expectantly at his. What did Theo expect him to do? he wondered. 'Why have you waited so long to tell someone?'

'We have a lady staying with us. A writer. She told me that Ann had told her about it, and I thought they might put Ann in prison, so I told her I hit Alan. They don't put children in prison.' It was matter-of-fact, calm. He might have been talking to his science teacher about an experiment, and how he expected it to work out. And they never do, John thought, remembering his childhood days in the lab. They never do.

'And?' he said. 'What happened then?'

'She told her husband and he didn't believe me.' Theo knew Will wasn't her husband yet, but it amounted to the same thing. 'He said I wasn't strong enough. But they said I must tell somebody the whole truth. Otherwise I'd get hurt. It's lucky they didn't believe me, isn't it, sir? Or they would have had to go to the police, wouldn't they?'

John sat down opposite Theo. 'Let me tell you what I want to do. Or rather, let me ask you. I need your permission. I will not go to the police about any of this: I give you my word. But there is someone I would like to talk to. If your account is correct, Ann needs help. She's carrying a terrible burden, and she needs to talk to someone. I'm not surprised she didn't go to the police, though they wouldn't put her in prison. She certainly didn't intend to kill him, and even if she had, there are ways of looking after women whose husbands are violent. Not that your father was, Theo,' he added quickly. 'He was a wonderful man, and a very good father and husband. Like all of us, like you and me, he had faults, and one of his faults was that, very occasionally, he used to lose his temper and behave in a way he shouldn't have. A lot of men do that. And probably quite a lot of women.

You don't hear about it because people love their husbands and their wives, as your mother and father loved each other, so they don't want to talk about it. That's why your mother didn't tell the police how it happened. They would have said, "Why did you hit him?" And she would have said, "Because I was frightened." "But why should you be frightened of your own husband, Mrs Wedderburn?"

'And the next day, in the papers all over the country, it would say, "Choirmaster Alan Wedderburn Savage Wife-batterer".' John found he was telling himself how it would have been, as much as Theo. 'None of us who loved and respected Alan would have wanted that. He was a loyal friend and a faithful husband and a fair and dedicated colleague. And a fabulous musician. I couldn't cope with having my faults put on the front page of the newspapers, Theo. God knows them, and that's bad enough. Ann did what was best for Alan, and best for you. Do you believe that?'

Theo nodded.

'But I would like your permission to talk to her about what you've told me. I think she should talk it through with someone, just as your friends thought you should talk about it. And, also, she should know you know. You shouldn't have secrets between you.'

Then John said the hardest thing he could remember saying for a long time. Almost as hard, in fact, as when he had told that girl, all those years ago, that he wouldn't see her again. He said, 'But it is up to you. I won't talk to her unless you say I can. And if you're not ready to decide, I will wait.'

They sat, in the stillness of the room, listening to the sounds of a Cambridge college on a Sunday afternoon. Undergraduates, coming back from an early lunch in a country pub, preferable to the cold, thin, buffet Sunday lunch of college, shouted to one another across the court, suggesting tea in one another's rooms at a later hour. Early winter tourists, who had wandered from the beaten track and found themselves lost in the backwaters of the kitchen yard, pointed out to one another in American accents how cute the English ruins were. Someone whistled, not a tune, but a sharp, vigorous whistle to call a colleague. The stairs creaked outside: a lone, diligent student returning to his rooms to work on an essay for the morrow. Somewhere, faint music played. John had deep reserves of patience, and could wait longer than most of the adults in Theo's life.

Eventually, Theo broke his gaze into nothingness, and said, 'Mmm?' as if John had prompted him to say something. He judged it was time to help the boy out. 'Would you like me to talk to her?'

'Mmm?' he said again.

'To Ann. To your mother.'

'Yes,' he said. Then nodded.

'Good,' John said briskly. 'Now, what time have you got to be in Chapel? Three fifteen? And can you go straight from here, or do you have to go back to school first?'

'From here, if I want.'

'Would you like to play a game? I've got something here . . .' John got down on his hands and knees and started searching in the window-seat, under his mullioned window. A few years ago, his parents had moved to a smaller house, and in the clearing up, his mother had asked his permission to throw away his childhood games. He had emphatically refused. He had brought them up to Cambridge, and stored them, dusty and unsorted, under the seat where undergraduates sat to drink their tea when they used his rooms for the crowded Christian Union meetings. So far, he had not had any call to use them.

'Mousey-Mousey,' he proclaimed triumphantly. 'Do you know how to play?'

Theo shook his head.

When they had the game out on the floor, and John had just caught two of Theo's mice with great alacrity and a whoop of triumph, Theo said suddenly, 'If Christianity's for bad people, why can't I pray?'

John stopped, his hand on the tumbler which had trapped the blue and yellow mice, whose tails stuck out beneath it like symbols of defiance.

'Can't you?' Theo shook his head. 'What sort of can't?'

'Someone said I couldn't.'

'Uh-huh. Who said that?'

'A voice.'

'Whose voice?'

'God's, I suppose.'

'Theo,' John said, shifting his position because his knee was digging into something under the carpet, 'I don't think God's voice would ever tell you not to pray.'

'What other voices are there?'

'Oh, there are lots. Lots of other voices. Do you remember Jesus in the Wilderness? Voices told him all sorts of stupid things. Luckily, he knew his scriptures, so he knew God wouldn't talk to him like that. And any voice that tells you not to pray is a voice you should take no notice of at all. You make a point of praying every day, whatever the voice tells you to do, and before the week is out, I bet you fifty pence the voice will have long given up. What's your full name, Theo?'

'Theophilus.'

'And what does Theophilus mean?'

'A friend of God. Theo means God. And the phil-bit is something to do with a friend.'

The chaplain shook his head. 'You could translate it "friend of God". The early Christians sometimes did. But the name is much older than Christianity. There's another translation, the original meaning, which is much more accurate theologically. "Friend of God" is a lot to live up to, and none of us is much good at it. Jesus told us we'd always fail if we put our trust in ourselves, and how good we are towards God. Remember the Pharisee who thanked God for making him such a good person? Jesus didn't think much of him.'

'What does it mean then, sir? My name.'

'It really means "loved by God". Whatever you do, he loves you. You could never be so wicked that you could use up all his love.'

'Amadeus!' the boy cried in delight. 'Alan told me I was named after the greatest musician who ever lived. I never knew what he meant!' Amadeus. Gottlieb. Loved by God. He remembered Ann's love, like the turtle dove, till all the seas ran dry. Presumably God really could love till all the seas ran dry. God would still be there when they did.

'I'll tell you what,' John said. 'We'll pray together before we go to Chapel. Right now, though, I want a go with those mice. Come on.'

It was a promise John didn't manage to keep. Within a couple of minutes, the undergraduate who lived next door to him, and his girlfriend, knocked on the door to ask if they could borrow some milk for tea. It was an idle quest: John's larder was worse stocked than any student's. But almost before they mentioned the milk, they were on the floor too, snapping the beaker down on the mice and proclaiming, 'A hit! A hit!'

They were all laughing and pushing and shrieking so much, that it was three sixteen before John noticed the clock, and pulled Theo to his feet and grabbed his gown as a couple more of his neighbours came to the door to investigate the noise. They left the four of them playing the game, John saying to them, unheeded in the uproar, could they pull the door to when they finished, please? He hadn't much hope that they would, nor that much of the game would still be intact when he returned.

'Come on then,' he said, making a mental note to ask Theo in a couple of days whether he'd managed to pray. He was only nine. John realised with deep satisfaction that he had four years of nurturing him before he moved on to his next school. And he would. He would. Theo was too precious, too special, to have his life dictated by hostile voices.

'Got you!' came a shout from his room.

'Did not! You did not!' cried the girl.

They ran down the stairs, so as not to be late for Chapel.

44

'Restore unto me the joy of thy salvation; and uphold me with thy free spirit' –

Psalm 51

Luckily, Will thought quickly. Within seconds, the spade was back in the porch, his handkerchief was out of his pocket, and he had wrapped it around the first finger of Caz's left hand and was holding it tightly.

'Sorry, Ann,' he said, as she came running in. 'Caz always makes a terrible fuss about nothing. She thought she'd cut her finger off, and would never be able to use a word processor again. It's barely scratched. Have you got a plaster? No, no, I'll do it. Just get the first-aid box out, and I'll do the rest. I'd get on much faster without her,' he continued. 'I'm going to shove a plaster on her finger and send her back to you.'

'Sorry,' Caz said, making a self-deprecating face.

'Here,' Ann said, putting a proper Sainsbury's red and white first-aid box on the table. 'Let's see.'

'I'm fine,' Caz said. 'I'll keep this hankie on for a minute, then put a plaster on. Do go on playing; it was lovely. Leave the door open, if you're happy to.'

'All right,' Ann said, smiled, and left them alone again.

Caz breathed out. 'You see,' she said, in an undertone.

'Yes,' Will said, getting a plaster, thoughtfully, out of the box.

'You'd have to go all the way round the table.'

'Yup.' He fumbled with the paper wrapper.

'He wasn't allowed in the house. How would he have got past

Alan? *Why* would he? You wouldn't, would you? You'd grab the nearest thing, as you just did. That fire extinguisher is not the nearest thing. It's right the other side of the room, by the door that leads to the hall. In fact, you can hardly see it from the back door, because it's tucked between the cupboard and the other doorway.'

Will nodded.

'So, you're grabbing the nearest thing . . .'

The piano started up again. It was different music, romantic, and louder this time, because the doors were open. Caz unpeeled the plaster, considered her finger, and stuck it on the side which would have been nearest the knife.

'And the fire extinguisher is only the nearest thing . . .' she continued.

'Caz,' Ann called from the sitting room, still playing. 'Do you like Rachmaninov?'

'Love him,' she called back. 'I'm just coming.' She kissed Will briefly, and left him to clear up the first-aid box, and come to his own conclusions. He stood in the middle of the kitchen floor, chewing his moustache, thinking as he did so that it was time he shaved it off.

'It would only be the nearest thing . . .' he said to himself, and stopped. Caz was right.

It would only be the nearest thing if you were coming in through the door that led to the house.

45

'Ann /æn/ (f.) Variant spelling of ANNE.
   English form (via Old French, Latin, and Greek) of the
Hebrew girl's name *Chana* 'He (God) has favoured me
(i.e. with a child)' –
   The Oxford Minidictionary of First Names

'Behold, thou desirest truth in the inward parts' –
   Psalm 51

That afternoon, after Evensong, John rang Ann. He hadn't
worked out what he was going to say, so when she answered,
he was taken aback.

'Ann Fitzwilliam.'

'Ann. It's John here.' Because everyone referred to her as Alan
Wedderburn's widow, John had forgotten she used her maiden
name, and for a moment wondered if he'd rung the wrong
number. In his confusion he didn't give his own surname,
which, with such a common Christian name, was an omission
he very seldom made.

'John . . .' She was searching. 'John who?'

'John Wright. I'm ringing from college.'

'John! I'm so sorry. I recognised your voice, but couldn't place
it for a moment. I was listening to the radio when you rang. Not
concentrating. Sorry.'

'My fault entirely. I wasn't concentrating either.'

They sounded like a couple of teenagers, he thought, too
embarrassed to say anything. With a slight shock, he realised
he hadn't really spoken to her, other than platitudes over mulled

wine after the carol service and at similar occasions, since Alan died, two years ago.

'Listen,' he said, 'I wanted to talk to you about something. I wondered whether you'd like to come to dinner?' He hadn't wondered that at all, but it suddenly seemed like a good idea.

'Tonight?'

'Er, yes, if you're free.' It was then that he realised the difficulty. Normally he would entertain in college. But he could hardly lean over High Table and enquire politely whether she had killed her husband by mistake one evening a couple of years back, intending to divert another row. He would have to take her out.

They made arrangements about the time and the place to meet, he hung up, and then he realised that he had never thought of her like that before. Before she had been Alan's wife; a chance acquaintance who turned out to have a pastoral problem he may or may not have been able to help her with. Now, extraordinarily, she was a woman he was taking out, and worrying where to take her.

When she turned up at his rooms at half past seven, she was dressed, rather surprisingly, in jeans and a large but very attractive floppy jumper. Clearly she was not expecting to dine in Hall. Relieved, he asked if a pub sandwich would be all right. He could afford something else; of course he could. But not easily. A modest restaurant meal was the price of a good new commentary on the *Book of Romans*, or the cost of sponsoring a child's education for several months in the Third World.

She hesitated, her mouth half open, so that he added, almost defensively, 'I was going to suggest McDonald's, actually, but I thought we wouldn't get much privacy.'

And then she laughed. It was the kind of laugh the poets describe as 'silvery'. She laughed for a good twenty seconds, happy, carefree, delighted, standing in his doorway where anyone could hear her, simply laughing at the thought of a cheeseburger and chips and strawberry milkshake.

Then she said, 'You're not full of male pride or anything, are you?'

'Not particularly,' he said. 'Why?'

'Can I take you out for a meal? A little Greek restaurant, or French café, or something. Do let me.'

'That would be lovely,' he said, genuinely delighted.

He was aware, as they left college, of her slight seniority. He was shifting his weight, finding his feet, still not quite balanced as to how to relate to her. She was no longer the wife of a senior colleague. She was the parent of one of the choristers: that would do. But why did they need to eat together in order to discuss her son? Wouldn't it have been more normal to have given her an afternoon appointment in his rooms? Perhaps, but then he couldn't have spoken to her that day. He wasn't sure what the hurry was, given that the issue had waited two years. But he was aware that he had wanted to talk to her immediately.

He followed her into Mikaila's. She had eaten there before, and knew the waiters, and asked for a table at the back, where it would be quiet and fairly private. She also knew what to order and what to avoid, and in the end decided for both of them, starting with seafood and a light white wine.

'I don't drink much,' he said, worried that she would order too much, and it would be wasted. He suddenly felt awkward, young, as if he were not used to eating out and she knew exactly what she was doing.

'Drink some, for me,' she said. 'I hardly ever go out for a meal with a grown-up. Theo and I have been alone too long.'

When he had thought about the conversation at all, he had expected it to come at the end of the evening, tucked in between the coffee and the bill, and dealt with just before they left. He had always known it would be awkward to bring up. Now, it seemed, he had no choice.

'It's because of Theo that I wanted to see you,' he said.

It seemed to him that a spasm passed across her face, so quickly he almost missed it. As if she had been on the point of forgetting some trouble, of being young again, and he had spoilt it.

And then he realised how difficult it was to start. What could he say that wouldn't ruin the rest of the evening? But that was why they had met, after all. What did the rest of the evening matter? Perhaps the only way to do it was as Theo himself would have done: come straight out with it, and see what happened.

'He believes that you killed Alan.'

She looked at him, her lips slightly apart, her eyes wide, and said nothing. He looked at her, and thought, She is beautiful. She is perhaps the most beautiful woman I have ever seen. Her skin is like milk, and her hair has the look of a schoolboy's horse chestnut caught in the autumn sun. Her lashes almost cover her eyes, and where on earth did that boy get his blond looks from?

'Oh,' she said at last. 'And did you believe him?'

'Yes,' he said. 'I did.'

The spell was broken. The waiter came and asked if the first course was acceptable. Ann requested a jug of water. Then she said, 'And?'

'And what?'

'And what is the purpose of this meeting?'

'I thought you might need to talk. If he's right, I thought you might be carrying a terrible load, alone. I wanted to say, I'm here if you want a shoulder to lean on. And I wanted you to be able to talk to Theo truthfully, without pretending something neither of you believes.'

'Being what?'

'That a stranger killed your husband. Rather than that his death happened because of the kind of person he was.'

For a moment, Ann was too angry to speak. What right had he, this clergyman who knew nothing of married life, to pretend an understanding of their relationship, to make a judgement? She took a drink of whatever it was in her glass, and looked across the restaurant at the couple at the next table. What she saw made her sad. She saw a man and a woman, about the same age, who sat opposite one other saying absolutely nothing at all. They were so obviously man and wife, they so obviously had nothing left to say to one another and another forty years in which not to say it, that she felt profoundly depressed. And, as quickly as it had come, her anger was gone. John was not judging her. He was not pontificating. He was stating what he saw as fact, and telling her, in effect, that it made no difference.

She looked at him. 'How do you see me?' she said.

'What do you mean?'

'Describe me. Tell me what I'm like, as if you were telling someone else.'

He picked up his wine glass by the stem, and swirled the wine around.

Without thinking, he said, 'You're beautiful. Your lashes nearly cover your eyes, and you have a soft, low, gentle voice. It's hard to imagine you doing an unkind thing, and I should think you are a lovely mother. The sort of mother one could confess anything to. I'd love to hear you playing the violin. You have hair like silk. You are older than I am, and yet I feel protective towards you. I have no idea whether this is what you wanted me to say, and I'm sure I shall regret it in the morning.'

She looked down at her food, skewered a mussel with a fork, and ate it. It tasted of nothing, and felt like rubber.

'Oh,' she said at last.

'What did you expect me to say?'

'I expected you to describe a latter-day Myra Hindley. You just said I murdered my husband.'

'I didn't say you murdered him. I have reason to believe you killed him. That doesn't change any of what I just said to you.'

'Doesn't it?'

'Of course not. Why should it?'

'Are murderesses beautiful?'

He reached his hand across the table to touch hers then pulled it away again, thinking to himself that he was not used to the wine and must be careful.

'I didn't invite you here to accuse you. I'm a priest. I honestly thought you might want some help and friendship.'

'You didn't invite me here at all,' she said, and smiled.

'You're right,' he said. 'I blush. I invited you out for a sandwich and a half-pint in some smoke-filled, crowded room, and you brought me here. I apologise.'

'What for?'

'I sense,' he said, 'I have offended you.'

'If so,' she replied, 'I have only myself to blame. If I could stand back objectively, I think I would realise you've paid me the highest of compliments. You think I've committed the worst of sins—'

'No,' he interrupted. 'Not by a long way.'

'And yet you treat me like a human being.'

The waiter hovered. 'I can't eat any more,' she said. 'Please will you bring us whatever else it was we ordered?'

'Yes, madam.'

John felt a pang at the thought of the wasted food, but he, too, could not face any more for the time being.

She took a drink of her wine. 'Did he bring the water?' he asked.

'I don't know,' she said. 'I think he forgot.' Suddenly, she looked very tired. Without warning, she said, 'I didn't kill him. I couldn't live with myself if I had. I loved him, love him, more than life. And he was my son's father.'

John nodded.

'Do you believe me?' she asked.

He shook his head, looking at the table and realising how confused he felt. Was it the wine? If so, why did people drink so much?

'Yes, at the moment, I do. But to believe you means I don't believe your son. And I find it hard to imagine that he could be mistaken.'

'Thank you,' she said. 'Funnily enough, I value that more than your believing me.'

They sat in silence till the waiter came again. When he had laid the dishes of steaming food in front of them, and gone away again, she smiled and said, 'D'you know, I don't want any of this.'

'It's difficult,' he said, 'isn't it?'

Suddenly, it was as if she had given in. 'Tell me,' she said. 'What did he say?'

'Who? Theo?'

'Yes. Theo.'

So John repeated back to her all that her son had said. He realised, as he did so, how much store he set by the boy's reliable memory; how difficult it was to explain the sequence of events any other way; how impossible it was that anyone else had killed Alan. How Ann herself had descended the stairs some minutes before Alan had died. How incriminating that was.

When he had finished, she said, 'Fine. I will tell you what happened, on one condition.'

'What's that?

'That you believe me. I'm not in the business of justifying myself. I don't want to defend my actions, and have you hum and hah. If that's not acceptable to you, you can go to the police now.'

'There's no question of that,' he said quickly, hurt.

'But I don't want to give you my version just to have you weigh the evidence.'

'Well then, you ask the impossible,' he said.

'Why?'

'You can't ask me to believe something before I know what it is I have to believe.'

'And you a man of faith.'

'What do you think faith is?' he asked, in his stride now, defending what he was used to defending several times a week. 'Believing, like the White Queen, six impossible things before breakfast? Faith *is* weighing the evidence, and coming to the most plausible conclusion. That is all I can agree to do. Tell me or not, as you wish. All I can promise is to decide on whichever I find the most convincing version. It's all I could manage for my Saviour, and it's all I can manage for you.'

Ann looked at the dishes in front of them, and began to spoon them out. It looked, and smelt, very good. Perhaps, after all, she didn't need to do anything other than have a good meal, and give him a good meal too. He was not going to do anything. He had said there was no question of going to the police. There was nothing she needed to do. She had no one to convince.

Except her son. He believed that she had killed the man they had both loved. She had some explaining to do there. And if she couldn't convince John, how could she ever convince Theo?

'It's ironic,' she said at last. 'Theo must have heard me going downstairs. I don't know whether you'll understand this.' She stopped, and smiled. 'I was going to say, "being a man," but it sounds so patronising, doesn't it'

'I rather like it, actually. It reminds me that there are things we don't understand about one another. Is that very old fashioned?'

'Probably. Probably frightfully incorrect. Anyway. I went downstairs.' If he hadn't known better, he would almost have thought she blushed, like a schoolgirl. 'I went into the downstairs loo. I always keep a bit of make-up there. Comb, eyeliner, mascara, stick of lipstick. I don't often use it, but I always keep it there. Silly. I never have time to go upstairs to put make-up on, and if I realise . . . I mean, sometimes, when I realised that Alan was about to come home, I would nip into the loo, and put a bit of make-up on.

'I remember my mother,' she said suddenly, 'used to put make up on. And I asked her why once, and she said, "For Daddy, and you children." And I can remember wondering whether she would wear make up if she went to prison.'

She stopped. This time, John did reach across the table and touch her hand.

'Go on,' he said. 'Finish telling me.'

'That's all really. I went into the loo, and must have spent a few minutes "doing my face", as they say. You can't hear anything because there's an extractor fan in there. It's really noisy. You sometimes don't even hear the front door bell. So that must have been when . . .'

It was the moment he had been waiting for. It had hit her. Her face changed colour dramatically, like a sky changing colour on a stormy night, and he half expected her to be ill, or to faint, or make some other demand on him that he wouldn't know how to meet.

'I know,' he said. 'Don't feel bad. You couldn't have saved his life.'

She had realised what he had seen a moment before. If they hadn't had a row, if she hadn't been anxious to please, if she hadn't gone into the loo to make herself look good for Alan, she would have walked into the kitchen when he was still alive.

'He would have killed both of you.' Somehow, John knew he was right on this. He knew that it had worked out better the way it was. Their row, her attempt to look attractive, the delay, had all been providential. It was too much of a fluke not to have been for the better. He had to believe it. Even if it wasn't true, he had to make her believe it.

'If you had gone in a moment earlier, Theo would have gone downstairs and found two corpses on the kitchen floor.' He stroked the back of her hand with his finger, and passed her

her glass of wine. 'Which might have been easier for you, but would have been tough on your son.'

She nodded slowly. 'Are you sure?'

John looked steadily at her. He very seldom lied.

'Yes,' he said. 'I'm sure.'

There was one other thing he wanted to tell her, though he shrank somewhat from doing it. Still, it would be common knowledge soon enough, to anyone who was interested.

'Whistler won't be around much longer,' he said. He wondered how much to spell out.

'Oh?'

'He's not very well.'

'I knew he was HIV positive,' she said. 'The police told me two years ago.'

'Worse than that, I'm afraid. When did you last see him?'

She thought for a long time. 'I don't know,' she said at last. 'He's the kind of person you think you're seeing all the time, but now you come to mention it, I suppose it's months.'

John nodded. 'He's in a hospice. I usually visit him once or twice a week. He's been there since August.'

'Will it be long?' Ann found she was strangely relieved. It seemed like the end of an episode. She had often told herself that she was not interested in revenge, or even justice, but, now that a far more powerful hand than hers had decided to execute it, she felt oddly satisfied. She wondered if this was ghoulish, if she ought to feel guilty for her lack of charity.

'Weeks, if that,' John replied. 'He suddenly became much weaker at about the beginning of term. I don't think he'll see Christmas.'

'I'll send him a present,' she said unexpectedly, wondering to herself whether she really would. 'He used to love my cherry cakes.'

John smiled. 'That would be kind.'

He walked her back home sometime later, and neither of them felt the need to say anything in particular. They had enjoyed the rest of the meal, even if they hadn't done it much justice, and they had felt as if they had known each other much longer than they had, and had been relaxed in one another's company. When he eventually delivered her to her house, she had hesitated, wondering whether to ask him in, just as he would have hesitated, wondering whether to accept.

In the end, he said, 'Would you come and dine in Hall with me sometime? The company can occasionally be pompous, but the food's always good.'

'Any time,' she agreed. 'Tomorrow?'

He laughed. 'Monday's not a good day. But let's go for it. And this time I'll pick you up. I'll be here at seven o'clock tomorrow.'

'Tomorrow,' she said. 'And thank you.'

'What for?' he asked.

She wasn't quite sure. 'I think,' she said, 'for believing in me when you didn't even believe in me. If you see what I mean.'

'It was a pleasure,' he said, truthfully.

She let herself into her empty, lonely house, shuddering slightly as her eye rested on the fire extinguisher, now hanging by the door which led from the kitchen to the rest of the house, moved, as it had been after Alan's death two years ago, to be near the hall, rather than near the back door.

46 ∫

'You great clot,' Will said, kissing his wife-to-be the night they arrived home in London, two years to the day after Alan Wedderburn had died. 'That fire extinguisher had a date on it. As well as the weight, incidentally. You, mucking about with scales and weights: more body than brain, aren't you, really? Specially in those amazing Italian pyjamas.

'That fire extinguisher was installed after Alan's death. And it was moved. You could still see the old bracket marks by the door to the porch, where the other one used to hang. If you'd looked for ten seconds, you would have seen it. Just where you would grab it, if you were an unsavoury intruder.'

'How the heck do you notice that kind of thing?' she said, amazed. 'Yow! that tickles. Get off.'

'Because I'm just the kind of boring, reliable man your mother would approve of, who has recently installed a fire extinguisher in our joint kitchen, and spent two hours fiddling about with the bracket, and Rawlplugs, and bits of Polyfilla. I think, on balance, these pyjamas look better on the floor.'

'And how does somebody as boring and reliable as you,' she said, 'get to be so very sexy?'

It was not a question he deigned to answer.

At least, not in as many words.

47 ∫

'O Lord, open thou my lips; and my mouth shall shew forth thy praise' –

Psalm 51

Theo Wedderburn lay in his bed in Mozart dormitory. He looked at the grey ceiling, wondering, as he did every night, whether that was a cobweb in the corner, there, or a crack in the paint. Occasionally, he heard one of the other beds creaking, as a boy turned, or pulled his duvet up to his chin. Every so often a door would open or shut elsewhere in the school, a car drive past on the distant road, or an adult's foot sound on the Tarmac outside.

He couldn't sleep. He often couldn't sleep, but he didn't mind. He liked to lie in the dark, thinking. He liked being at boarding school. He liked going home, as well, of course, but he always looked forward to the beginning of term, his own bed in school, the routine, the hard work, especially in the choir. He hoped Ann wasn't too lonely without him. He felt guilty, sometimes, that he had left her behind. He wondered whether she would marry again, and then frowned, trying to imagine what it would be like.

Then he thought of Alan, and a tear rolled down his cheek.

Something was different. What was it? When he thought of Alan, he didn't usually cry. It felt good to cry, easy, comforting. Then he remembered. Mr Wright had told him. He hadn't believed him at first, had thought Mr Wright had made it up to make him feel better, but then they had talked to Ann about it, together, and he had believed. She hadn't done it. She really hadn't. And that meant he hadn't either. They had both loved Alan, and they missed him, and now Theo could think about his father without that awful weight pressing on his chest, and he could cry.

After a few minutes, he got out of bed and went out into the corridor. If Mrs Havent saw him, or even Miss Henrietta, he might get into trouble. So he went to the bathroom, because that was allowed. He went into one of the toilets, and locked the door, and put the seat down so he could stand on it, and opened the window.

It was a clear night, and there were hundreds of stars. The more he looked, the more there were to count.

I wonder where Alan is, he thought, as he looked at the stars. Dear Lord Jesus, he said, before he could stop himself. He had tried not to pray, since his experience in Chapel, with the nasty voice. But this time there was no voice. Dear Lord Jesus, he said again, as an experiment. Silence. He smiled. He could pray again. And now he knew Mr Wright was right, and he would always be able to pray, for the rest of his life. Funnily enough, now that he could pray, he didn't know what to say. It didn't matter. He didn't need to say anything.